Birdsville

Evan McHugh's previous books include *Shipwrecks: Australia's Greatest Maritime Disasters; Outback Heroes; Red Centre, Dark Heart* and *Outback Pioneers*. He writes a weekly column, 'Dry Rot', in the *Sunday Mail* and has written for television and radio. He is married and, usually lives in Sydney, but has spent the last twelve months in Birdsville, learning that what he didn't know about the outback could fill a book.

Birdsville

My year in the back of beyond

EVAN MCHUGH

VIKING
an imprint of
PENGUIN BOOKS

VIKING

Published by the Penguin Group
Penguin Group (Australia)
250 Camberwell Road, Camberwell, Victoria 3124, Australia
(a division of Pearson Australia Group Pty Ltd)
Penguin Group (USA) Inc.
375 Hudson Street, New York, New York 10014, USA
Penguin Group (Canada)
90 Eglinton Avenue East, Suite 700, Toronto, Canada ON M4P 2Y3
(a division of Pearson Penguin Canada Inc.)
Penguin Books Ltd
80 Strand, London WC2R 0RL England
Penguin Ireland
25 St Stephen's Green, Dublin 2, Ireland
(a division of Penguin Books Ltd)
Penguin Books India Pvt Ltd
11 Community Centre, Panchsheel Park, New Delhi – 110 017, India
Penguin Group (NZ)
67 Apollo Drive, Rosedale, North Shore 0632, New Zealand
(a division of Pearson New Zealand Ltd)
Penguin Books (South Africa) (Pty) Ltd
24 Sturdee Avenue, Rosebank, Johannesburg 2196, South Africa

Penguin Books Ltd, Registered Offices: 80 Strand, London, WC2R 0RL, England

First published by Penguin Group (Australia), 2009

10 9 8 7 6 5 4 3 2 1

Text copyright © Evan McHugh 2009

Cover and text design by Karen Trump © Penguin Group (Australia)
Cover photograph by Karen Brook
Map by Pamela Horsnell, Juno Creative Services
Typeset in 10.75/16pt Sabon by Post Pre-press Group, Brisbane, Queensland
Printed and bound in Australia by McPherson's Printing Group, Maryborough, Victoria

National Library of Australia
Cataloguing-in-Publication data:

McHugh, Evan.
Birdsville / Evan McHugh.
9780670072712 (pbk.)
Country life–Queensland–Birdsville–Anecdotes. Birdsville (Qld.)

920.71

penguin.com.au

To Michelle

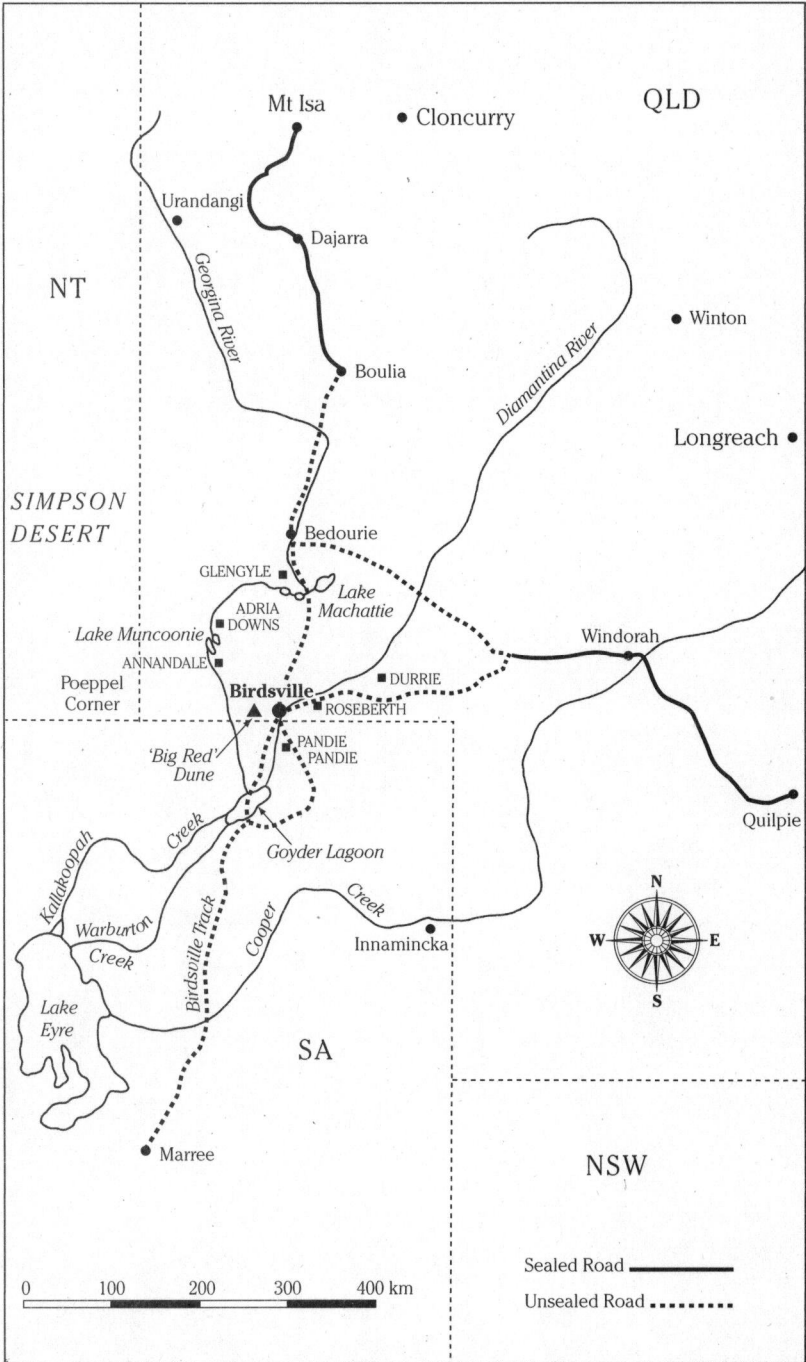

1

FURTHER OUT

If you want to polarise your friends, moving from inner-city Sydney to an isolated outback town like Birdsville is the kind of extreme tree change that'll do it every time. Most will tell you with remarkable honesty that you're out of your mind. A very few will salute your sense of adventure. In both cases they'll invite you to one last dinner before you go because they're sure you'll perish in the remotest corner of the Australian outback.

In the days before we showed the doubters we were serious about moving to Birdsville, we fed like kings. There were lavish meals in restaurants of every description – Italian, Thai, Middle Eastern, modern Australian, Japanese, Vietnamese and Thai again (because we were really going to miss it). We enjoyed a succession of 'last suppers' across a city that boasts one of the most diverse and sophisticated dining experiences in the world, while answering a stream of questions about what we were facing in the back of beyond.

'How many restaurants are there?'

'Only one.'

'How many supermarkets?'

'The nearest is 650 kilometres away.'

'Mobile phones?'

'There isn't a phone tower in the entire Diamantina Shire.'

'Internet?'

'Via satellite.'

Then, while sitting in a restaurant watching the surf roll in at Bondi, there was the big one: 'Why Birdsville?'

This, after all, is the town where, in 1882, a policeman committed suicide after a woman spurned his marriage proposal, and his colleague, Sergeant Arthur McDonald, noted in the police station's journal, 'Sub-Inspector Sharpe shot himself on the police station verandah this afternoon. Another hot day in Birdsville.' It's also not far from the spot where, in 2005, a woman's body was found with her vehicle just a few kilometres from the Birdsville Track. She'd run out of petrol near a water tank, but eventually starved to death, while following the advice to 'stay with your vehicle'. The roof of her car was dented where she'd been jumping on it, trying to signal motorists passing only 5 kilometres away.

The Birdsville Track was one of the most infamous stock routes in one of the harshest environments in Central Australia. In 1901, drover Jack Clarke was struggling along the drought-stricken track south of Birdsville with 500 bullocks when his men saw a huge cloud above the horizon ahead. 'If it's rain, we're blessed,' he said. 'If it's dust, we're cursed.' The ensuing dust storm all but buried the men, their horses and the bullocks. In their panic some beasts gored others to death. Others were scattered into the desert and lost. When the dust cleared, more than 400 head had perished.

Birdsville is also in the middle of the habitat of the most venomous land snake in the world. The venom from one bite of the inland taipan (*Oxyuranus microlepidotus*) could kill a hundred people. It's 400 times more venomous than a cobra. The taipan also goes by the name fierce snake because, apart from its deadly bite, locals reckon it's always in a bad mood. But that's not all. Officially, Birdsville holds the record for being the hottest place in Queensland. Cloncurry claims a record temperature of 53.1, but that was recorded in 1889 on non-standard equipment. In 1972, in Birdsville, the temperature officially reached 49.5.

Despite all this, Birdsville manages to attract between 20 000 and 40 000 tourists a year. Some turn up just to down a beer at the pub that's become the symbol of the outback. Just as the Sydney Opera House is synonymous with Sydney, and the Eiffel Tower with Paris, the Birdsville Hotel immediately identifies the back of beyond. The town is also the gateway to the Simpson Desert, a mecca for four-wheel-drive enthusiasts seeking adventure among the giant red dunes and claypans of one of the country's most arid regions. It's the centre of a cattle industry with stations among the biggest in the world. And each year the Birdsville Races attract thousands who drive and fly from all over Australia to camp in a dust bowl, bet in a dust bowl and watch horses gallop in a dust bowl. Even the slogan for the races is 'The dust never settles'.

All this we knew. It was enough to fill a couple of pages. Like the overwhelming majority of Australians whose lives revolve around cities, we were sufficiently confident of our world view to believe that's all there was. But as we contemplated spending a year in such a place, we began to suspect that what we didn't know could fill a book.

*

In the days before 'the big goodbye' my wife, Michelle, a serious foodie, started stocking up on the 'necessities'. She bought Thai curry pastes, Asian and North African spices, jars of olives and tomato passata, anchovies, salsa verde, pasta, noodles, Arborio rice and dozens of other items in bulk. As the mountain of food (and cookbooks and appliances) grew, I started worrying about how we were going to transport all of it over 2000 kilometres of country roads in our newly purchased four-wheel drive and off-road trailer.

Not that I was in a position to complain. This was the woman who had already endured major hardships on previous ventures.

At the top of the list were mountains. Windswept crags, snow-blasted peaks, frozen and scorched highlands, she'd followed me up the things from Central Australia to the west coast of Ireland. When I suggested she quit her well-paid graphic design job to spend a year discovering what life is really like in the outback, she had just one question.

'Any mountains?'

'Just sandhills.'

'I'll consider it.'

Convincing Michelle turned out to be the easy part. Organising everything else took months. We researched vehicles and settled on a Toyota LandCruiser that we soon dubbed the Truckasaurus as we attempted to squeeze the enormous beast down narrow city streets and lanes. It only got bigger when we added a bullbar to the front. We organised babysitters for our boat and cat, stored most of our possessions, rented our humble home for an exorbitant Sydney price and arranged somewhere to live in Birdsville.

Trickiest of all was explaining to my various clients – a news-paper, international airline and book publisher – that moving to the end of the earth didn't mean disappearing off the edge of it. 'It'll be business as usual,' I assured them, as I tackled the technological hurdles involved. Who was I kidding? If I couldn't service their needs the way I did in the bosom of the inner city, the worst-case scenario would see us retreating with out tails between our legs to the nearest place with broadband Internet. Given that the only Internet cafe in Birdsville had closed and the town's library was being renovated (and only had dial-up anyway), the nearest broadband was in Windorah, 400 kilometres away.

Access to modern technology may have been the deal breaker, but moving from the inner city to the outer outback was fraught with other unknowns. How would people like us, who got up at around 7.30 a.m. and went to work as the mood took us, survive in a place where people got up with the sun and went to bed when it got dark? As urban dwellers we were accustomed to showering in the morning so we smelled nice when we went to the office. In the outback they showered when they got home to get the sweat off before bed. Even shaking hands with outback people was an issue. My soft city hands were a dead giveaway that I'd never done a hard day's work in my life. When you shook hands with people in the outback, they had skin like bark. And sometimes it wasn't just the blokes.

On a fundamental level we were utterly different to the people we were going to be living with and trying to get to know. My hopes of experiencing and writing about outback Australia would be derailed if we were measured, found wanting and dismissed. Success or failure depended on the generosity of the people we met. Would they warm to us? Would we to them? In my experience, 'interesting characters' are often only interesting in small doses. To spend a whole year in a place where the only topics of conversation were cattle and drought could feel like an eternity. Would we be able to listen politely for that long or would we become like a friend at a dinner party who yawned at the person talking next to him and said, 'Sorry, I'm just waiting for you to say something interesting'?

As the days ticked down to our departure, the sleepless hours increased. Lying awake, my mind churned through the things still undone and the things that could go terribly wrong, like snakebite, death from thirst and mechanical breakdowns. And what about the things we knew nothing about? After a few nights of lying awake at 3 a.m., I discovered that reciting poetry to myself provided enough distraction to induce a few hour's sleep. I learned *The Man from Snowy River* in its entirety, plus *The Bush Christening* and Slessor's *Beach Burial*. For local colour, I memorised the song 'The Diamantina Drover'.

In the last week, the reality of what was involved in moving to one of the most remote towns in the world hit like an outback dust storm. Every loose end had to be tied up because nipping back to deal with anything left undone would be too time-consuming and expensive. With tenants signed up to move in, there was no room to shift our departure deadline.

The last twenty-four hours were a blur of packing, with the added pressure of making sure every plate, cup and sensitive electronic device was padded to survive a 2000-kilometre drive, the last 300 kilometres on rough dirt roads. With the distances and the dirt road involved, hiring removalists simply wasn't an option.

On the day of our departure, we packed the Truckasaurus and trailer with clothes, computers, herbs and spices. When the load didn't sit well, we pulled everything out and packed it again. Whatever bric-a-brac was left in the house we distributed among neighbours. Then we headed into Sydney's peak-hour traffic. It was 5.30 p.m. on 1 May 2008. If everything went to plan, we wouldn't see traffic, peak-hour or otherwise, for at least a year. The adventure had begun.

*

If the signs are anything to go by, the outback begins in central New South Wales. We drove through Dunedoo, The Gateway to the Outback, refuelled in Nyngan and continued towards Bourke. There the signs proclaimed The Heart of the Outback. We were still more than 1000 kilometres from our destination.

Cunnamulla . . . Quilpie . . . The further we drove, the more 'outback' it felt. By now The Big Smoke was already a distant memory. We were beyond those regions where the fields were fenced and the paddocks grassy and studded with trees. We were in red-soil country with stringy mulga bushes and the occasional tuft of grass.

Beyond Windorah, the scenery changed again. Country folk sometimes complain that in the city they can't see the sky. Of course fragments are always visible, away up between the tops of the buildings, but out past Windorah you can understand what they're talking about. Out here, the sky seemed to have swollen to immense size, pressing the earth into a flat golden-grassed plain. A few red dunes hovered in mirage on a distant horizon. The road was a ribbon of heat-baked tar stretching out to the edge of the world. We noticed that we could drive 100 kilometres without seeing another car.

There's an expression used by bushmen to refer to the region we were entering. As European settlement expanded, those hoping to take up land were always obliged to search for it 'further out'. When they reached the limits of the land suitable for agriculture, settlers seeking to escape civilisation, such as it was, referred to going 'further out'. Now the expression refers to the country of Central Australia, the places as far from the capital cities as it's possible to get. The land nearer cities and towns is 'closer in'.

An hour west of Windorah the bitumen came to an end. The country became steadily more barren. We were passing through the Sturt Stony Desert, still on cattle properties, but much of it was red gibber rock country and not much else. In places the gibbers stretched to the horizon, without so much as a tussock of grass. It was hard to imagine how anything could survive. Yet in the distance we noticed a dingo trotting away from the road. It wasn't in a hurry, but kept up a constant pace while glancing back at us over its shoulder. Was it hoping we'd break down?

As we drove on, the sand dunes became more frequent. Road signs warned to 'Keep Strictly Left' as we approached their summits. Finally, driving over one of them, we came upon the Birdsville Racecourse. It sat on a broad plain devoid of vegetation. In the distance a collection of corrugated-iron sheds and buildings had a forlorn, abandoned look. Beyond them, a line of trees marked the course of the Diamantina River. A water tower and a large antenna protruding above them signalled the presence of the town.

Where the road from Windorah joined the Birdsville Track, it became bitumen again. It crossed the Diamantina River, a succession of deep red-brown pools, then a parched floodway, before crossing a cattle grid and making a dog-leg into the town. The main street comprised two strips of tar divided by an equally wide strip of dirt. On the first corner the Birdsville Clinic was a modern building. Alongside it was the much older Australian Inland Mission Hospital, now a museum. There was a school, the ruins of the Royal Hotel, a couple of vacant blocks of land, the community hall, and a petrol station and post office. On the right was the iconic Birdsville Hotel. It faced the airstrip and a handful of small aircraft. On the other side of the airstrip was the police station, and then the dunes began again.

We stopped at one of the town's two petrol stations to pick up the keys to our new home. Apparently we were expected. 'You're the writer,' the woman behind the counter replied when I introduced myself. 'Welcome to Birdsville.'

Her name was Dia. We'd spoken on the phone when I discovered the satellite dish for my Internet connection had been 'delivered' to a vacant lot across the road from the service station. She'd been kind enough to collect it for me. The station was also the town's general store. Dia, a middle-aged Dutch woman travelling from job to job around Australia, gave us a quick tour of the store, explaining that it was expensive, but good for essentials and if we ran out of anything. We decided it would be cheaper to order things in.

Dia went into the office to tell her boss, Nell Brook, that we'd arrived. Nell and her husband, David, owned the Shell service station and part-owned the Birdsville Hotel. Their company, Brook Proprietors, also owned four cattle stations in the Channel Country of south-west Queensland and South Australia, plus a small property near Goondiwindi.

David's family had lived in the area for three generations, but Nell was born and raised in South Africa. A tall, elegant woman, she welcomed us very graciously, but beneath the surface was an unmistakeable strength. She struck me as a woman definitely not to be toyed with. She told us that we should have taped cardboard on the back windows of our car to protect them from stones. Unfortunately, our first lesson in outback travel was the discovery that a rock had bounced off our trailer and smashed one of the windows.

*

Birdsville, population seventy on a good day, is so small there's little private accommodation, let alone a real estate agent to manage it. The Diamantina Shire Council owns and manages houses and townhouses for its employees and the town's largely itinerant workforce. Through the council we'd rented a one-bedroom townhouse, site unseen. We'd peered at it in the satellite view on Google Maps and been told there was a fridge, washing machine, bed, lounge, table and chairs. There was a small yard where I might be able to indulge my passion for gardening. The rest was a leap into the unknown.

At the end of a cul-de-sac evocatively titled Gibber Court, we found the block of townhouses that was to be our home for the next year. None of the houses had numbers, so we pulled up in front of the one that looked least inhabited and tried the key. Inside, our first impression was 'cosy'. The combined lounge, dining and kitchen area measured 7 × 4 metres, much smaller than we were used to. There was a separate bedroom, bathroom and laundry. The building itself had wide eaves to provide protection from the summer sun. Apart from a clothesline, the backyard was bare dirt. Our new home/office seemed liveable, but one thing we couldn't help noticing was the dust. A thin red film coated every surface, even though we'd been told the place had been thoroughly cleaned before our arrival. It was even inside the cupboards and drawers.

In the window frames it was more than a film. The slides were almost choked with the stuff. It was hard to imagine what kind of dust storm could create such an accumulation, and leave a coating even in the backs of cupboards.

After the dust, the next thing that caught our attention was the view. From the kitchen window we saw red gibber rocks that looked hot even in the mild weather of late autumn. They sloped down to the town's billabong, which shimmered through the coolabahs. Beyond the billabong was a broad dusty plain dotted with the occasional tree and extending all the way to the horizon. There, a long white sand dune edged the sky. Whenever we filled a kettle we'd be reminded where we were: Birdsville, legendary town in the Australian outback.

*

Birdsville's story stretches back long before all memory. Millions of years ago it lay beneath the sea. After the sea retreated, the land was fed by generous rains that brought forth such an abundance that giant ancestors of today's marsupials, Australia's megafauna, flourished across the land. The country grew drier, the megafauna died out, and powerful winds formed the extraordinary dunes that extend from Western Australia to Queensland.

The south-western corner of Queensland became the domain of many Aboriginal peoples – Wangkangurru, Yarluyandi, Wangka-madla, Mithaka, Yawarawarrka and Karangura – desert peoples, survivors among sands, claypans, gibbers, and rivers that ran dry more often than not. Their songs are of drought and flood, fire and storm, starvation and plenty. Their Dreaming – a knowledge of country reaching back thousands of years – extends far beyond the borders of their homelands. Creation stories talk of Uluru, 1000 kilometres west across the dreadful wastes of the Simpson Desert. Their ancient trade routes reach south almost to the sea.

Due to the rapid spread of smallpox brought by the first settlers, some tribal groups were in decline long before Europeans reached their lands. The first explorer to reach south-west Queensland was Charles Sturt, attempting to find the geographical centre of the country in 1844–45. His name survives in Sturt's Stony Desert. Beyond present-day Birdsville he entered Munga-thirri, the land of sandhills now known as the Simpson Desert. He wrote of it in his *Narrative of An Expedition into Central Australia*:

> From the summit of a sandy undulation close upon our right, we saw that the ridges extended northwards in parallel lines beyond the range of vision and appeared as if interminable. To the eastward and westward they succeeded each other like the waves of the sea. The sand was of a deep red colour, and a bright narrow line of it marked the top of each ridge . . . familiar as we had been to such, my companion involuntarily uttered an exclamation of amazement when he first glanced his eye over it. 'Good heavens,' said he, 'did ever man see such country!'

Sturt was forced to retreat and barely survived. The next explorers to enter the region weren't so lucky. Robert O'Hara Burke and Charles Wills passed near present-day Birdsville during their ill-fated expedition of 1860–61. Their attempt to traverse the continent from their depot on the Cooper Creek near Innamincka to the Gulf of Carpentaria was successful, but when they returned to Cooper Creek they were too exhausted to follow other members of the expedition who'd left the depot the same day. Burke and Wills died among an abundance of bush foods in a good year along the Cooper. Only one of their party, John King, survived with the help of the indigenous population.

Despite the explorers' reports of desolation and misery, land-hungry 'run hunters' soon saw plains of plenty. Legendary drover

Nat Buchanan and his companion Edward Cornish actually found
the tracks left by Burke and Wills along the Diamantina River only
a month after the explorers had passed through. In 1866 William
Landsborough named the Diamantina River after Diamantina Roma
Bowen, wife of Queensland's first governor.

The pressure for grazing land was still not sufficient to see country as remote as that along the Diamantina taken up. Elsewhere in
Australia, land was being devoured by voracious speculators and the
population was being swelled by gold rushes in nearly every state.
Then in 1870 the grazing potential of south-western Queensland
was demonstrated in spectacular fashion when Harry Redford and
his mates stole a thousand head of cattle from Bowen Downs Station
in central Queensland. He drove them down the Thomson River and
Cooper Creek, through open country to South Australia, where the
cattle were sold. Not only did Redford get away with such an auda-
cious duffing, he pioneered the first Channel Country stock route to
Adelaide, opening a new market for Queensland cattle.

Within a decade stock were coming down the Cooper or following the more reliable waters of the Diamantina. Old Roseberth
Station (north of the present-day town) was established in 1874 or
1876 (sources vary). Also in 1876 pioneer Robert Frew set up Had-
don Downs and Cadelga (east of Birdsville). Shortly after, with a
Melbourne backer, he formed Pandie Pandie. A depot was established there by a man named Matthew Flynn, near what was known
as Diamantina Crossing. In 1879 the depot was bought by P. Burt
and converted into a store. Two years later, in 1881, the Queensland
government reserved four square miles around Burt's store for the
town of Birdsville.

The pace of expansion was swift and for the indigenous population it came at a terrible cost. All around south-western Queensland
the evidence of prior possession can be found – camp fires, wood and
mulga shelters, ceremonial circles, grinding stones and axe heads.

Some sites are remembered for the extreme violence that the loss of country involved. Nevertheless, indigenous people have survived and around Birdsville most now identify as Wangkangurru.

The other peoples who once populated the area are remembered by a very few of the oldest members of the region's indigenous community. Even the academics who scramble to gather the last seeds of knowledge before they're lost forever are growing old. On the road into Birdsville we'd met Emeritus Professor Luise Hercus, an 82-year-old linguist from the Australian National University who's been studying the disappearing desert languages of Central Australia since the 1960s. Hercus, a German émigré, has a face deeply lined by many summers spent scouring the Australian outback, gathering knowledge of people who are now little more than names on a map. She was on her way to Birdsville to attend the sixtieth birthday of Aboriginal elder Don Rowlands. She also wanted to see Linda Crombie, one of the last speakers of the Wangkangurru tongue, herself bed-ridden and struggling to remember the songs and stories of a culture that was already in decline when she was born.

*

By dusk we'd unpacked the vehicle and made a reasonable start on settling in. I'd tried the telephone and found it wasn't working. In my lengthy conversations with Telstra they'd said if I heard a dial tone I could call them during business hours and it was a simple matter to switch the service on. As for the Internet, the satellite dish was installed on the roof and the modem had a reassuring bank of flickering blue lights, but when I plugged in a wireless router and tried to access it with my laptop – nothing. I still had Sunday to get the thing working, so we decided we could afford to go for a walk along the billabong.

As the sun went down behind a distant sand dune, thousands of white corellas flocked to the trees along the water, which got me thinking about the origin of the town's name. One explanation is that it was a corruption of 'Burt's ville', the name of the original storekeeper. Another was that Robert Frew (also a storekeeper) named it for the abundance of birdlife around the billabong and the sometimes broad reaches of the river nearby. As the corellas set up a raucous chorus punctuated by the cries of whistling kites and the aark of Australian ravens, the latter seemed more believable.

That night we had dinner at the Birdsville Hotel. It was the best restaurant in town, being the only restaurant in town. The food was more than a surprise. Most Australian pubs have two choices: steak, chips and salad, or steak, chips and vegies. But here there was massaman beef on a bed of rice, barramundi (with salad or vegies) and kangaroo with a quandong sauce. You could still get a steak, but someone in the kitchen was clearly capable of more. It wasn't cheap and the meals weren't the country portions we'd enjoyed from the Blue Mountains to Windorah, but they were better than we'd expected.

After dinner we moved into the front bar for a nightcap. The bar had the usual memorabilia that passes for rustic charm in country pubs: old hats, stubby coolers with the names of various 'characters', 'dekcuf teg' stickers, and endless photographs of people who for all we knew were alive, dead, longingly remembered or long forgotten.

We ordered a couple of beers and took in the atmosphere, wondering what it was about the place that made it so iconic. It was like country pubs anywhere. Most of the customers weren't locals. They were tourists who were looking around like us, trying to spot an authentic outback character and only seeing people like themselves. Maybe we'd just had a long day, but it felt like we were missing something.

We finished our beers and headed back to Gibber Court, where we laid out our camping mattresses side by side on the bedroom floor.

There'd been a stuff-up with the furniture and there wasn't a bed. Not that it mattered much. After a six-hour drive, major unpacking and settling in, we slept the sleep of the exhausted.

The next morning I got up to make the cups of tea we always have while sitting in bed listening to the ABC news. I thought, this feels just like home. While I jiggled the teabags I glanced out the kitchen window. A wedge-tailed eagle flapped down and landed in the paddock next door. The huge bird strutted about, spooking the ever-present ravens and giving me an unexpected thrill. I thought, this is nothing like home!

After breakfast Michelle got to work on making curtains with the fabric she'd brought with her. I grappled with the mysteries of getting the Internet, wireless router, satellite modem and laptop talking to each other. After an hour I was reduced to swearing at the technology, 'Work, you bastard.' At the back of my mind was the growing realisation that if it wouldn't work, there was no-one within hundreds of kilometres who could help me. Without a phone, I couldn't ring anyone. I didn't even have dial-up. There was no backup.

My mind couldn't quite comprehend the intractability of the problem. 'If it's busted, get it fixed' had always worked before. Now all I could think about was that if I wasn't online to my clients by the following morning, I'd be in big trouble. If I couldn't deliver work reliably, I'd ultimately be forced to leave – going bankrupt in Birdsville wasn't an option. If this was what being isolated meant, it sucked.

Michelle was under less pressure. She had some freelance work on her books, but nothing urgent. She was otherwise unemployed and could take the year off if she pleased. That wouldn't be a problem in a big bustling city with lots of friends, but out here? She planned to do some photography, and she was developing an interest in jewellery making, but she was a little fearful that she might go out of her mind with boredom.

We beavered away at our respective tasks until coffee o'clock, me cursing user-friendly systems without a pop-up screen that read 'To fix whatever's wrong, click OK' and Michelle turning our humble lodgings into a home. There was no chance we'd forget to stop for a break because force of middle-aged habit meant both our watches had the alarms set for 11 a.m. to remind us. Of course, only good coffee would suffice. In our experience most coffee beyond the urban fringe tends to be made by people who either don't know or don't care about good coffee. To this end we always travel with the requisite ingredients and equipment. For Birdsville we'd stocked up with three kilos of the house blend from our favourite coffee supplier (and had details on their mail order service), but before we dipped into our precious supply, we wanted to give Birdsville a go.

Just down the street was the Birdsville Bakery, which also operated as a cafe (no Internet, I'd already checked). The bakery was a giant corrugated-iron shed with a broad verandah supported on rough bush timbers. Inside, the walls were decked with the usual tourist postcards and hand-drawn cartoons of outback fauna, such as cockatoos dressed in suits with the caption 'boss cockies'. The centre of the room was given over to a life-sized windmill, its blades decorated with an Aboriginal dot-painted rainbow serpent. The windmill was hung with all manner of rustic outback gimmickry: dog traps, whips and greenhide ropes. The decor didn't fill me with confidence.

We fronted the counter. 'A long black and a flat white, please,' I said to the diminutive woman who was there to serve us. On the side of the counter I noticed a pie warmer. Behind the counter I could see ovens and sundry baking equipment, which suggested the bakery actually baked the pies it sold. In my book, a good pie is even rarer than good coffee. There's a place in Sydney that gets my tick, another in Paris, and that's it. The Birdsville Bakery had some interesting pies in its selection – curried camel, kangaroo and claret, butter chicken – but it also had the yardstick by which all pies are measured: chunky beef. I decided to give one a try.

While the woman behind the counter made our coffees we sat at a table with the pie. Before we could start eating, a middle-aged bloke in a dark blue work shirt detached himself from a group at another table and came over to us. 'G'day, folks,' he said. 'Where you from?'

My usual response to such a question would be 'Do I know you?' followed by 'We'd appreciate some privacy'. But we were in unfamiliar territory, so I said, 'We're from Sydney, but we've just moved here.'

'Ah, you're the writer,' he blurted and thrust out his hand. 'Dusty Miller. Welcome to Birdsville.'

Dusty was solidly built, with an impressive moustache and equally impressive paunch. He had the powerful grip and rough hands I'd been expecting. I wondered how much typing it would take before I got a callus on as much as a fingertip. We introduced ourselves, and Dusty introduced the woman behind the counter as Teresa, his partner. She was the opposite of Dusty – slender and delicate, and with a hint of an English accent.

We exchanged the usual pleasantries while she finished making our coffees. Then Dusty moved off to do his hail-and-well-met routine with some other customers. I focused on the pie. 'So what do you think?' Michelle asked, well aware I fancied myself a pie aficionado.

'It's actually pretty good,' I replied. 'Nice pastry. The beef is actually chunky, and the sauce is delicious.' It was certainly better than I'd have expected from a bakery in the middle of nowhere. Of course the place had the usual signs spruiking the virtues of their pies. Don't they all? Not many live up to their promise.

Now for the coffee. I gave it a sniff. 'At least it's not burnt,'

I muttered to Michelle. A taste. 'Mmm.' It was proper, freshly ground coffee, made with an espresso machine. It's easy if you know how, but disastrous if you don't.

'How's yours?' I asked Michelle. Her tasting ability was better than mine.

'We can come here again,' she replied with a smile.

What a relief. The pub made a pretty decent meal. The cafe made a pretty decent coffee. The transition from the city to the bush might not be such a shock after all.

That afternoon, with the modem and router still not working, we embarked on our first tentative expedition and broke the number one rule of outback travel: setting off for a drive in the desert without telling anyone. We headed west out of town, towards the sand dune called Big Red, armed with a GPS that beeped every time we hit a bump and struggled to recalculate our location. We drove for about half an hour through country almost bereft of vegetation. The ground was bare dirt, gibbers or sand dune. Here and there was a tussock of spinifex or a stunted bush. Yet as the sun sank towards the horizon, bathing everything in soft golden light, the dunes glowed and the few struggling trees became a translucent green. Flights of pink and grey galahs flashed and turned above the red rock and sand.

Two-thirds of the way to Big Red, we decided we'd gone far enough. We turned down a track off the main road, followed it to a dune and decided to go for a stroll. That was another no-no, but I thought, what could possibly happen to us within sight of the main road back to town? It was May, a pleasant afternoon. You'd have to be a complete muppet to perish in such conditions. Even if we got bogged in sand, we wouldn't be that far from help.

What drew us on was the desire to explore a dune close up. We clambered up the shifting red sand to the summit. Just the feel of it was fascinating. It was perfectly dry, incredibly fine sand, almost silken to the touch. Nearly everything that moved across it left an impression. Here was a beetle's track. There was a small lizard's. Elsewhere were the splayed claw prints of small birds – landing, a couple of hops, then gone again. On top of one flat section there looked to be the prints of a large goanna – a series of claw marks with a dragging tail – except they stopped abruptly. It was some larger bird, a hawk perhaps.

We marvelled at the plant life, almost all of which was new to us. The more we explored, the more we found. There was an extraordinary diversity. Peering closer, many plants were in flower, their tiny delicate petals exposing buds of pollen. We'd heard it hadn't rained in the area since the beginning of the year, four months earlier. It didn't seem to bother the plant life in the dunes. It carried on regardless.

We decided not to break the second rule of the outback – don't drive at night – and headed back to town before it got dark.

That night I endured the fitful sleep of someone who had to work the next morning, but still didn't have their satellite Internet working. I lay awake wondering what setting or configuration I hadn't set or configured. I wished I'd been around when the technician had installed the dish so I could have enlisted his help. Now I was pondering the possibility that whatever was amiss was some complex technical issue requiring someone who actually knew what they were doing.

I rose early to continue grappling with technology. I tried all the obvious things several times again. And then – it started working, for no obvious or apparent reason. One moment, nothing; the next, emails were downloading. Favourite websites were popping up when I clicked on them.

'It works!' I shouted in triumph to a still-slumbering Michelle. 'The Internet works!'

A muffled 'Hooray!' issued from the bedroom.

The sense of relief I felt as I composed an email with the subject line 'Business As Usual' brought home just how powerful technology could be in overcoming isolation. Soon responses were bouncing back from every corner of the world, some expressing astonishment that we were in such a far-flung place.

Later that morning, I went to see the mechanic at Birdsville Auto about getting a new back window for the Truckasaurus. Patrick was a young, solidly muscled bloke with short, dark hair. He looked tough, but when he said, 'We'll be needin' to order it in,' he spoke with a soft Irish lilt.

'I'm guessing you weren't born and raised here,' I offered.

'No. I'm here on a working holiday. My girlfriend and I were workin' as ringers on Cordillo Downs until I let slip I was a diesel mechanic. I've been here ever since.'

'So you've traded the forty shades of green for forty shades of brown,' I said.

He laughed. 'Very much so.'

He asked how long I was in town and I gave him my year in Birdsville spiel.

'Really,' he said. 'I picked you for a tourist when I saw you lock your car.'

'Locals don't lock their cars?'

'Why would they?' he replied. 'If you stole a car, where would you go? And when they caught you, you'd cop a good floggin'.'

'Good point,' I said. 'By the way. Do you do the rescues if people get stuck in the desert?'

'I'm supposed to,' he replied, 'but I haven't done one yet.'

'If you do, is there any chance I could tag along?'

'No worries,' he said. He may have had an Irish accent, but he'd picked up the local expressions.

My watch beeped. Caffeine time.

At the bakery, as we had our coffees, it dawned on Dusty that we were a rarity in a small town that relied on the tourist trade – regulars. He came over for a yarn. Michelle mentioned she was looking for any job that was going, like pulling beers in the pub. Dusty suggested there was a job as an admin assistant in the school, although how much assistance a school of nine pupils needed wasn't clear.

He also had plenty of advice on ordering groceries. We knew we could order supplies from various supermarkets, but he got a lot of his fruit and veg from his own fruiterer and had it sent up from Adelaide. He thought it was better quality.

When we suggested we'd hoped to offset some of the food costs by growing our own vegies, his face lit up. 'You're into gardening?'

'I love gardening,' I replied. 'I've got a mate who works on a gardening magazine who's been researching what we can and can't grow and how to do it. He's mailing up all kinds of seeds, fertiliser and shadecloth so we can start our garden.'

'I can probably help you there,' Dusty said. 'Come out the back and I'll show you my vegie patch.'

He led us out the back door and there, caged to protect it from dogs, rabbits and crows, was a lush expanse crammed with broccoli, silver beet, tomatoes, Italian parsley, basil and rocket. On the other side of an assortment of takeaway food trailers and refrigerated trucks he had a huge pumpkin patch. I'd met my first Birdsville gardener. But there was more.

'Come and see my Sturt's desert peas,' he said.

Sturt's desert pea (*Swainsona formosa*) was the grail of my gardening hopes here. Birdsville has a climate perfect for the plant that is South Australia's stunning floral emblem. It was originally discovered by William Dampier on his trip up the coast of Western Australia in 1699 and named *Clianthus dampieri*.

Dusty took me out the front where an area to one side of the footpath was fenced off. There, amid an assortment of plants, small seedlings were starting to put out shoots in all directions. Dusty had grown them from seed, which meant he had a black belt when it came to cultivating difficult-to-grow Australian natives.

'When they're in flower, the tourists love 'em,' he said. 'They gather round and twist themselves into all sorts of angles to take photographs.'

Little did he know I was fighting the urge to do exactly the same.

That afternoon, the twice-weekly mail plane arrived. Two hours later the mail was available for collection from the Mobil petrol station, which doubled as the post office. Narelle Gaffney was Birdsville's formidable post mistress. I'd spoken to her prior to our arrival, while tracking the errant satellite dish to its eventual resting place in the vacant lot. On the phone she'd struck me as someone who knew the ropes intimately, but regarded explaining them to someone in Sydney as a waste of her time. It was only when I'd mentioned that we were about to move to Birdsville and were getting mail redirected that she cut me short.

'What's your address in Birdsville?' she asked.

I gave it to her.

'All your mail will be here when you arrive,' she said.

Meeting her in the flesh, she was just as I'd imagined – in her late fifties with neat, tightly curled hair and the unflinching demeanour of an outback woman who'd spent her life tackling adversity head on. Her expression suggested that she didn't suffer fools gladly.

'Hi, I'm Evan,' I introduced myself brightly.

Her eyebrow lifted ever so slightly. I was sure I could hear time's winged chariot pulling up outside. 'What can I do for you?' she asked.

'Err . . .' Damn! A wasted syllable. 'My mail please?'

She turned to her pigeonholes. There was a gratifyingly large post, or so I thought. That should impress her. She handed it over without a hint of emotion, impressed or otherwise.

'Thank you,' I said. I was about to start rummaging through

my mail when something told me it wouldn't do to waste space at Narelle's counter. Tucking my tail firmly between my legs, I scuttled away, thinking that if the Birdsville billabong ever dries up, the bottom will be found strewn with fools.

That night Michelle and I went for a walk down the main street. We started at the western end, at one of Birdsville's oldest buildings, the Courthouse, built in 1882 from locally cut sandstone. It was a classic Queensland building, with verandahs down three sides and a high tin roof. Out the back was an old tin shed, separate from the other buildings. It used to be the Aboriginal trackers hut. It looked basic in the extreme, but in 1921 the Sub-Inspector of Police reported on the accommodation that 'any further expense in connection with the trackers stationed in this district would be exorbitant and unnecessary'.

From the front step of the Courthouse there was a view across the airfield to the pub, the oval and the old part of town. Birdsville is one of the few places in Australia where you can land in a plane and taxi almost to the front door of the pub. Walking down the main street, you can pass a few parked cars and a few parked planes.

The Birdsville Hotel (built in 1884) used to be one of three in town. Tattersalls is long gone, but the Royal Hotel (built in 1882) remains, the building a derelict shell. At the turn of the nineteenth century, the town boasted a population of over a hundred – stockmen, cameleers, fencers, doggers (wild dog shooters), and customs officials gathering duty on stock crossing the border between Queensland and South Australia. Federation in 1901 meant the end of border taxes between the states, and towns like Birdsville suffered as a result. Photographs from the 1920s show a handful of scattered buildings sitting on a dusty plain devoid of vegetation.

Now, where once there was a saddlery, blacksmith, five stores and other businesses, there are just the two service stations. There are almost as many vacant lots as there are buildings. Looking at the partially collapsed walls of the partially roofed Royal Hotel, with its weathered posts and piles of rubble, the place feels more like Hiroshima than the outback.

The Royal was derelict even in 1923 when nursing sisters Grace Francis and Catherine Boyd became Birdsville's first bush nurses and turned the pub into a hospital called the Brisbane Home. Theirs was one of the most remote and difficult postings in the Reverend John Flynn's Australian Inland Mission. The conditions they endured through summer and winter were appalling, but they and those who followed were determined to provide health services to the outback even if it meant great personal sacrifice. The Brisbane Home was still operating in 1929 when the Flying Doctor Service (begun in 1928) was extended to Birdsville. That year the town also received a pedal wireless, the first direct link with the outside world.

Past the Royal, where the Brisbane Home operated for fourteen years, there's a park with the town's war memorial and a playground. Next to that is another milestone in the provision of outback health services, the Birdsville Hospital. Originally built as the Birdsville Nursing Home in 1934, the building was a vast improvement on the tumbledown pub. When it caught fire and burned to the ground in 1951, the current building was erected on the site.

The hospital operated until 2005 when health services in Birdsville were taken over by the Diamantina Council and the North and West Queensland Primary Health Care Service. Their new clinic is right next door, where two or three Remote Area Nurses are supported by the Royal Flying Doctor Service, which makes regular visits and stands ready to evacuate emergency cases at any time.

*

Late autumn in Birdsville was turning out to be nothing like what we'd expected. There was no danger of perishing as we breakfasted on our front verandah in warm sunshine. Even the flies were little more than a nuisance. On Wednesday we played our first game of tennis, marvelling at the dust that kicked up when the ball hit the concrete surface. We couldn't complain, though. It was free to play.

As the days passed we became more familiar to the locals. A casual g'day on first meeting progressed to an exchange of names and 'Yes, I'm that writer bloke.' Driving around town, a passing wave became a common courtesy.

Towards the end of the week, our walks tended towards the rodeo grounds. I'd timed our first full weekend in Birdsville to coincide with the town's annual rodeo, but during the week, things were already starting to happen. Trucks were unloading stock. At night, we fell asleep to the sounds of distant cattle. In shafts of morning light, dust rose over the plain.

2

TRADITION AND DUST

Most educated city people have been raised on a steady diet of preventing cruelty to animals. It pretty much goes with the same territory as save the whales, no dams and hug a tree. Rodeos? Tsk-tsk. Never mind that we knew nothing about rodeos. Our minds were made up.

On Friday night we took our preconceptions to the Birdsville Rodeo – at least, I did. Dusty had corralled Michelle into helping the Social Club run the catering van, so I wandered over on my own to watch the animals suffer. Sure enough, in one of the chutes a horse had decided that it wasn't going to wait before it got down to business. Puffing and snorting, it half-reared even as the ringers manoeuvred to secure a harness around its belly. It was lashing the air with its hooves. Its would-be rider stood above it, a foot on the top rail on either side of the furious beast below. Looking in through the bars, I could see a wide eye glaring defiantly. The horse bucked and kicked out, reacting to the merest touch. A cloud of dry dust rose, catching in my throat as I watched the animal struggle when anyone and anything got too near. It only got worse when the rider tried to settle on its back.

'Coming up next is "J",' master of ceremonies Don Rayment told the crowd of a hundred or so that had congregated around the beer tent and food caravan. 'His family has produced some of the most respected horsemen in western Queensland. For generations they've been renowned for their abilities. It'll take something pretty special to buck him off.'

No-one told that to the horse. The gate hadn't opened and it was already bucking. 'J' was lifting off and standing on the railings as the beast reacted strongly to any suggestion it might be ridden. Then, for just a moment, the horse settled, J got on and the gate was flung open. The animal celebrated its freedom with an almighty leap into the arena. Still in midair it twisted its body then arched its back. The wild contortion flicked the rider high into the air. The horses' hooves still hadn't touched the deep dirt of the arena, yet the much-fancied rider was already off. They hit the ground more or less at the same time, but in two different places. The horse took off one way, bucking and kicking out its considerable rage. J picked himself up and started shuffling off to repair his somewhat tarnished pride.

The embarrassed silence was broken by Don Rayment. 'I guess he's from the exploring side of the family.' Hoots of mirth came from around the crowd.

The next event was the bullock riding. Anyone could have a go, win a few bucks or break a few bones. Bullocks are quite different to horses, but what they have in common is a reluctance to be ridden. An assortment of ringers, labourers and council workers put life and limb on the line for a moment of body bruising excitement – the locals were queuing up. There were few takers among the tourists scattered among the crowd.

'Next is Patrick, from Birdsville Auto,' Don Rayment announced. Sure enough the mechanic was nervously settling on a bullock's back while his girlfriend, Olivia, a fine-featured Irish lass who nevertheless thrived on outback life, got into position to get a photo he might cherish forever. Birdsville's policeman, Neale McShane, offered her some advice: 'Don't wait to try and get a good shot. The moment that chute opens, take the picture.'

Good call. The bullock burst into the arena, a brown and white ball of thrashing Hereford. The camera flashed not a moment too soon as Patrick promptly became airborne. He hit the ground like a sack of Irish potatoes. Later he said he'd only been on for a second, but even that left him hurting all over.

As the event continued, I made it Bullocks 10, Riders 2. I have to admit I was on the bullocks' side, for very worthy reasons, but I was starting to feel sorry for the humans. They were doing most of the suffering. After the last buttock was bruised and the last ego dented, the crowd adjourned to the refreshment area to eat, drink and socialise.

I noticed a young Aboriginal stockman front the bar. On his neck the word 'Dieri' was tattooed. The Dieri are a tribal group from around Marree, down the Birdsville Track in South Australia. People had come from far and wide. Indigenous and non-indigenous people mingled freely. On first impressions, the community seemed to be more integrated than any I'd seen in country Australia.

The following morning the rodeo got down to serious business. Western Queensland, northern South Australia and the Northern Territory are home to an event based on the traditional method of branding cattle in the bush, called bronco branding. It's nothing like any other rodeo event, and rarely seen anywhere else, but it's hugely popular 'further out'. A whiteboard for the first event listed teams with evocative titles: Desert Leirs, Redrock, Morney Plains, Stock Camp, Camel Catchers, Adria Downs, Durham, Stonehenge, Mumpy, Georgina Sam, Nappa Merrie and Roxborough. The names didn't mean much to me, but they had an authentic outback ring.

Bronco branding begins quietly enough, with a rider guiding his or her horse through the middle of a herd of yarded cattle. The cattle mill and push to keep away, but the rider just keeps moving among them. He or she bides their time until, in a blink, a rope flashes above the horse's neck and is thrown at a passing calf. If it misses, the rider gathers the rope, coils it and resumes the slow ride through the herd. If the calf gets caught, things get busy.

Bleating, bucking and kicking, the calf is dragged from the herd. It's a bigger catch than most fish, with a lot more fight. The struggling calf is pulled up to a timber structure called a bronco panel, horse and rider working hard to get it to just the right position. Two ground crew rope the calf by a fore and hind hoof, securing it with turns of the rope around the posts of the bronco panel, and throw off the head rope. Then with the calf kicking dust and fury in their faces, they and a third ground crewman flex their muscle against the calf and tip it on its side. With the hooves secured, the beast can't rise, allowing the third crewman to brand the animal using a brand dipped in paint. While they're doing all that, the rider is already among the herd again, searching for another 'unbranded' calf.

Little calves are no match for powerful horses that know all about bronco branding. Bigger calves take the stockhorse on, even as the head rope tightens around their neck. Their tongues loll and eyes bulge. Sometimes the horse can't budge them and the impasse is resolved when the stubborn calf collapses. Then the judges swoop in with the ground crew to release the beast before it comes to harm.

To an outsider, it was hard to follow what was going on. Fortunately, there was no shortage of people who could explain the subtleties. Between rounds I wandered over to one of the judges, Allen Hubbard, manager of Galway Downs, to find out what I could. It turned out I'd asked the right person. Allen was an older gentleman and neatly turned out in his moleskins, shirt and broad-brimmed hat. He was one of those outback types who somehow manages to stay neat and clean despite spending the day in a yard full of cattle and dust.

'This is the original method of branding calves in outback Queensland,' he told me, 'especially on the very big properties with a limited number of yards. There was a bronco yard at every water, consisting of the panel enclosed by a wire fence. Before that there were open bronco camps – they had no yard at all. The men had to hold 'em, and they'd cut one side of a forky tree and put a line over it and use that. They were called hot-rod bronco camps. With no yard it was a very laborious job. After a few hours cattle got sick of staying in camp and they took a lot of holding. Then they come up with the bronco yards and there's still a lot of bronco yards on the stations today, probably only used for overnighters, or camping in.'

Modern bronco branding started about twenty years ago when revered bushman R. M. Williams, who'd experienced bronco branding on the big stations in his younger days, realised it was becoming a lost art. Modern yards and cradles had all but replaced the old technique and very few old hands could still do it. Williams decided to do something about it.

Allen explained: 'The method today is authentic, but turned into a sport. Everything they use is genuine – the greenhide ropes, the panels. You see them pulling low down on the horse with a collar or breastplate. The idea was that every cleanskin beast had to be pulled up. Got a big bull or something, the horse can pull a bit lower, hasn't got the high purchase on him. In the mob you'll see everything – cows, calves, bulls. When they mustered around the water, they yarded everything. There was no way of drafting off so that's why you have a mixture of cattle in the yard.'

The event is timed, with penalties for rough handling, incorrect branding and roping, among other mistakes. I asked about the rules.

'This is the singles we're having here. You have to catch three calves. The first calf has to be caught in two and a half minutes and three calves have to be branded in six minutes. For novices it's three and eight. In the doubles two horses pull them up – still the same ground crew, three men, but they have to catch five calves. The first calf has to be caught in two and a half minutes and all five within six minutes. The doubles is the most spectacular event because it's quick and fiery and you've got two horses pulling up.'

The judges are a little bit lenient with the novices. They encourage people to have a go, give them extra time and let them get away with a few minor things. Afterwards the judges will give them a few tips and pointers. Not so in the singles and doubles.

Said Allen: 'A good performance is three calves in under three minutes – brands and everything. The record is held by a fella called Wayne Geiger, works for me at Galway Downs near Windorah. With a ten-second penalty he pulled 'em up, branded and completed everything in one minute and forty-nine seconds.'

The ropes are a work of art themselves. 'David Morton, they like his ropes. It's the tightness of the ropes, the tighter you can get them, the better. Old Herb who works for me, he's a good rope maker. They all have different methods. Some use a bit more fat on the hide when they pull them up and tighten them. They test them by the fall – some cast better than others. A fella here a while ago had a very loose type of rope. That's a very hard rope to catch with, too soft and sort of saggy. You want a rope that'll cast out, hold its shape. You don't want a stiff rope, but you want a good firm one. Charlie Rayment was another good rope maker. And Jimmy Nunn.'

Ropes are made from the hides of 'killers' – the cattle that are slaughtered to feed the stockmen.

'Some makers have a preference for Herefords as their hides are heavier than Brahmans',' Hubbard explained. 'A lot of them prefer a white hide, too. They think it has a more even thickness. Some go for roans.

'The strands they cut, the greenhide, are roughly three-quarters of an inch wide. [Three or four strands are then plaited to make the rope.] They do shrink, but some are cut a little bit smaller. The catching rope is roughly 30 feet [9 metres] long. You'll notice they don't swing it round like they do in the movies. They just place the rope on one side then they throw it across the horse. That's always been the method of throwing the greenhide rope.

'Leg ropes, everything, are made in the same way. The hind leg rope is always a bit longer than the front leg rope. It's probably 10 or 15 fifteen feet, while the front one's about 12. Chain on the rope is a hobble chain with a swivel end so it'll twist and turn around and won't get screwed up.'

There's no formal process in becoming a judge, but years of experience in the bush plays a big part. Hubbard reckoned he'd been around stock camps since he was seven years old, mostly on big western Queensland properties. Eventually someone asked him to become a judge. 'When you get asked you sort of get stuck with it.'

There's no age limit for participants. Kids as young as seven can do the branding; some of the title-holders are in their seventies. All-female and mixed teams compete. Until recently, Don Rayment's father, Charlie, was competing in his eighties after having a triple bypass. He was also a war hero. He served aboard the battle-cruiser HMAS *Australia* in World War II when it was hit by six kamikazes during a series of battles in the Pacific.

According to Allen Hubbard, the only limitation to participating in bronco branding is lack of experience. 'It's a little bit difficult if you're not brought up in that way of life because you seem to get hurt. There's also an old saying, there's no dog like an old dog. He knows what to do. He doesn't get hurt and doesn't get in the way because he's always in the right place at the right time. The same goes with a man. In this game you see some of the old fellas who don't seem to do much, but they're quick and effective and get the job done.

'Some fellas make it look very easy. They know when to throw the rope. What they do is throw across the horse and catch the calf on the opposite side. If they're right-handed they catch him on the left side because that's where they pull from. They usually get the calf as it walks back past them. You throw the rope out in front of them and they walk in. There's a lot of skill and a lot of practice in being a good catcher.

'Also, when you catch a calf you can get the rope caught up in your horse's hind legs. You've got to know which way to ride the horse. If the rope gets caught up in their legs, a lot of horses will play up bad and buck or throw themselves on the ground, and that's bad – someone could get hurt.'

Allen ran through some of the best bronco branders. 'Peter Klein-Smith, Jimmy Nunn, Herb Geiger, Mick Bishell. There's probably ten old fellas who had a go there today who are very experienced and very skilled. Old Jimmy Crombie is a great old catcher; he's probably in his seventies. David Morton, the big man there, has been a very experienced catcher. Reared up all his life in the stock camps, and that's all he's known since he was a child.'

Allen explained that bronco branding wasn't the only uniquely outback rodeo event. 'They have what they call the station buckjump where they ride conventional saddles, not rodeo saddles, and they crack a whip while the horse is bucking. In the old stock camps, you never questioned any horse you were given. You just got on him. Out in the flat he could buck you, he could do all he liked and you just had to wear it. That was part of the life. You accepted that.

'And there's the bullock riding, too. Often in the big camps we'd pull up the big micks [mickey bulls], and a lot of the young fellas would jump on, grab 'em by the tail and ride them away for a bit of fun. And then they'd jump off. It was just for a bit of sport.'

When the next round started I was able to watch with a more educated eye. The aimless strolling of the horse became manoeuvring with a purpose. And there was a calf, walking back past the horse. There went the rope. Good catch. Mind you, it still looked pretty rough on the calf. Later, I talked to Dalene Brook, the delicate-featured 33-year-old daughter of Nell and David, who was responsible for marketing their organic beef production. Dalene explained that looks could be deceiving. 'Every one of the cattle in there is the very best the stations can muster,' she said. 'That's because they know all the other cattlemen are watching. But there's no way the owners would let their best stock get knocked about.'

As it happened, all the cattle were from one of her parents' properties, Adria Downs, which was managed by Don Rayment, the ring commentator. He was watching everything. Now that she mentioned it, the Herefords milling about did look extremely fit and healthy. I'd expected that anything grazing in semi-desert must be a half-starved, forlorn-looking beast.

'If there was a drought,' she said, 'they would lose condition, in which case the rodeo wouldn't be held. But at the moment there's plenty of feed around. Birdsville gives people the wrong impression. It's up high, above the river, so it's stony and dry. Most people find it hard to believe that out at dad's property, Adria, on Lake Muncoonie, there's grass as far as the eye can see.'

'You've had good rains?'

'A flood. The lake is slowly drying up and as it does the grass comes through.'

She explained how her father constantly monitored river levels on stations upstream of Adria, and could predict the effect any flood would have when it reached his property.

'The stations aren't circumspect with information that might help a potential rival?' I asked.

'Everyone usually helps each other,' Dalene replied. 'About the only time things get difficult is when they're in the pub and they've got a few rums in them.'

That evening, the bronco branding finished and the bullock riding began. This really was cruel . . . for the riders. The previous night the bullocks seemed to be full of fight but now, after a day of being bronco branded, the bullocks took the gloves off. The finest beasts in the Diamantina, round-bodied and rippling with muscle, were in no mood to be ridden. Most of them flicked their riders off like flies. Riders who managed to stay on for a couple of bucks found themselves staring at the steel bars surrounding the arena, right before being thrown into them. One young lad came off just as the animal threw itself down. He managed to land beneath a thrashing Hereford bullock. It occurred to me that you never see a bookie at a rodeo event. I thought I knew why.

Another bullock reminded me that all these cattle were hand-picked. After throwing his rider into the dust he stood in the middle of the ring, puffing and prancing first one way, then another. He was like a prize-fighter looking for more challengers. He owned the arena, a magnificent animal, even to my untrained eye.

The judges eventually declared a winner, but it should have been one of the bullocks. Nevertheless the prizes were awarded and the crowd retired to the beer tent and Dusty's takeaway food van, chatting animatedly about the day's adventures.

One last feat of cattle handling remained, though it almost went unnoticed. Out beyond the glare of the arena spotlights, Don Rayment, who'd been running events and performing the role of announcer since eight that morning, quietly walked into the bronco branding arena and opened the gate to release the herd into the holding paddock, where bales of feed were waiting to reward them for their exertions. After opening the gate, he circled around the tightly bunched cattle. At a point on the opposite side of the herd, he stopped, stood and waited. Slowly, the herd started to move. One by one, they walked quietly out through the gate. Rayment didn't speak, shout, wave his arms or throw dust at the cattle. His presence alone was enough. To someone like me, who knew absolutely nothing about handling cattle, it seemed a remarkable skill. Yet no-one around me gave it a second glance.

While I was learning about rodeos, Michelle was making her own discoveries about hospitality and catering. Dusty had asked if she'd help him in his catering van. She'd worked almost all day serving customers, making coffees and snacks. When I went over to see how she was going, she told me Dusty had offered her a job. We'd been in Birdsville exactly one week.

Dusty had asked if she would take over as his baker. Young Ben, the current baker, who was also living in the townhouse next to us, was keen to return to his family in New South Wales.

'A baker?' I said. 'What are the hours?'

'Start at 4 a.m., finish around eleven,' Michelle said.

If there's one thing I know about Michelle, it's that she's definitely not a morning person.

'You're not seriously considering it,' I said.

'Maybe I can help out at the front counter,' she replied. 'Dusty and I could share the baking.'

'It's worth a try,' I said, 'though only if you don't have to get up at four in the morning.'

3

THE CHANNEL COUNTRY

The day after the Birdsville rodeo, I went along to a presentation Dalene Brook was giving in the Birdsville Hotel. It was about a group of outback women who had made an overseas trip to promote the Channel Country's Organic Beef Export Company (OBE). To an outsider, beef producers in the Channel Country selling their cattle as 'organic' looks like little more than clever marketing. On their giant properties it's impossible to spread chemicals over thousands of kilometres anyway, so their beef was organic by default, wasn't it?

Dalene's presentation began with a video showing Hereford cattle grazing extraordinarily lush pastures. It looked like they'd never left the well-watered English county after which they'd been named. Yet the video was shot 100 kilometres west of Birdsville in the Simpson Desert. The day before, when Dalene had mentioned 'grass as far as the eye can see', I'd imagined scrawny beasts in straggly brown fodder that had forced its way up through dry, crusty earth, not fat beasts up to their bellies in verdant feed.

When the video ended, Dalene outlined the Channel Country's dynamics. 'In Australia we're very fortunate to have this region,' she said. 'If you think of other countries, they all have mountains in the middle so when it rains the water flows down into the oceans, taking all the nutrients with it. In Australia all the mountains are closer to the coast, so when it rains the water flows inland. In Queensland it flows into the Channel Country. For millions of years it's been doing this and leaving all the good things in the soil. So when we talk about what the cattle graze on, we're suggesting they graze on grasses that have a very high nutritional value.'

She maintained that because the cattle fatten naturally there's no need for supplements or hormones. The area is also free of disease and parasites, which means cattle can get by without chemical treatments. To take advantage of the situation, thirty Channel Country producers, mostly husband and wife properties, have gone to the trouble of getting themselves certified as organic. They've formed a company, OBE, and taken their organic beef to the world.

In their experience, it's not enough to tell people, 'This is good, you should buy it.' So the pitch includes the Channel Country, a place so far from anywhere and anything that there's no threat of pollution, infection (mad cow, bird flu) or other contamination. OBE isn't just organic, it's *Channel Country* organic.

To help get the message across, in 2008, eight women who were part of the OBE supply chain visited Hong Kong and Taiwan on a promotional tour. Some were wives of producers and station managers. Others, like Dalene, were from the marketing side. Several had never been out of Australia.

Doing business in Asia was a steep learning curve for many, from coping with minute accommodation to the etiquette of exchanging business cards. The constant press of humanity was a challenge for these women who'd be lucky to see a handful of people in a month. They started to miss they sky. What they did see of it was grey with pollution.

For Judy Rayment, wife of Adria manager Don Rayment and an expert on the National Livestock Identification Scheme, it was an opportunity to see the beef that left their station on trucks (most for processing before export, some exported live) sitting on supermarket shelves on the other side of the world. Compared to Australia, the portions were tiny. Packages of only 100 grams of meat sold at $10 each. Yet Hong Kong women were queuing to buy the beef she'd helped produce.

It gave Judy a sense of pride, but it wasn't long before she was yearning to be back at Adria. 'After a few days I just wanted to go home,' she told me afterwards. 'I wanted my husband, I wanted my space. It was an interesting experience, but I really missed home.'

On their tour the women did press interviews, photo shoots and attended meetings promoting their product and Australia. Some had never spoken in public before, but were soon answering questions about animal welfare, life in the outback and how cattle survive when they roam freely to graze instead of being kept in feedlots and fed by hand. Following the trip, Hong Kong sales of OBE beef doubled almost overnight.

Population density and space were not the only contrasts the OBE women noted. They visited an organic garden cooperative where tiny plots 1.5 × 2 metres were rented to people who came every weekend to nurture their little gardens. Every plant was individually cared for.

Dalene Brook found that awareness of organic products was high, but that most people had no concept of beef production, particularly in outback Australia. 'One guy who took us to dinner,' she said, 'his three children had never walked on dirt. If they've grown up like that and never even seen a cow, they just don't have any comprehension of it.'

I wasn't about to admit that when it came to understanding cattle, I was with the Chinese and Taiwanese. And like them, I had big plans for the tiny patch of bare dirt out the back of our house.

As luck would have it, I was on my way home when I noticed an Aboriginal neighbour pulling buffalo grass runners out of his front lawn. He had an enticingly large pile. I walked over to him.

'Hi, I'm Evan,' I said.

'I'm Harry,' he replied. He was very thin, but his face lit up with a brilliant smile as he shook my hand. 'You're that writer bloke.'

'That's right. I was just wondering if you had any plans for those runners.'

'You want 'em?'

'If you can spare any . . .' I tried not to sound too eager.

He gave me the lot – that is, after a tour of his garden. He had sweet peas, bougainvilleas, desert roses, lobelias, a couple of eucalypt seedlings and a struggling lemon tree. Harry turned out to be Harry Crombie, brother of Jimmy Crombie, who'd been pointed out to me at the rodeo. Both were sons of Linda Crombie.

Harry was another of Birdsville's keen gardeners. It transpired that he had plenty of time for his interest because he was off work.

'I've got prostate cancer,' he explained with remarkable candour. 'I've been getting treatment in Townsville. I'm just waiting to hear if it's in remission.'

Despite his medical condition, Harry was easygoing and cheerful. Like most gardeners he was also happy to share his knowledge and give me a hand with my garden if I needed it.

We got talking and Harry started telling me about Joe the Rainmaker, who'd been featured in John Heyer's 1954 film about Birdsville, *The Back of Beyond*. 'He lived in a humpy house,' he said, 'down by the river. Whenever it rained he'd be down there singin' and singin', all the time that it rained. He used to get the government ration and if he ever left that humpy house us kids'd get in there and steal his raisins. We used to love those raisins. We were little terrors. He got so that when he got his rations he wouldn't leave the place if us kids were about.'

I was learning that in Birdsville there's no such thing as a short conversation. Eventually I took my runners home and started working out where I was going to put them. I decided to plant them in a line from the back verandah to the clothesline. I figured that when the runners filled out it would be better to walk on grass than on dirt or mud – if they grew, that is.

Harry and Dusty both reckoned that the only soil that would grow anything in Birdsville was red desert sand. They said the local dirt was practically sterile. There was a pile of sand on a vacant lot near our house. That afternoon I borrowed a wheelbarrow from another neighbour, Carlos, and toiled back and forth with load after load. Soon I had enough to plant my runners and lay out a garden bed along the back fence.

Gardening in Birdsville would be easy if everything you planted grew like the various Channel Country grasses. Alas, for plants accustomed to temperate climates and conditions there were endless obstacles. For starters, there were no worms to nurture the soil. There were no bees to pollinate flowers. Even the desert sand was leached of almost all nutrients. Its best quality was that it could absorb and retain moisture. Then there was the question of heat. The sun in winter was relatively benign, but the shadecloth around nearly every garden bed signalled the burning fury that was to come in a few short months.

A care package of seeds, soil improving nutrients and 20 per cent shadecloth had already arrived by mail from my mate back in Sydney. After burying and watering my lawn-to-be (I used river water from the garden tap in order to save the precious water in the rainwater tank), I decided on my first plantings. First to go in were rocket, lettuce, tomatoes, radicchio, Chinese cabbage, spring onions, basil, Italian parsley, sage and thyme. I later erected a frame over the garden bed to support the shadecloth.

At the end of a remarkably busy first week in Birdsville, we went out to Big Red to watch the sunset with Dusty and Teresa from the bakery. We took parmesan, brie, taggiasca olives, a couple of dips, a bottle of wine and a couple of beers. As we drove out there I noticed the cattle – big fat Channel Country Herefords.

. On top of Big Red we laid everything out on a folding table and set up the chairs in time to watch the sun disappear into the desert. The scene would have been tranquil and serene but for three vehicles that were taking turns trying to climb the far dune. They took long run-ups, the high-revving of the engine carrying clearly across the plain. As the air cooled even the drivers' voices reached us from more than a kilometre away. At last, one vehicle reached the summit, the achievement met with cheers from below. The next vehicle eventually got up, then the third.

'They must have let their tyre pressures down,' Dusty said gruffly. 'You'll get a lot further that way.'

With the vehicles gone, all we could hear was our own voices and a flock of corellas down among the mulgas at the base of Big Red. To the west, dune after dune stretched south-east to north-west from horizon to horizon in a landscape of silent grandeur. Here and there a straggly tree, a clump of spinifex, a lump of sand or stretch of claypan was suffused with golden light. No-one felt compelled to echo Charles Sturt and exclaim, 'Did ever man see such country!'

As the others chatted and snacked, I got up and walked a short distance away. Without the distractions of conversation and cheese, it was easier to sense the beauty unfolding before us. The clarity of the light, subtle variations in green, grey and silver vegetation, the improbably red sand against a pure blue sky was so quiet it felt timeless, changeless and utterly remote. It had been like this for thousands of years. It might always be so. I was a mere flicker on its surface.

When the sun disappeared the sky still glowed red, orange and gold. On the eastern horizon shadows of purple and mauve began to rise. As the light in the west slowly faded, the face of Big Red caught and reflected the remaining luminescence. The sand seemed to shine from within.

It was an effort to go back to the food and my companions. Eventually I sat down and had some brie, but something of the experience seemed to linger on. 'It gets inside you,' I'd heard some of the locals say. I was beginning to understand what they meant.

The next morning Michelle had to start work in the bakery at 8 a.m. It was only 100 metres from our house, but after breakfast I walked her to her new job. Dusty caught me kissing her goodbye at the door.

'What a romantic fellow you are,' he observed in an embarrassingly loud voice. I slunk away. At eleven o'clock I went back for morning coffee, not knowing whether Michelle would be allowed time off to join me. In her previous job she could come and go more or less as she pleased. I wasn't sure what kind of taskmaster her new boss might be.

'You're back!' Dusty bugled. 'You only said goodbye to her three hours ago.'

I blushed and muttered something about elevenses.

'Mate,' he went on, 'I have to tell you Michelle's a bloody godsend. I really mean that, and I'm an atheist.'

It was good to hear things were working out. Writing is a necessarily solitary endeavour, and for the last week Michelle had been tiptoeing around my artistic temperament like Daniel in the lion's den, but even the tiptoeing had been getting on my nerves.

Michelle was working out the back. There was a sign on the counter that said 'Ring bell for service'.

'Dusty?' I asked. 'If I ring this bell, will Michelle come running to serve me?'

He grinned. I rang the bell, and Michelle indeed came running.

'Yes,' she said. 'Can I help you?

'How much for this bell?'

'It only works in the bakery,' she muttered darkly and went off to demonstrate her new-found skills with a coffee machine.

Dusty introduced me to a bloke who was standing at the counter. Geoff Morton was manager and part-owner of Roseberth

Station. His cattleman's paw grasped my soft writer's hand. What a giveaway.

By way of conversation I tentatively asked if Geoff might be a descendant of Lyle Morton.

'He's my father,' Geoff answered.

Lyle's story was linked to the first health service in Birdsville, and the whole outback for that matter. 'Am I right he was the first —'

'European child born in Birdsville who survived,' Geoff finished my sentence. 'He's still alive, retired in Toowoomba.'

Lyle owed his existence to the first bush nurses who were sent to Birdsville by John Flynn in 1923. Up until then the mortality rate for the few European children born in the Diamantina district was 100 per cent. Two children born in the town the year before had died, as had two older children living at Annandale Station, north-west of the town.

When Lyle was born, in May 1924, he was delivered and cared for by the bush nursing sisters Francis and Boyd. They saw all the town's children through an outbreak of bronchial pneumonia later that year and by the time they were relieved, late in 1925, all the town's children, including baby Lyle, were thriving. It was an enormous tick for the new service. The nurses were the forerunners of the Royal Flying Doctor Service, launched in 1928 – the vanguard of John Flynn's vision to provide a 'mantle of safety' throughout the outback. The success of that vision was embodied in people like Geoff Morton, whose father's life (and therefore his own) may have depended on it.

Michelle brought our coffees out from behind the counter and we found a table. To my surprise, Geoff asked if he could join us. I wasn't about to refuse the man whose 5000-square-kilometre property completely surrounded Birdsville. Like David Morton, his cousin, who part-owned and managed Pandie Pandie to the south, and David Brook, who owned Adria to the west (and other stations), he ran a property that was the size of a small country. It was hard not to think of such men as Mary Durack had: kings in grass castles.

Geoff was in his mid-fifties, brown-skinned from years in the sun, and with piercing blue eyes. He was starting to show his age with grey hair around the temples, but he still had arms that would make Popeye jealous. At the rodeo I'd seen him in the station buckjump, glued to the saddle and cracking his whip with wild abandon. The crowd had loved it.

As we sipped our coffees and enjoyed our pies, I asked if fuel prices were making it hard to run such a big station. At that time, diesel was close to $2 a litre. It turned out that this was just one of Geoff's problems. 'Getting good workers is the big challenge,' he said. 'The previous CEO of the shire got a job in a mine in WA. He's paid $100 000 a year just to drive a dozer, without any of the stress of running the shire. But when he goes, everyone moves up a rung. Then there's no-one at the bottom. That's where we have a problem – getting people to come in to do the basic jobs around the place.'

We'd already noticed the employee shortage around the town. The shire had a 100 per cent employment rate, and many people were working more than one job. Michelle had been snapped up in a moment. Dusty was running the bakery and the town's power station. He also went out on desert rescues. Gus Daffy worked in the pub but also refuelled aircraft. John Hanna worked in the pub, did maintenance jobs, refuelled planes and ran the power station when Dusty was away.

The problem was even more acute on the stations. 'When we need something done now, we employ contractors,' explained Geoff. 'Most of the year we shut down and just pop our heads up when we need to. We usually work it around mustering. We brand new calves around the beginning of the year. We muster and turn off bullocks around the middle of the year and again just before Christmas.'

'You work in the heat of summer?' I asked, trying not to sound like I thought doing so must be folly.

'All year,' he answered. 'You know, after it gets into the 40s, it doesn't seem any hotter no matter what the temperature. It's just hot.'

In between times he said the cattle were left to 'paddle their own canoes'. It seemed an odd expression. I couldn't imagine cattle canoeing and from what I'd seen of the country there weren't many places where they could.

Even with the station 'shut down' there was still plenty to do. Geoff drove or flew hundreds of kilometres checking that dams, pumps, fences and yards were all maintained and working properly.

When I asked what markets his cattle went to, he answered with typical cattleman pride, 'They're the best prime bullocks you'll ever see, although no-one in Australia will ever know what they taste like. Every one of them goes to export for the Asian market. People don't understand this is some of the sweetest country around. I once put out vitamin supplements, years ago, for the stock to lick. They never touched 'em. Didn't need anything. It's that sweet. In places you can see the things are still out there, untouched.'

When I mentioned how I'd been impressed when Don Rayment was handling cattle in the bronco branding yard just by standing to one side, Geoff understood immediately. 'And if he'd stood a metre one way or the other, it wouldn't have worked. They'd have gone every way. When you're mustering, a length of a motorcycle can make all the difference. You know from experience. You can really see it from the air. And don't I let them know it if someone stuffs it up! [The plane has radio communication with those on the ground.] It can mean starting again and that takes time, and if you've got a plane in the air and people on the ground it costs a lot of money.'

Mustering by plane and motorbike had been major developments in the outback. Before the 1960s, it took many more people to run a station like Roseberth. Now with a plane, a couple of bikes and yards with wide wings, cattle could be mustered with a handful of people.

'Doesn't that assume the cattle haven't become completely wild, having never seen a human being?' I queried.

Geoff disagreed. 'Cattle aren't by nature wild. Men make them wild. Cattle are usually pretty quiet.'

We talked about what happened when the mustering was finished. Gone were the days when mobs of up to a thousand made their way down the Birdsville Track to the markets in Adelaide. In fact the track was defined by the cattle. Not long after Harry Redford pioneered the route along the Cooper to Adelaide, it was found that the waters of the Diamantina were more reliable for droving stock. It and the Georgina soon saw mobs travelling from waterhole to waterhole, and eventually bores were sunk to provide a more reliable supply.

'They all used to go down to Adelaide until the 1960s, but then as the Asian markets developed they switched to Brisbane,' Geoff told me. 'That's why the road that should be sealed is to Windorah. Sealing the road to Bedourie was a waste of money because no-one goes that way. Everything comes and goes along the Windorah Road [officially known as the Birdsville Developmental Road].'

As we sipped our coffee and I wished I'd brought my voice recorder, I asked Geoff if he'd noticed any effects of global warming in the Channel Country. In his opinion, nothing had changed. 'We've got records at Roseberth going back to the 1930s and it's the same as ever. It's a seven-year cycle. Four bad years, two we're breaking even, and then there's one where you really make your money. Every year I make a profit, but it's not a real one. Often it's from selling off cattle to save them, rather than because they're ready. People say it's the worst ever at the moment, but they forget it's been terrible before this.

'You can look at the land, and there are signs that in ancient times there were droughts that lasted a hundred years,' he paused for a moment. His knowledge of the property he'd lived and worked on his entire life ran deep. He seemed to weigh up whether he'd revealed more than he meant to, then went on. 'There's an old creek bed on Roseberth that's now covered in dunes. The creek used to flow one way and you can see how it kept the dune back. Then there was a drought that must have lasted a century and the dune got established and now the creek can't get through any more. That suggests a far worse drought than anything we've got now.'

I told Geoff that I'd thought dunes moved constantly. 'The tops of them move,' he said. 'They change all the time. Sometimes you'll go out along our southern boundary, and we've got dunes out there that are bigger than Big Red, and the fences are almost completely buried. So you bolt on new pickets and raise the fences up, and then you go back and do it again. The next thing you see is a fence post 20 feet high because the dune's shifted away.

'Have a look out at the airport. The dune at the far end keeps coming back. The council spent a fortune shifting it out of the way and a couple of years later it was back. So they spent another fortune, but this time they carted it away. A couple of years later, it was back.'

*

The bakery usually got quiet after lunch, which meant Michelle was given the afternoon off. It gave her time to start grappling with the logistics of placing a grocery order. There were two choices. She could buy from the supermarket in Quilpie, 650 kilometres east, and have it trucked out by Bonsey's Transport. Or she could buy from supermarkets in Adelaide, 1200 kilometres south, and have it brought up on Tom McKay's Trackfreight. Dusty used Trackfreight, so she decided to go with Adelaide.

She made a few phone calls and found a Woolworths that put together shopping orders and delivered them to Tom's depot for a $20 fee. Tom then charged $12 per box brought to Birdsville. The arrangement added about 50 cents to every item on the shopping list. It was a hefty premium for the privilege of living in the outback, and not for the last time we thought people in the city would scream if they had to put up with this.

Placing an order was a trial in itself. To find what she wanted, Michelle looked up the Woolworths home shopping website. The site compiles your order and delivers it to your door if you live in a major capital city. The service doesn't reach anywhere near Birdsville, but the site does list most of Woolies' stock and its prices. Michelle painstakingly went through the items. When she found something she wanted, she cut and pasted the description to a spreadsheet. The shopping cart on the site could create a shopping list, but it was more trouble than it was worth to print it out in a form that would make sense to the people who filled our orders.

When she had the shopping list ready on her laptop, she emailed it to me and I used my laptop's fax capability to send the order to the supermarket (it didn't have email). When the supermarket filled our order it debited our credit card.

All orders had to be in by 9 a.m. on the Monday of a week when Tom was doing a trip (twice a month in winter or once a month in summer). The orders were delivered to the depot on Wednesday. Tom left Adelaide on Wednesday afternoon or Thursday morning, arriving in Birdsville Thursday night or Friday morning. The schedule was subject to alteration if the Birdsville Track was closed for any reason.

This complicated arrangement was quite a shock for Michelle, an inner-city shopper accustomed to dropping in to a supermarket on the way home from work three or four times a week. Now we had to think about what we wanted to eat at least two weeks in advance.

Tom's service could deliver dry goods, vegetables and frozen foods (his truck had a refrigerated section), but we worried about the procedure for picking things up when he arrived. As it happened, the first time the truck turned up, Dusty simply drove up to our house with our dry food. He told us if anything was missing we should check at the pub. It would probably be safe in their cold store. Forewarned, we went over for the unloading of the frozen section. Outside the Birdsville servo several vehicles were gathered. Gus was on the pub's forklift, shuttling back and forth.

Over the ensuing months we were to have our groceries brought to our door by whoever was around when various parts of the truck were unloaded. They grabbed whatever was unloading and ran it around town delivering every box that had a name on it. It turned out to be just one of the ways that people in the little community helped each other out.

4

OUTBACK RESCUE

Negotiations over the back window of the Truckasaurus had reached the point where Patrick thought he'd have to order one in from Japan. I decided to see if my research skills could help out. After making a few phone calls, I located one in Mackay, halfway up the Queensland coast. A couple of extra calls later, and a mate in Sydney who'd chucked in a career as a futures trader to become a less-stressed courier agent had organised to have the window picked up.

Narelle from the post office had explained that everything couriered would eventually arrive in Quilpie, where it would be transferred to the same delivery service as the post – the twice-weekly MacAir plane or Steve Bonsey's truck. If our windscreen made it onto the plane, it might well arrive in a couple of days. If not, it might be a couple of weeks until the truck made the trip.

As predicted, the package made its way down the coast to Brisbane then out to Quilpie in under three days, tracked all the way by my mate. He rang to tell me that it should be on the plane that afternoon. And . . . it was! Considering Narelle's warning and the 3000-kilometre journey involved, we couldn't help feeling we'd won a small victory. We drove around the corner from the post office to Birdsville Auto to deliver our trophy only to find the mechanic, Patrick, was waiting for us.

'I've been trying to reach you. We're going out to recover a vehicle 20 kilometres past Poeppels Corner. Would you like to come?'

Poeppels Corner was 160 kilometres west, in the Simpson Desert at the intersection of the Queensland, Northern Territory and South Australian borders. Of course I wanted to go – getting there meant taking a track called the QAA Line, considered one of the most challenging four-wheel-drive routes in the country.

'When are you going?'

'Now. We're heading over to Neale's then we're on our way. You can go with him.'

Neale was the local policeman, Senior Constable Neale McShane. It took five minutes to grab a swag, food and water, and get to the police station. Patrick and his girlfriend, Olivia, were already there, tying down gear in the back of their four-wheel-drive ute and on the recovery trailer. Neale was putting the last of his camping gear into the police vehicle, a bush-bashed LandCruiser. I noted with satisfaction that it was exactly the same model as the Truckasaurus. After all our research and shopping around, it felt like we'd chosen the right vehicle.

It was just after 5.30 p.m., but there was no thought of waiting until morning. The intention was to tackle the dunes of the Simpson Desert during the night with the goal of reaching the stranded vehicle, which had burnt out its clutch, before making camp. We rolled out of Birdsville with the sun in our eyes and reached Big Red as the sun was going down. We paused for a moment to lower the air pressure in our front and rear tyres to 20 psi.

When we were ready to go, Neale turned his UHF radio to the channel used in the desert, channel 10. 'Vehicle westbound over Big Red,' he said, to warn anyone who might be coming up the dune from the other direction. Neale engaged high-range four-wheel drive before taking a run at Big Red and hitting the sand with the engine revving near 4000. The vehicle bounced and jolted, the steering wheel jagging savagely in his hands. Hanging on for grim death in the passenger seat beside him, I mused that this experience clearly demonstrated the value of a seatbelt. As the vehicle gradually lost momentum, though still bucking and bouncing, Neale dabbed the clutch, blipped the throttle and shifted down. The revs stayed up and the momentum held as we neared the top. That's where it got tricky.

There was a flat section, then another small sand hillock. Neale accelerated and hit it at speed. Just before we reached the top he backed off the throttle long enough for me to glimpse a sky rich in the rosy golds of an outback sunset. Then our momentum carried us over the lip. 'So this is what it feels like to drive off a cliff,' I thought as we dropped. I'd heard about someone coming over the top too fast, the vehicle digging its nose in when it hit the other side, then rolling end over end down this very dune. Fortunately, we hadn't managed to launch ourselves into space. The far side of the dune swung into view. All Neale had to do was arrest our slide down the other side and we'd both get to live. Despite being accompanied by our own private avalanche, he managed to keep the bonnet pointing down the slope. We rolled down onto the flat to give Patrick room to follow us over.

Then it was on to the second of several hundred more dunes. The next one was even bigger than Big Red. A couple of days before, watching the sunset with Dusty, Teresa and Michelle, I'd seen that party of three vehicles struggle to get over it. Some people we'd met at Big Red admitted they'd failed to get past it. They'd given up their hopes of driving across the Simpson Desert at only the second dune.

Neale tackled the monster dune first. I can't tell you how fast we were going because I was too stiff with fear to look at the speedometer. It seemed very fast. As we hit bumps of hard, compressed sand hidden beneath the softer drifting sand, the vehicle bounced wildly, slewing from side to side. As we climbed, Neale again shifted down to maintain momentum as we approached the summit. Just to make things interesting, there was a deep hole in the sand where the track should have been. A sidetrack darted sharply off to the right to avoid it. As we neared the summit, I wondered if Neale had seen it. Fortunately he had, but when he jagged to follow the track he lost speed. With the engine screaming and the tyres spinning, we were only just moving forward. Then the track grew less steep and we picked up speed. We were over.

'Gee, I hope Patrick can make it with that trailer,' Neale said as we coasted down the other side.

We found out a few moments later.

'I didn't make it up that one,' his voice came over the UHF radio. 'I'll have another go.'

We sat in the police car enjoying the colours of dusk. Then Patrick came back on the radio. 'I've managed to jackknife the trailer. Can you come and give me a hand?'

Neale sighed. 'I was really hoping he'd make it,' he said.

We turned around and headed back over the dune. With the weight of the vehicle propelling us, we began sliding down the slope and only just stopped in time to avoid hitting the stuck ute and trailer. Sure enough, the trailer was skewed right off the side of the track, the trailer bar almost at right angles to the ute.

I couldn't begin to imagine how we were going to get Patrick out. The police car couldn't winch him up the slope we'd just climbed. It seemed the only way we could get the trailer straight was to physically lift it back onto the track.

And that's just what we ended up doing. Unfortunately, the trailer wasn't the type that takes piles of leaves to the dump. It was the kind used to carry large four-wheel drives. It was *very* heavy. The four of us started bouncing and pulling at it, shifting it a few centimetres at a time. We paused for breath after half a dozen pulls then had another go. When the sand built up in front of the four tyres on the trailer's double axles, we grabbed shovels and dug it out. Then we coaxed the trailer a few centimetres closer to the track. We eventually discovered that digging extra sand away from the tyres made pulling it sideways easier, but we were tiring fast.

Then Neale had an idea. He jumped into the police car and manoeuvred it off the track, down past the ute and trailer. He did a U-turn across the face of the dune, putting the vehicle at such a lean I was glad I wasn't in the car with him. Then he came up below the trailer. He grabbed a snatch-strap and connected it to his vehicle's front recovery point ring. Patrick shackled the other end onto the back of the trailer. Now we could use the police car to help with the pulling. With a bit more digging, and a lot more grunting and straining, we finally got the trailer back behind the ute.

Now Patrick could reverse back down the dune. He started up and rolled back. In a moment, he was sliding, with no control. He got 50 metres down before the trailer jackknifed again. Neale moved up with the police car. Olivia and I moved in with our shovels. It took thirty minutes to get the ute off the dune, by which time it was dark.

'Righto, Patrick,' Neale said when we were all at the bottom of the dune. 'You want to give it another go?'

'I think I should give it a bigger run-up this time,' he said.

Neale and I stood beside the police car at the bottom of the dune that I was starting to think of as the nemesis for desert adventurers. As Patrick and Olivia turned and headed far out onto the large smooth plain between Big Red and the dune, I did a quick mental calculation of how long it was taking to get over one dune and multiplied it by the many dunes ahead of us. It worked out to be a very long night.

Patrick's headlights were just a dot out on the plain when he commenced his second attempt. As he got closer, the engine's roar got higher as well as louder. By the time he reached the base of the dune, the trailer rattling and banging and his headlights and driving lights lashing wildly, he was a juggernaut.

The ute hit the bottom of the dune with extraordinary violence, bouncing and crashing up the long slope. It and the trailer slithered up the rough track like an enormous metallic snake, losing momentum as it went. He couldn't have been halfway up before it was clear he wasn't going to make it. The vehicle was slowing noticeably and the summit was still far above. Patrick got past the point he'd reached on his first attempt, the ute's engine howling, but he was down to a crawl. A little higher and the vehicle began to dig in. He stopped before he got bogged.

Neale and I watched from the bottom as Patrick started backing and sliding down the dune, the brake lights glowing in a cloud of red dust. The trailer slithered along behind the vehicle for a while and then jackknifed. We knew what to do. Back up we went. Neale and Patrick attached the snatch-strap. Olivia and I did our digging. My soft writer's hands were blistering up nicely, but there was nothing to be done about it. Fortunately, we'd perfected the art of extracting a jackknifed trailer from a sand dune, and it only took a few minutes to get the ute back down onto the flat.

It seemed unlikely that the ute and trailer were going to conquer Nemesis Dune, but Patrick was undaunted. He drove back out into the middle of the plain, turned, his headlights shining at us, and charged at the dune again. As the ute hurtled towards us like a runaway train, Neale was barracking beside me, 'Come on, Patrick! Come on!'

Out beyond Birdsville, Neale's words had great resonance. More than fifty years ago, the mailman of the Birdsville Track, Tom Kruse, was the star of John Heyer's film *The Back of Beyond*. In a memorable scene, he charges a sand dune in his Chevrolet Blitz truck. As he does he beats the side of the vehicle, exhorting it to make an extra effort, and growls, 'Come on! Come on!'

Over the years, the Birdsville Track has been upgraded substantially. The treacherous Inside Track has been supplemented with a less flood-prone Outside Track, which although unsealed is usually suitable for two-wheel-drive vehicles. As such, the era of epic battles to service the needs of people in this part of the outback had passed. Or had it? Standing at the bottom of Nemesis Dune, Neale's words were an echo of Heyer's film. The circumstances may have changed, but the challenge of the sandhills was still there, especially when it came to rescuing tourists stuck in the desert. I couldn't help feeling I was having that much-sought-after thing, an authentic outback experience. Watching the ute hit the bottom of the enormous sand dune for the third time, apart from all the digging, it was thrilling to make the connection.

As the lights of the vehicle illuminated the billowing dust above us, Neale and I willed Patrick on. To no avail. He started to bog once again and was forced to stop. He slithered back down; the trailer jackknifed. We dug him out and pulled him down. Unnoticed in all the digging, the blisters on my hands burst. After his fourth and thankfully final attempt, they started to bleed.

Neale suggested Plan B. It turned out there was a long way round to the site of the breakdown. It involved heading back over Big Red to Birdsville, then driving 200 kilometres down the Birdsville Outside Track to Warburton Crossing, where we'd camp for the night. In the morning we would drive 200 kilometres up the less-duned Warburton Track to Poeppels Corner.

The first challenge was getting back over Big Red. We decided to take the dune at a lower point a kilometre south, called Little Red. It wasn't as high as Nemesis Dune, but when Neale tackled it in the police car we knew we were going to have trouble. We hit very soft sand at the top of the dune and the vehicle all but stopped. When the front wheels got over the lip of the dune we were barely moving, even though the engine was revving furiously, sand and dust flying all around us. Then, with a slight dip, the vehicle's angle changed, we picked up speed, and with a sigh of relief from both of us, we were over.

'Patrick won't make it over here,' I said.

'Hopefully we can winch him,' Neale replied.

Sure enough, Patrick's ute bogged about 10 metres short of the summit. Once again, Olivia and I dug the sand out from around the tyres while the boys hooked up the cable from Neale's winch.

As I dug, I reflected on how much I'd looked forward to Birdsville, and to a publishing project that was more 'hands on' than my usual research work digging through aged reference books and newspaper clippings in musty libraries. After two hours of digging sand, those libraries began to look pretty attractive.

Winching the ute was a tricky business. With the extra baggage of the trailer, it tended to stay where it was and pull the police car towards the edge. While Neale worked the winch I stood on the police car's brake while revving the engine to give more power to the winch. Patrick tried to help with some drive from the ute, but had to be careful not to dig its tyres in. When the police car got too close to the edge, we stopped, payed out some more cable, reversed the police car back from the edge of the dune, then took up the winching again.

Eventually we coaxed the ute over the dune and, with a sigh of relief, headed back to Birdsville to refuel for the 800-kilometre round trip that lay ahead. Back in town I debated whether I'd already had enough of digging, blisters and bouncing over sand dunes to make a warm, comfortable bed look very appealing. With considerable effort I decided to see it through.

One of the rules of outback travel may have been 'Don't drive at night' (it's not a question of will you hit a kangaroo or cow, it's a question of when), but rescue missions are the exception. Fortunately, the 200-kilometre drive down the famous Birdsville Track turned out to be an anticlimax – the only things that appeared in the headlights were a red kangaroo and some cattle on the road. For me the disappointment was that the scenery along the way was invisible. The track itself was in remarkably good condition, smooth and well-made. Back in Birdsville, people had said it was more like a dirt highway than a track, and I had to agree.

Nevertheless, this was one of the most famous roads in the outback. It had once been the difficult and dangerous stock route for millions of cattle on their way to the railhead at Marree, 500 kilometres south, and bound for the markets in Adelaide. It was also the route used by Afghani and Indian cameleers, whose trains of up to a hundred beasts wound slowly over the dunes and stretched across shimmering gibber plains, carrying goods and supplies between the two towns. As recently as the 1950s, even the police patrolled this area on camels, moving through country far from any road to search for missing persons or stock thieves. It was also a place where the unwary or ill-prepared still perished.

'About four years ago, a woman died just out there,' Neale pointed out into the darkness, referring to the death I'd already heard about. 'She didn't have a radio or sat phone. She eventually starved to death.'

The woman had set off on a camping holiday in April 2005 and was reported missing in June. She was found at the end of October. Newspaper reports referred to 'skeletal remains'. In February of the same year, another vehicle, a yellow Ford Laser, was found abandoned on the edge of the desert near Big Red. The owner, who left what can be construed as a suicide note in the vehicle, has never been found. The car is still outside the police station in Birdsville.

It was almost 1 a.m. when we found the Warburton Track, and it really was a track – narrow, corrugated and potholed. Where it crossed Warburton Creek, it dropped sharply into the dry creek bed then climbed up the other side. Once again, wearing seatbelts ensured we didn't hit the roof on the bigger bumps.

On the far side of the creek we found a place to camp. Neale turned on the side lights of the police car to illuminate our campsite then he, Patrick and Olivia rolled out their swags. Neale took a spot beside the police car. Not having camped in a swag for years, I'd have felt safer between him and the vehicle, but I wasn't quick enough. Olivia and Patrick rolled out their swags on top of the trailer. They didn't say what was on the ground that they didn't want to spend the night with.

I'd assumed that after everything we'd been through we'd go straight to bed. But no, Neale and I gathered firewood while Patrick and Olivia cracked a few beers and began meal preparations. Soon we had a fire going, and were tucking into plates of chops, bread and tomato sauce. After the meal we sat around in deckchairs, talking. I was exhausted, yet despite a long night of digging and driving, none of the others seemed tired. 'Have another beer, mate,' they said every time I suggested I might turn in. There was no way I was going to let them think I couldn't hack the pace. We didn't go to bed until three.

For reasons best known to my overtired mind, I kept imagining the footfall of a wild camel. They were common in the area and I feared what might happen if one wandered into our camp. The upside was that after the fire died down, I could look up and see a night sky dusted from horizon to horizon with billions of stars. The others were asleep and all of the night's immensity was mine alone to contemplate. There were no camels.

Eventually I drifted off, although had I known that in his swag Neale was being bitten by what he thinks was a scorpion (he didn't tell me until months later, when it still hadn't healed), I wouldn't have slept at all. Either that or I'd have curled up on top of the trailer with Patrick and Olivia, no matter how much of an imposition it might have been.

Despite the late night we were all up at dawn. I kindled the fire and soon the billy was boiling while we rolled up our swags. After a cuppa and a bowl of cereal, the sun peeked over the horizon and we headed off. Poeppels was still 200 kilometres to the north.

The track at first crossed Clifton Hills Station. It was sandy but there were few dunes. In the distance a soft white dune floated like an improbable sculpture on the shimmering plain. Its smooth surface was like skin and the voluptuous rise and fall of its curves was surprisingly sensuous. Perhaps I was more tired than I realised . . .

As we left Clifton Hills and entered the Simpson Desert Regional Reserve, the colours and landscape shifted. What I'd thought had been desert became even more forlorn. What trees there were looked like they'd been burned, but no fire could travel through such sparsely vegetated country. It could only be the sun, scorching them leafless and leaving them charred. We negotiated a handful of small white dunes then came to a claypan. The surface of the pan was perfectly smooth but for the tyre tracks of motorists who'd decided to break the monotony of their drive by risking becoming bogged in the midst of such desolation. The road followed the eastern side of the claypan. On the western side an immense red dune presented a formidable barrier to the Simpson Desert beyond.

It's ironic that a place so dry should be named after a washing machine manufacturer. A. A. Simpson sponsored Cecil Madigan's 1939 expedition that was to traverse the heart of what became known as the Simpson Desert, from Andado Station on the western side 500 kilometres to Birdsville on the east. The names associated with the expedition were part of the legend of the outback. Truck driver Tom Kruse delivered the men and supplies to Andado. The camels were selected with the help of Bejah Dervish, one of the greatest of Central Australia's cameleers. Bejah had been invited on the expedition as cameleer, but at seventy-six was too old for such an undertaking. His son Jack went instead. Said Madigan in his book *Crossing the Dead Heart*: 'In Jack Bejah and Tom Kruse it was felt that we had the best camel man and the best outback motor driver the country could provide, and time proved that our confidence in them was justified.'

We drove on along the Warburton Track, following a dingo's prints for kilometre after kilometre. There was no sign of tyre tracks and it looked like no-one had come this way for months. We were now well into the Simpson Desert, but still nowhere near the edge of Constable McShane's area of responsibility. As Birdsville is the nearest police station to the south-east corner of the Northern Territory and the north-east corner of South Australia, he has authority to act in all three states. He is responsible for an area of nearly 250 000 square kilometres – a single policeman for 3 per cent of Australia's landmass. His beat is slightly larger than the state of Victoria, or the United Kingdom.

Neale was a heavy-set bloke in his mid-fifties, with short-cropped greying hair. Despite all our efforts on the dunes the night before, his police uniform, which he'd worn throughout, was still neat and tidy. As he drove along the rough track, his driving skill became abundantly clear. When a corner turned out to be tighter than he thought, he didn't panic. He just kept turning without touching the brakes, even though the wheels on my side were off the track. The vehicle ran a little wide, which was worrying for me, but it was of no consequence in a place where there's nothing to hit. And it was a lot better than if he'd hit the brakes, which could have caused the vehicle to roll.

Neale's driving was punctuated by an occasional heavy sigh. I wondered if it was prompted by some haunting memory from his thirty-two years as a policeman, first in Victoria and then Queensland. Perhaps he was pondering the logistics of helping the people out beyond Poeppels Corner with a rescue vehicle that couldn't pull the skin off custard. Most likely it was a response to the tedium of driving that was such a big part of his job.

At least he was happy to talk about his life as we sped along. He'd been raised in Byron Bay, on the north coast of New South Wales, and still had a house there. He'd worked in locations as exotic as

Cooktown, ploughing through mud to rescue cyclone victims, dealing with the after-effects of storms that cut power to the entire community, and trying to teach locals and visitors that crocodiles really should be taken seriously. He'd gone on to become Prosecuting Sergeant at Charleville. The job, however, took its toll.

'I was getting tired of puttin' away low-lifes,' he explained. 'Some of the sex cases were pretty terrible, you know. Then I saw the job in Birdsville. It was advertised three times before I put my hand up. It meant taking a demotion, but there was a remote location allowance and a lot less stress. And there's a lot of other things you can do to make up your income.'

Multi-tasking was a familiar story in the outback. Apart from his police duties, Neale was Birdsville's weather observer, locust counter, meter reader and telephone box–money collector (the town has six public phones). He was cleaning the school until they found someone else to do it. All things considered, some of the locals reckoned he was the highest-paid uniformed policeman in the state.

He was married with three children, but his wife was still living in Charleville, where their youngest son was finishing high school. His daughter was at university. His eldest son had spent three years travelling and was settling down to a building apprenticeship.

At around eleven we stopped for what Neale called 'smoko' in a small grove of Georgina gidgee (*Acacia georginae*). They had to be tough to survive in a place like this, but they were not only alive, they were in flower. The police car was making good time, but the ute was labouring with the trailer and we kept having to stop to wait for Patrick and Olivia to catch up.

While we stood in the shade of the gidgees, sipping soft drink, Neale gave me the first of many helpful pieces of advice. 'Watch out for these trees,' he said. 'A lot of people turn around and get a stick in the eye. You've always got to be careful, especially out here. You always need to be thinking about what you're doing because you're a long way from a hospital if you get a serious injury. If we have to evacuate you it can take a long time and get very expensive.' (It costs the RFDS around $7000 to make an emergency flight to Birdsville.)

The road continued north and entered a maze of small red dunes. A couple proved a bit of a challenge for the police car, but after we'd knocked the tops off, the ute managed to cross them easily. The police car was literally cutting a road for the rescue vehicle following behind.

Near Poeppels Corner we missed the turn-off to the French Line road (named after the French Petroleum Company that cut it through the dunes as part of oil exploration in the 1960s) because the sign had been souvenired. When we realised we'd come too far, we doubled back and worked out where it was using the police car's GPS. The turn-off climbed from the Warburton Track straight up the face of a very steep dune.

It took one attempt in the police vehicle for us to realise this dune was going to be too much for the ute and trailer. Neale and Patrick decided to leave the ute and drive the police car the remaining 20-odd kilometres to the stricken vehicle. Patrick parked the ute on the edge of a claypan and locked up in the cab any rescue equipment that might prove tempting to passers-by. While he was doing that I collected a litter of water bottles that were strewn about the track. They were all full and must have fallen from a vehicle as it tackled the steep dune at the start of the French Line.

'You're a good fella for doing that,' Neale said.

'I reckon the desert looks better without 'em,' I replied.

The French Line's first dune turned out to be the hardest. The police car barely made it up, especially now that it was crammed with four people and the gear Patrick and Olivia didn't want to leave in the ute. After that it was a couple of easy dunes to Poeppels.

'We might as well take a look,' Neale said as he turned off to the car park. 'You might never come back here again.'

No-one argued. We'd been travelling for the last eighteen hours to get this far. A few minutes more weren't going to make much difference to the people we were rescuing.

At the car park we came upon a 'tag-along tour'. Neale knew the leader of the tour, Harry Osborn, and the owner of the vehicle that had come along for support, David Cox, from the Mount Dare Hotel. Mount Dare was the first fuel, food and beer stop on the other side of the Simpson.

Harry and David had come across the desert from the western side and were headed for Birdsville, via the route we'd originally planned to take, the QAA Line. When it came to four-wheel drives, Cox's little vehicle was remarkable. It had very wide sand tyres, with 'bead locks' that meant they could be deflated to very low pressures that gave even more traction crossing the dunes. The bead locks reduced the risk of pulling the tyre off the rim when the pressures were so low.

Harry, David and their guests were a bit surprised to see the police car pull up, but Neale soon explained what we were up to. The tag-along tour had passed the broken-down vehicle and confirmed it was less than 20 kilometres from Poeppels. Being at the intersection of three states naturally led to the tag-along people making jokes about being able to escape from Neale by making a run for it out of Queensland. Neale happily joined in.

'Nah,' he said with a grin, 'I can chase you wherever you go. And if I can't, I'll make a phone call and they'll be waitin' for you wherever you go.'

He was right about that. When I'd asked him about home security in Birdsville, he'd explained that the last time they'd had a crime was two years ago, when someone stole radios and driving lights from several vehicles. The thieves could only go one of three ways: 200 kilometres north to Bedourie, 500 kilometres south to Marree or 400 kilometres east to Windorah. The time it took to drive to any of those places was ample for the police at the other end to set up a road-block for the suspect vehicle. As it happened, the car didn't turn up.

After a while, the Marree policeman began to wonder if the thieves might have had some car trouble. He went for a drive up the Birdsville Track. Sure enough, he found them pulled over on the side of the road.

'Those fellas weren't real bright,' Neale said. 'The one thing they didn't steal was petrol.'

It wasn't long before the tag-along people at Poeppels asked if they could get their pictures taken with the Birdsville policeman. Neale was only too happy to oblige. He posed for photo after photo, smiling broadly. When it came to police public relations, Neale was pure gold.

While he charmed the tourists, the rest of us finished taking our own photos and climbed back into the police car. I sat looking at David Cox's capable-looking vehicle. When it came to vehicles towing other vehicles over dunes, his looked the real deal. After a while, I turned to Patrick. 'Do you reckon there's any chance David could use his car to help us?'

Patrick sat in the car for a couple of minutes. Then he opened the door and strolled over to have a chat with David.

When Neale was finished shaking hands and having his back slapped he came back to the car.

'What's Patrick doing?'

'Negotiating,' Olivia replied.

Patrick came back. 'He has to talk to Harry,' he said.

David's first responsibility was to accompany Harry's tour, but Harry was good enough to spare him and his vehicle for a couple of hours to help us out. David, who'd brought his toddler daughter and brother with him, said he'd finish his lunch and be right behind us.

Beyond Poeppels Corner the dunes weren't particularly high, but they were crammed together in groups of a dozen or so. In places the red cores of the dunes were exposed, the almost rock-hard sand carved by the wind into pillars and treacherous holes. From time to time we came to another claypan. Like the dunes they stretched into the distance to the south-east and north-west.

After 15 kilometres of driving up dunes, sliding down the other side, then tackling the next, the novelty was wearing off. Apparently, the scenery continued like this for hundreds of kilometres. Although I'd managed to achieve two of my ambitions for desert driving (up Big Red and out to Poeppels Corner) within my first two weeks in Birdsville, my third goal, driving across the Simpson, was rapidly losing its appeal. The dunes were relentless. All of us started searching the road ahead for any sign of our stricken travellers. They couldn't appear soon enough.

At last, at about one o'clock in the afternoon, we caught the glint of vehicles in the distance. We slipped down the face of yet another dune and turned into a campsite with three vehicles. Up on the next dune, we saw the people we'd struggled for twenty hours to reach. They were playing golf.

While introductions were being made, Patrick ducked under the broken-down vehicle and confirmed that the clutch had gone. The owner, Graham, a retired lecturer from Toowoomba, and his wife Adrianne, insisted that they hadn't been riding the clutch or doing anything that might burn it out prematurely. The hundreds of dunes the vehicle had traversed had simply taken their toll.

It couldn't have helped that the vehicle was crammed with gear. There was no room in the back seats for passengers. Even the space in the two front seats was reduced by maps, books, binoculars, radios, a GPS and a plethora of other 'must-have' equipment. The roof racks were jammed with canisters of extra fuel, tyres, shovels and more gear.

Graham, Adrianne and their friends had been planning to drive all the way across Australia to Broome, in Western Australia, which to a degree justified their heavy loading, but there's a limit to how much a vehicle can take, especially when it's working hard in rough terrain. Under the circumstances it might have paid to go without a few luxuries, such as the golf clubs.

When we'd been equipping the Truckasaurus for a year in Birdsville, we'd compiled a long list of all the things we could get for it: driving lights, electric winch, snorkel, HF radio, awning, fridge, suspension lift kit, diff locks, tailgate tyre holder and so on. Talking to people in Birdsville before we bought anything, we'd limited ourselves to a bullbar, a UHF radio, a compressor for pumping up tyres, a puncture repair kit and a snatch-strap. After the experience of driving out to Poeppels Corner there was only one more thing I wanted: a proper shovel (to replace our folding shovel, which I now realised was little more than a toy).

The good thing about rescuing folk with all the luxuries was the tea and delicious fruit cake we were offered while waiting for David Cox to turn up. The milk for the tea came fresh from the fridge installed in the back of the broken-down vehicle. We sipped and snacked while trying to lighten the load in Graham and Adrianne's vehicle by piling what we could into the police car or the other vehicles (which were planning to continue across the desert).

David Cox's vehicle turned out to be a godsend. After he'd hooked up, we set off ahead in the police car and listened on the UHF radio as Graham and David talked to each other. 'That was easy,' Graham said after the first dune. It was the same after the next, and the next. It took less than an hour to tow Graham and Adrianne's car back to the trailer. On the last dune Olivia and I hopped out of the police car and waited on top to get some photos. As David's vehicle climbed the dune, towing 2 tonnes through sand, his tyres didn't spin once.

Getting the vehicle onto the trailer proved more difficult. First, the trailer winch wouldn't work, so David had to shackle back on and tow the vehicle onto the trailer. When it got to the top of the ramp, it looked like it wouldn't fit. There was a moment where it seemed we'd just driven 400 kilometres only to find we didn't have the right trailer. A closer look revealed there was a centimetre to spare on both sides. We just had to get the vehicle dead centre.

Once the car was on the trailer the next job was to cover the entire front end with padding to stop stones being thrown up and damaging it. A section of carpet from the ute went over the bonnet and windscreen. Groundsheets were spread over them, folded down the sides of the vehicle, and taped and tied down.

We were ready to go, but Patrick was feeling nervous. 'I'm not sure how we'll go gettin' over some of those dunes with a car on,' he said.

It was late afternoon and there were some tricky spots along the 200-kilometre route ahead of us. 'Mate,' I said, mustering all the experience I'd gained in twenty-four hours of desert rescuing, 'I've got meself a shovel and I'm not afraid to use it.'

And with that we were off, the police car in the lead transporting Graham and Adrianne. Olivia was with Patrick in the ute.

The first sticky bit was a red dune not far from the turn-off to Poeppels Corner. The track climbed up the face at an angle then turned right sharply at the top, to avoid a steep bluff of sand. We got up it in the police car, but knew that it was going to be a tester for Patrick. Fortunately, we could radio to him to tell him exactly which way to go when he hit the top. We stopped clear of the dune and got out to see how he'd go.

Patrick charged the dune, a brave thing to do with the added weight of a vehicle of around 2 tonnes sitting on the trailer behind him. As he hit the bottom of the dune and commenced the climb, the trailer appeared to be steering the ute as much as the ute was steering the trailer. With the engine revving to the max, Patrick reached the top of the dune and turned blind to follow the track. He went a touch too far and grazed a tussock, reducing his momentum.

As the trailer topped the rise, sand spurted from the ute's tyres and it began to sink. He cut the throttle before he was completely bogged. A metre more and he'd have made it.

'Almost,' Neale said. 'I reckon we can snatch you the last bit.'

The principle of the snatch-strap is similar to a rubber band. If the recovery vehicle was simply connected to the bogged one by a static tow rope, when the police car started pulling, its tyres would just spin. Instead, the snatch-strap (made of a material similar to that used in seatbelts, but with a great deal of stretch) is shackled between the two vehicles. Neale backs up to the ute so there is plenty of slack. He then accelerates away, gaining momentum. As the webbing pulls tight, the energy builds up in the strap, eventually creating a pull so great that the ute springs forward, even with another vehicle on a trailer behind it.

The process sounds dangerous and it is. If the strap snaps or a shackle connecting it to a vehicle comes off, the sudden release of energy into a wildly whipping strap can be lethal for both drivers and any bystanders. It's a similar story with winching – where the rescue vehicle is anchored and uses brute force applied to a steel cable to pull the other vehicle free. Those of us who could were standing well clear.

On Neale's first pull the ute only moved a few centimetres, but it was better than nothing. As Neale reversed for another go, I grabbed the snatch-strap and pulled it in to keep the slack away from his rear tyres. On the next pull, Neale was a touch more aggressive and the ute popped out like a cork from a bottle. We unbolted the snatch-strap, threw it in the back of the ute and we were on our way.

The next couple of dunes were easy, and then there was a long stretch of track with no dunes at all. The sun was setting as we passed the long claypan we'd seen in the morning. Golden light shone over the distant dune and broad expanse of the claypan. We paused to take photos while Patrick caught up.

It was dusk, night hues rising in the east, an orange sky fading in the west, when we got to the next difficult stretch. There were no dunes, but the track traversed long stretches of deep, fine white sand. Each one threatened to sap the ute's momentum. On one stretch we'd stopped on firmer ground and watched as Patrick almost made it, only to bog metres from us on a slight rise. We hooked him up, dug a bit, and pulled him out. Then it was on to the next dune.

One of the curious features of the track was that there was no sign that we'd driven along the same road that morning. There'd been only a light breeze blowing all day, but it had shifted the superfine sand enough to obscure our tyre marks. That morning I'd thought a vehicle couldn't have been on the road for months. Now I realised that vehicular tracks could disappear in a matter of hours.

After dark, the lack of tracks threw us into confusion. We were driving along when we came to another dune, barely 5 metres high, and the road disappeared. We pulled up and climbed the dune to see where the road had gone. On the other side, at the bottom of the dune, was the track. During the day the wind had drifted the sand to completely cover the way over.

We radioed Patrick to tell him to wait for us to clear this dune first. He was some way behind. When we saw his lights, Neale flashed the police car's lights to show him where we were.

Quick as they come, we heard Patrick joking on the radio: 'The min min lights! They're scarin' me!'

'You better give this one a good run-up, Pat,' Neale told him. 'We'll let you know when we're clear.'

Neale gunned the police car's engine and we scampered up the face of the dune. As the wheels dug into the incredibly soft sand, and the vehicle slowed, Neale shifted down to keep the revs up and we made it to the top. We slid down the other side and pulled up well away from the dune.

'Reckon he'll struggle on that one,' I said, getting out to watch his attempt. Neale radioed Pat again and gave him a heads-up about the conditions.

From the far side of the dune we heard the rising roar of the ute's approach. The dust floating in the air from our passage over the dune brightened in the intensity of the ute's driving lights. Then came the crash and rattle of the vehicle as it hit the base of the dune and charged up, headlight beams slashing the night sky. The whine of the engine didn't drop as Pat kept the power on all the way. Then the ute and trailer literally exploded through the top of the dune, lights and sand and dust spraying in all directions, landing on the other side with a bone-jarring slam. If there was any more spectacular sight in the desert, you could sell tickets.

'That was incredible!' I shouted as Patrick and Olivia, somewhat shaken by the experience, tumbled out of the vehicle. 'Patrick the human spear!'

However, conquering the dune came at a price. Patrick checked the trailer and saw that the heavy-duty tow-ball mount had almost sheared off the back of the ute. If it went completely, which was quite likely with more dunes ahead, the trailer and vehicle would be stranded. Patrick was undaunted. He pulled a piece of chain out of the ute, jacked the trailer up and used it to shackle the trailer's draw-bar directly to the ute's chassis. When he lowered the jack, the chain took up the strain, reducing the load on the tow-ball linkages.

A bit further on another dune gave us trouble. Patrick gave it every-thing, but backed off a touch as he got to the top, rather than have 5 tonnes of combined weight airborne again. He lost momentum and while the ute made it over, the trailer and vehicle were left hanging on the far side. Patrick couldn't reverse, and it was unlikely we'd pull the heavy trailer up and over with the police car and snatch-strap.

'We'll have to dig the top of the dune out,' I said. Admittedly, all I'd learned about desert rescue so far was how to shovel sand, so I was surprised when my experienced colleagues agreed with my assessment. The job was made more difficult by the fine, almost liquid quality of the sand – as we dug, it slid back in. So we had to start by clearing the sand back from the sides of the trailer before digging it out from around the trailer bar and wheels. We used the two shovels from the ute, and one that belonged to Graham and Adrianne, and dug until the whole bar was free. When anyone got tired, someone else took over. My blisters opened up again, but by now I was so tired I barely noticed.

At last we thought we'd dug enough. The police car was hooked up and ready to go. We all retired to a safe distance as Neale accelerated away. The snatch-strap pulled tight. The police car slowed then stopped. The trailer didn't budge. The angle of the ute relative to the trailer meant it tended to pull the trailer down, into the dune, rather than up and over it.

'More digging, people,' I said, getting stuck in with the shovel. Olivia was on the other side doing the same. Graham was digging beside me. Neale took over when I tired; Patrick took over when Olivia did. We moved a prodigious amount of sand. Only then did we have another attempt at snatching Patrick through.

The first attempt shifted the trailer a few centimetres, but at least it *did* shift. Neale reversed up to the ute, and got ready for another snatch-strap run. Again the trailer moved a few centimetres. Now it was far enough forward that we could scoop a bit of the sand that had piled up down the face of the dune. He charged off again and this time when the trailer moved, the whole face of the dune in front of it moved as well.

'You're moving mountains, Neale,' I called. 'Give it another go.'

We didn't bother with shovelling. We watched as Neale reversed, then powered down the dune, letting the equipment do the work. The ute and trailer pulled free.

'Thank goodness for that,' said Olivia, as she flipped her shovel back into the ute. As I did the same, a thought struck me.

'Olivia, what's it been like going over all those dunes in the passenger seat?' I asked her.

'On that last one,' she replied, 'I was determined to keep my eyes open.'

It made me realise that at times she must have been terrified, yet she hadn't said a thing.

The dunes got easier after that and when we got to the boundary of Clifton Hills Station, we knew we were through the worst. While we held the gate open, waiting for Patrick to catch up, I remarked to Neale, Graham and Adrianne, 'I never imagined I'd say this, but gee I'll be glad when we get back to the Birdsville Track.'

After what we'd just been through, they all agreed with me.

It was after 10 p.m. when we reached the Track. From there it was a slow crawl back to Birdsville. Neale looked exhausted, but when I offered to help with the driving he told me I wasn't allowed to drive the police car.

The heavy load on the trailer meant Patrick couldn't keep up with the police car, so from time to time Neale stopped so he could catch up and we could be sure he was okay. At one of our stops we saw another vehicle heading towards us. The vehicle, an odd-looking little bus, pulled up when it saw a police car beside the road, in the middle of the night, in the middle of nowhere.

'Any trouble?' asked a bearded face dimly lit by dash light.

'We're waiting for a vehicle coming up behind us,' Neale explained. 'Where are you off to?'

'Just looking for a place to pull over for the night,' the driver said.

'Anywhere along here will be fine,' Neale said. 'Just make sure you're well off the road in case anyone driving along loses control. You want to be out of harm's way.'

'Thanks for that,' the driver said.

'You on your own?' Neale asked.

'No, I've got a hitchhiker with me.'

The driver continued on his way, little realising how much information the local policeman had managed to glean from a quick chat.

It was after 2 a.m. when we rolled into Birdsville. We passed the pub, locked up and completely dark. 'Looks like we've missed happy hour,' Neale said.

There'd been several times during the last few hours when a beer would have gone down very easily. Now all I wanted was bed. When Neale dropped me at home I left my gear in his car. It could wait until tomorrow. Neale took Graham and Adrianne around to the police station where they could sleep in the barracks. I went inside and showered off some of the dust and grime of the last forty-eight hours.

When I finally crawled into bed, Michelle muttered in the darkness, 'How was the rescue?'

I managed to say 'exhausting' before falling into a very deep sleep.

The next morning, Michelle had to walk to work on her own. It was all I could do to make it down to the bakery for eleven o'clock coffee. After that I went around to see Patrick about the Truckasaurus's window.

'How did you sleep last night?' he asked when he saw me.

'I was so tired,' I replied, 'but when I got in, Michelle wanted to have sex. I said, "Okay, but just for one hour".'

He looked at me in disbelief, and then burst out laughing.

'How about you?' I asked.

'We went out on another rescue this morning,' he replied. 'A vehicle towing a trailer on the Birdsville Track hit some bulldust and bent its chassis.'

I'd already been impressed by the stamina, persistence and ingenuity of the outback people I'd met. The thought of Patrick going out again when he must have been exhausted raised him even higher in my estimation.

Meanwhile, all the rescues meant the Truckasaurus's window was slipping down Patrick's list of priorities. Things were even worse for Graham and Adrianne, who had to get a new clutch freighted out. A clutch is very heavy, and might not be permitted on the plane. To make matters worse, Patrick and Olivia's visas were about to expire and they had to fly back to Ireland in a couple of days. Patrick was the only mechanic in Birdsville capable of replacing a clutch. If the clutch didn't make it on the plane, their vehicle might be stuck in Birdsville indefinitely. Around town they became known as the Maroonees.

5

BUSH PILOT

Back in Birdsville, Michelle was taking to the hospitality industry like a duck to water. When she got to work at eight, she started slicing fresh loaves ready for the first customers. When the doors opened, she served at the counter, made coffees, cooked breakfasts and prepared sandwiches. Every morning at eleven I went down for my coffee break, which I was learning all the locals called 'smoko'. I had tried all of Dusty's pies and liked them so much that I couldn't resist having one with my coffee. Between the temptations of the bakery and the lack of exercise – back in Sydney I used to race yachts up to four times a week – my waistline was expanding.

Like the pub, the bakery was one of Birdsville's social hubs. It saw a regular stream of locals, many of whom helped out when the place was busy by taking their cups and plates and washing them up. It was a common sight to see Neale, Birdsville's policeman, doing the dishes in the kitchen.

A steady flow of tourists came and went, and Dusty said it was shaping up to be a good season. One morning two colourful carloads pulled up at the bakery. The men looked like Arab sheiks, dressed in kaftans and red-and-white head scarves. They were from Yemen and really took a shine to Dusty's curried camel pies. They bought an entire tray to take with them.

On another afternoon Michelle got talking to a young pilot, Luke Pedersen, who flew the two-day mail run from Port Augusta to the stations along the Birdsville Track and beyond. He was at a loose end, overnighting in town before doing the return leg in the morning. Michelle invited him to come with us on a drive to some hills north of town to watch the sunset. Rather than sit in the pub twiddling his thumbs, Luke jumped at the chance.

As we drove I asked him about his job. He flew what is considered the longest postal route in the world, more than 2000 kilometres. It took him two days a week to provide a service that had once taken the mailmen of the Birdsville Track weeks on horseback, by camel or truck.

Luke had none of the 'she'll be right' larrikinism one might expect of a bush pilot. He was a well-groomed young man with the quiet intensity of someone who has his goals clearly in sight. As we drove along, and he talked about his life, it became clear that he'd experienced a steep learning curve.

He was originally from Brisbane and had always dreamed of flying. When he left school, though, he didn't have the patience or the substantial amount of money required for pilot training, especially without the guarantee of a job at the end. He travelled overseas, returned to do a business degree then found work in finance. Nearly ten years later there was just one problem. 'The longer I spent in the office,' he said, 'the more I watched the aeroplanes flying past the window thinking "gotta be me".'

Two years later, aged twenty-eight, he qualified for his commercial pilot's licence. A year later, in 2007, he landed his first job as a pilot. Aerial mustering. I did a double-take. 'Your first job was aerial mustering?'

'It's a lot of people's first job,' he replied, as though it was nothing special. 'It's remarkable the number of hours that a lot of the kids mustering out here would do. But the hours are insignificant compared to the difficulty of the work they're doing.'

'Isn't it one of the most dangerous kinds of flying there is?'

'Outside aerobatics, definitely. Some of it is aerobatics, but it doesn't have to be. The people who teach you, most of whom are station managers who've been around for a long time, will say that you don't need to be on the cattle all the time. Basically, if you put noise behind them, they will move. Planes will only work in open country. You need choppers for thick stuff, so obviously if the ground cover is dense you wouldn't even try it with a plane. If the cattle are stubborn, sure, go in and bomb them, come back off and circle around behind them for a while until they're moving in the right direction.

'After you've been in on the same mob of cattle five, six, seven times – and it's not like in a chopper where you can just sit on them – you get one crack then you've gotta come right back around and then find them again and then have another crack.'

'How low do you fly?'

'Between 10 and 700 feet.'

'Ten?' I couldn't help sounding incredulous.

'I was seriously worried I was going to rip a wheel off on one of the cow's heads last year,' he replied. 'And that was one of those points where I just thought, "Okay, ease up. Take a deep breath. Have a drink of water." One of the boys flying this year demolished a wing on one of the planes. I don't know how he managed to land, but the wing had dents all the way down the leading edge so it was probably branches rather than cattle. He was a very lucky boy. If you hit something with your wing and you're in a high-wing plane, there's more chance of doing serious damage as the rest of the plane is obviously lower. The managers out here have seen a lot of people die. Kidman's [the cattle company he worked for] had a fleet of Cessna 182s. By the time I got there, there were none left because they'd all crashed. So the rules are written in blood I guess.'

We turned off the road onto a track that consisted of a couple of wheel ruts. We hadn't gone far when we encountered a short stretch of sand. It was so insignificant I drove onto it without much thought.

We bogged. I engaged four-wheel drive. We stayed bogged. My heart sank at the thought of getting on the radio to all and sundry in Birdsville and begging someone to rescue me. I was sure there'd be sniggering.

Then Luke said, 'I think we might have to let some air out of the tyres.'

Out we climbed and lowered the pressures. I was nervous as I put the Truckasaurus in gear ready to drive out of the bog. This time, though, the tyres didn't spin. I drove straight out. Too easy, as they say in the outback.

Luke's first posting was the 7500-square-kilometre Kidman-owned Naryilco Station, just north of the New South Wales–Queensland border. The company's senior aviator, who trained new pilots, was based there. 'About a week after I arrived he went on holidays for a month,' Luke explained. 'So I sort of flew around, building up the hours I needed before I could be sent off.'

While he learned what he could, Luke also had to come to terms with the outback lifestyle. He was city born and raised, his only experience of the outback a 'salt-of-the-earth' grandfather who'd been a cattle station manager. Through him Luke had a sense of what the country and people were like, but nothing could prepare him for the reality, especially when he started work in January, the height of summer.

'It was quite a shock arriving at Naryilco because they hadn't had any rain for a very, very long time,' he said. 'It wasn't until about four weeks after I got there that the skies opened, and that was on top of another flood that was already coming down the Diamantina. We had people over for a Friday night barbecue and they couldn't leave for about eight days. They were stuck there in the clothes they were wearing. Quite amazing. The airstrip washed away so I couldn't fly them home.'

Despite this introduction to the outback's extremes he adapted quickly. It didn't take him long to realise that rather than being remote and lonely, the station was a remarkably social place to be. People were passing through doing odd jobs. Miners prospecting on the property stopped in for smoko. People who'd worked on the station in years gone by dropped in to catch up with old friends. Hardly a day passed without someone new showing up.

As far as the dangers were concerned his bosses emphasised the importance of drinking lots of water to combat dehydration in the severe heat. The message was reinforced when he had to pick up a couple of ringers who'd tried to tough out the conditions and ended up collapsing. Their organs were shutting down and the Royal Flying Doctor had to evacuate them to hospital.

While the heat on the ground could be life-threatening, it could be even hotter in the stuffy interior of a small plane.

'One of the first mornings in Naryilco it was only 6.30 a.m. but when I got in the plane it was already 38 degrees. The sun was barely up. But it's a different heat to the coast. It's not so oppressive, but it'll sneak up on you if you don't look after yourself.'

On another occasion, flying into Birdsville, he said the plane was cool enough while he was at altitude, but as he began to descend it got hotter and hotter until the cabin was like an oven. As soon as he landed and the plane was taxiing slowly, he popped the door open. As fresh air flooded in he marvelled at how cool it was. Then he pulled up to the fuel bowsers, where Gus Daffy was waiting to refuel him. 'How's it going?' he said.

'Bloody hot,' Gus replied. 'It's 44 in the shade.'

We stopped on top of a hill with a view over gibber plains dotted with waddi trees. We got out our deckchairs. While Michelle swung into catering mode, I set up the folding table.

'Gee, you guys certainly know how to do things,' Luke said as he tucked into some of our treasured store of cheeses.

'Of course,' Michelle replied, opening a container of olives.

After being accredited for aerial mustering, Luke was assigned
to Glengyle. 'The most exciting part of my week was seeing the big
plane [a twin-engine Beechcraft Baron] come in, and racing to the
landing field to pick up the mail. We'd be looking forward to things
from home, care packs and whatever.'

He realised that flying the mail run would be a good next step in
his aviation career, so he went into the Mt Isa office of West Wing
Aviation, the company that runs the service, and said, 'What do I
need to do to get a job here?' Over the next six months he studied
and trained until he was qualified to fly twin-engine planes and rated
to fly on instruments. Then he gave them a call and they hired him.

The route begins in Port Augusta, South Australia, where he picks
up some of the mail for the run. Then he flies 220 kilometres to
Leigh Creek to pick up more. From Leigh Creek it's 225 kilometres
to Merty Merty Station, 100 kilometres to the town of Innamincka,
150 kilometres to Durham Downs in Queensland, 145 kilometres
to Cordillo Downs in South Australia and 160 kilometres to Birdsville. He usually gets there around 12.30 and has lunch, refuels and
picks up the mail for Glengyle and Durrie (pronounced 'do-ree') stations. In the afternoon he flies the 100 kilometres to Durrie and 125
kilometres farther to Glengyle before flying 135 kilometres back to
Birdsville for the night. On the second day he takes a more direct
route south, 130 kilometres to Clifton Hills in South Australia, 100
kilometres to Cowarie Station, 50 kilometres to the Mungerannie
Hotel, 80 kilometres to Etadunna Station, 40 kilometres to Dulka-
ninna Station, then 180 kilometres to Leigh Creek to drop the return
mail off before returning to base at Port Augusta. On the outward
journey he flies 1225 kilometres. Out and back it's 2160.

The number of stops and the short distances between them means
Luke is always busy – taking off, setting up for a cruise, landing,
unloading mail or making radio calls logging his flight in and out with
safety authorities. He reckons he doesn't have time to get bored.

'It's a great job,' Luke said. 'It probably doesn't appeal to a lot of people, but having flown out here all of last year and on four of the stations that I drop the mail to anyway, I already knew half the people on the run. This is like my social outing for the week – seeing all the people on the mail run, bringing them anything extra that they need, stopping for a cup of tea, having a chat. When I was on a station I got quite a kick out of going down to the mail plane and having a chat to the pilot and seeing what's going on in town or wherever they're from. And now I'm the pilot.'

Luke said he'd flown in a few unpleasant sandstorms and that in summer the turbulence can get quite violent, but it's nothing his plane can't handle. The only real drama is when there are floods. Most stations have dirt strips which turn to slush when it rains. Early in 2008 he couldn't land at any of them. He could only land at Birdsville and the oilfield runways at Moomba and Ballera (they fly their own mail in, but stations can drive there to pick up their own mail if the roads are open).

'Have you ever had a major emergency?' I asked.

He shook his head. 'I've never lost an engine, or been unable to lower an undercarriage. I've never hit the ground, yet. I say "yet" because I think it's probably wiser to expect that at some stage it will happen. I had a friend who was checking a fence last year and he was checking it very closely, you could say. His front wheel hit a rock and bounced him up into the air . . . further into the air. Tall rock. Probably not even that tall a rock.

'At Macumba last year we were mustering and it was actually quite a smooth day. It was probably the only air pocket I hit all day but it was a doozey. I went straight onto the roof. Took me totally by surprise. Your feet and arms are flailing about – nothing's on a control – and you're thinking what just happened? Fortunately, it was at a reasonable altitude – 500 feet or so.'

As we sat on top of the hill watching yet another glorious outback

sunset spread colour across an enormous sky I had one more question. After two years living and working here, what did he think of
the outback? His answer was immediate.

'I love it. I can understand why people from the outback are shirty
with people from the city because on the whole they have no concept
of it. Once you realise just how social it is and how many events do
take place and how insignificant an eight-hour drive is out here, it
does change your perspective quite a lot.

'Like the Qantas pilot I met a couple of weeks back. He and his
partner own a resort now, two and a half hours south-east of Dar-
win, and he said when he was building his hours, this is what he did.
He was all through Birdsville and Doomadgee and Burketown and
down south at Innamincka and all through the middle, the Northern
Territory. And that's where he's retired to after having an extremely
lucrative career at the very top end of aviation.'

6

ANOTHER DAY, ANOTHER RESCUE

Only days after we'd pulled Graham and Adrianne out of the desert, Patrick got called out again. A dozen dunes past Big Red a four-wheel-drive ute with a camping box on the back had all but snapped in two. Once again, Neale and I headed for Big Red in the police car. Patrick went out with the ute. This time, though, he unhitched the trailer before we tackled the dune. He got over it without trouble then scampered up Nemesis.

It wasn't long before we sighted the broken-down vehicle. It was on top of a dune that wasn't particularly high, but was quite steep, so Neale accelerated to hit it at speed. We'd just started climbing when there was an almighty crash. Underneath the soft sand there was something extremely hard – a real car breaker.

'Gee, Neale,' I said. 'That felt like a rock. Do you reckon that's what snapped the car up there?'

'Yup. Good chance it was.'

Up on the dune the stricken vehicle was an extraordinary sight. The chassis had split almost all the way through. It would have done except the owners had propped their spare tyres under the rear to stop it falling on the ground.

Neale pulled up and we got out. I tried to ease the tension with some humour. 'So what seems to be the problem?' I asked. The for-lorn couple didn't so much as smile.

Patrick pulled up and immediately inspected the damage. It turned out the chassis had sheared right through on one side. On the other side a thin sliver of metal was the only thing keeping the vehicle in one piece. To me it looked a wreck, but Patrick thought otherwise.

'We'll weld it up and see how we go,' he said.

There didn't seem to be any way the vehicle was going anywhere, but we began unloading it anyway. As we did it was obvious how much this couple had prepared for their trip into the desert. Everything was neatly organised and laid out so it was readily accessible. It reminded me of all the months Michelle and I had spent planning, researching and organising our trip. This couple, Wayne and Mary, had clearly done the same thing, only to see their trip of a lifetime come to an abrupt end a dozen dunes into their adventure. I regretted having been so flippant when I met them.

When the back of the vehicle was empty we got two high-lift jacks, propped them at the rear corners and raised it up. When the two halves of the vehicle were aligned, more or less, Patrick set to work with a portable welding kit. The rest of us retired to a safe distance to watch the sun set. As the moon rose over the dunes, the rescue scene was bathed in serenity – except for the welding sparks that could have ignited the fuel tank and sent Patrick up in a ball of flame.

Finally, the job was done. The vehicle didn't look very straight and few of us thought it would get far. We loaded most of Wayne and Mary's gear into the police car and ute to lighten the load on their vehicle, then we set off.

Neale and I took bets on how many dunes they'd get over before the welding gave up, but to our surprise the couple drove the car over the first dune, then another, arriving at Big Red without mishap.

We decided to take the easy way over Big Red and headed 3 kilometres south to Little Red – it's actually the same dune, just a lower section. Neale cleared the dune without incident, followed by Patrick, but Wayne and Mary's vehicle struggled in the steep, deep sand. Neale winched them up and over. Now they had a clean run to Birdsville where they could join the growing number of maroonees.

We later learned that the vehicle had been written off, but that the insurance company refused to pay out on it. They said the damage was caused by metal fatigue. I was starting to think that the best way to experience the Simpson Desert was in the police car. Certainly the number of vehicles suffering serious damage suggested that the Simpson should only be attempted as a necessity. Many locals said they'd never been to Poeppels Corner. I thought I understood why. It wasn't as though getting rescued was a cheap undertaking. At $4 a kilometre and $40 an hour, a rescue over a couple of hundred kilometres could soon reach into the thousands.

*

The night that Patrick and Olivia had their farewell drinks at the pub, the clutch for the original Maroonees, Graham and Adrianne, still hadn't arrived. Patrick's imminent departure meant that even if the clutch did arrive, there'd be no-one within several hundred kilometres who could install it.

The Brooks, owners of the service station, were searching for a new mechanic, but it wasn't easy to find someone who had the skills and inclination to relocate to such a remote town. As a stopgap, they hired a young Canadian, Corey, who was working as a ringer on Adria to come in and do basic jobs. Corey wasn't a qualified mechanic, but Patrick had given him a crash course on routine tasks such as repairing tyres.

Patrick's departure also meant there was no-one to install our back window. I'd gone around to the Mobil service station (aka the post office) to see Narelle's husband, Barry, who ran the automotive side of their business. With Barry, you could get a puncture repaired or you could talk local politics, because he was also the Diamantina Shire's Deputy Mayor. He was also the local agent, ground crew and baggage handler for MacAir.

Barry, who'd lived in the Diamantina Shire for all of his nearly sixty years, was a thin man, freckled from a lifetime's exposure to the fierce western sun. He could recall the days when the town lacked the amenities that were now taken for granted. He remembered when there was no air-conditioning at all, and when it only operated while people had their generators running. He remembered when the radiotelephone was replaced, in 1976, with a modern telephone system that allowed people in the town to hold a private conversation for the first time. Even the flies had changed, he reckoned. In the days before the sewerage system was modernised, they spread disease from the septic systems. Now they were 'clean flies'. They were still a nuisance, but they wouldn't kill you.

Barry knew all this and more. One thing he knew was that he couldn't fix the window on the Truckasaurus. We were running out of ideas for getting it repaired. If we couldn't get it done in Birdsville, where could we go? Not having a back window wasn't a big problem, although the plastic we'd taped over the hole only kept some of the dust out when we were driving. It was one of those nagging little things that added to our growing understanding of what isolation really meant.

Two days later, it was my birthday. My present consisted of a cup of tea in bed because there was nowhere in town to buy anything more lavish – that is unless I wanted a sticker that read, 'And the angel sayeth unto the shepherd, "XXXX off, this is cattle country"'. At least when I went for morning coffee at the bakery, the ever-thoughtful Teresa was waiting for me with a birthday cupcake.

That night, a Friday, was happy hour at the pub – a brief interlude when beer wasn't sold at tourist prices. 'Happy' was probably overstating things, but 'less disgruntled by the prices hour' doesn't have the same ring. Most of the locals took the opportunity to finish the week with a bit of a get-together.

News travels fast in a small country town. We were walking across the oval when Nell and David Brook spotted us from the pub's verandah. When we got closer, they started singing happy birthday. At the bar, there were best wishes from all the locals we'd got to know in the three weeks we'd been in town. People bought beer and wine and wouldn't let us return a shout. There were the Brooks, the Gaffneys, the Mortons from Roseberth and Pandie Pandie, Blue the plumber, the Doyles, the schoolteachers Katrina and Jay, Harry Crombie and his brother Jimmy, and a dozen more people we'd been introduced to.

'You two have really settled in well,' Neale the policeman said as he handed me a beer. I had to agree. We already knew more people than we'd ever known in our own local back in Sydney.

After the congratulations quietened down I got talking with David Brook. I'd first met him a year before, while researching our projected year in Birdsville. In a ten-minute conversation he'd given me enough leads for several books. David was sixty, Birdsville born and bred. He can be seen as a toddler in the film *The Back of Beyond*.

Only a few years after the film was made, David's mother died and David became sole heir to his father Bill's cattle property, Adria Downs. He and his late father built the business over decades and today Brook Proprietors is the tenth largest landowner in the country, with Adria Downs, Kamaran Downs, Cordillo Downs and Murnpeowie Station (plus a small organic holding property near Goondiwindi) covering a total of more than 30 000 square kilometres.

From my first meeting with David, he'd struck me as being just like his fellow western Queenslanders, though with something that set him apart. Even though he spoke like them, dressed like them with his battered old hat worn over thinning hair, and was as outgoing and friendly as the next bloke, there was more to him than met the eye.

Despite leaving school at sixteen, David was acutely intelligent, and worldly. In addition to his cattle and business interests, he'd been elected to the shire council when he was twenty, and served on it for thirty years, thirteen of them as mayor. He'd been secretary of the Birdsville Race Club for decades.

I mentioned to him that I'd had an interesting chat with Luke Pedersen and we got talking about aerial mustering. David had been doing it for years and explained some of the tricks involved: a burst of throttle here, a low turn there – the manoeuvres that get cattle moving in the desired direction. I said that it sounded like hard work.

'You can be up there for six hours, which can be quite tiring,' he said. He explained that to operate at peak efficiency the planes only land when they have to refuel. 'You don't feel tired when you're up there because you're concentrating so much, but afterwards it really takes it out of you.'

It surprised me that David still flew. He was the head of a major pastoral operation, the lynchpin of its success, yet he chose to engage in one of its most dangerous aspects.

'Well it is dangerous,' David admitted, 'but not if you're experienced. People do get killed, but I couldn't make someone do what I wouldn't do myself. And I suppose after what happened to Deon [his son, who was killed in a helicopter crash in 1998] I feel that even more strongly. Anthony [another son, manager of Cordillo Downs] flies a bit, but I still do most of it myself.'

As he spoke, I noticed a photo of Deon mounted on the wall behind him. We'd been in Birdsville long enough to learn that many of the decorative items that adorned the pub had stories behind them or associations of special significance. The dozens of hats directly above the bar belonged to people who'd lived in Birdsville for at least a year. The fourteen hats and photographs on the wall opposite the bar belonged to locals who'd died.

The picture of Deon showed a smiling young man who looked like he didn't have a care in the world. The cause of his helicopter's crash was never ascertained. He wasn't mustering at the time; he was simply flying from one station to another. Evidence at the crash site on Mt Leonard suggested that his chopper hadn't suffered a mechanical malfunction. There are several theories on what might have happened, but they're only theories. The coronial enquiry returned a verdict that there was a sudden loss of control (it could have been something as simple as a bird strike) from which he was unable to recover.

Deon is buried in one of several well-tended graves in the Birdsville Cemetery. His grave is surrounded by a grove of eucalypts that can easily be seen from the pub verandah. On the edge of town, road signs give the distances to Deon's Lookout, a memorial and scenic rest stop on the road halfway between Birdsville and Windorah, not far from the crash site. From the Birdsville Hotel to the cemetery and on to the country around Birdsville, David and Nell were literally surrounded by reminders of their son. They were far from being unwelcome. You didn't have to talk to them for long to realise that ten years after his death, he's never far from their thoughts.

*

After four weeks in Birdsville, the Maroonees had finally got their clutch. Now all they had to do was get their car to a town where it could be installed. That meant putting it on the rescue trailer and taking it up to Mt Isa, 700 kilometres north. But how to get the Birdsville Auto ute and trailer back to Birdsville? As we still had to get our window fixed, a plan was hatched whereby we'd take the Truckasaurus to a window specialist in Mt Isa, then Michelle would drive it back and I'd drive the ute and trailer. When Dusty's partner, Teresa, heard of the plan, she asked if she could come too. She'd been in Birdsville since the start of the tourist season two months earlier, and jumped at a chance for retail therapy, hairdressing and the like.

We set off early in the morning, hoping to get to Mt Isa that day, stay overnight, and return the next day. We couldn't afford any more time since Michelle and Teresa represented two-thirds of Dusty's workforce.

The first leg of the journey was a 200-kilometre mix of dirt and sealed road to Bedourie. In places, the gibber plains were completely treeless and it was like driving across the surface of the moon. Midway between the two towns were the ruins of the Cacoory Station homestead. A sign explained that the former Kidman property had been abandoned as unviable. The isolation can't have helped, but the signage also mentioned that the site was now part of Roseberth. It turned out that the country around Cacoory was viable for cattle-raising after all. As Geoff Morton explained, it was a matter of knowing how, and being prepared to survive years of hard times.

The town of Bedourie is the administrative centre of the Diamantina Shire. At 95 000 square kilometres the shire is one and a quarter times the size of Tasmania yet has a population of 307 (according to 2006 census data); in 2001 it was 326. There are three towns in the shire: Birdsville with a claimed population of 100 (it's more like sixty-six), Bedourie with 140 and Betoota, population zero.

Betoota used to have a population of one, but the sole inhabitant, Ziggy Remienko, died in 2004 at the age of eighty-eight. Ziggy (also known as Simon) migrated from Poland in 1950 and worked as a grader driver until 1956, when he bought the Betoota pub for $6000. From then until 1997 he ran what was arguably the loneliest pub in Australia – 200 kilometres from anywhere, all of them on rough dirt roads.

Betoota had once been a customs depot on a stock route from Queensland to South Australia. (It was like the Birdsville Track, but not as famous. Farther south it is identified as the Strzelecki Track.)

In the 1880s Bettoota had three pubs, a police station, a store and a post office. After Federation the town's population ebbed away. When Ziggy retired at the age of eighty-two, he was the only person there. He continued to live at Betoota until 2003. As his health declined he was moved to Birdsville, then to a nursing home in Charleville. When he died he left the pub to the Brook family. He was buried at Betoota, his grave marked by a large stone behind the now closed and slowly decaying pub.

The road north of Bedourie is sealed almost the entire 200 kilometres to Boulia, in part due to the road-building efforts of the Diamantina Shire. Between the two towns you enter the tropics, but you wouldn't know it from the countryside. There's no sign on the road and the gibbers and black-soil flood plains are all of a kind. Only on the last 50 kilometres into Boulia, where the vegetation becomes less sparse and straggly, and ghost gums put in an appearance, do you feel that you've finally left the arid zone.

The big sky country changes again at Dajarra, 150 kilometres north of Boulia. A jagged range of hills rises behind the town (whose population is almost entirely indigenous) and rocky outcrops appear along the road. Closer to Mt Isa the soil takes on a spectrum of colour – yellow, orange, white and green – that hints at the mineral wealth of this region in Queensland's north-west. Even on the outskirts of Mt Isa the road is only a single lane of tarmac and when two vehicles approach both have to drop their passenger-side wheels onto the verge to pass. When a truck comes, it's better to pull off the road completely to avoid flying rocks.

After only a month in Birdsville, Mt Isa came as a shock. In June 2008 it was riding high on a mining boom. It was also the subject of international media condemnation thanks to its mayor's comment that 'beauty-challenged' women should move there because the town's large proportion of single men meant even they would find a partner. An investigation was also under way into high lead levels in the bloodstream of local children, but the town's residents had split over concern for the health of their children and concern for the health of the town's major employer. The town's skyline was dominated by the smokestacks of the mine, its buildings perched among piles of tailings on the side of a deeply scarred hill.

The first thing we did was take the Truckasaurus to a windscreen repair shop. We'd already rung the repairers to ensure they could do the job as soon as we arrived. In the process we'd discovered that mentioning you were from Birdsville and on a tight schedule could work wonders. When we got to the repair shop, they were waiting for us.

While they did their stuff, we went to town. There we shopped as we'd never shopped before. As we rushed from place to place, I learned first-hand why country people often look busy when they're going about their business in town. We had lists of things to do, appointments to keep and items to buy, and an afternoon and morning to do everything before we had to be back on the road. As the day wore on and our window of opportunity shrank, we scheduled our efforts around the closing hours of various outlets in order to squeeze in every last minute of shopping.

Only after all the retail outlets had closed and we'd picked up our newly dust-proofed Truckasaurus, could we catch our breath. At that point we discovered that the only thing stranger than having working mobile phones was the opportunity to choose which restaurant we went to. Back in Birdsville, Ruth Doyle (who, with her husband Ian, used to run the caravan park) had recommended an Italian and a Chinese restaurant. Sitting in the Red Lantern that night I decided she'd given us a good tip. Then a thought struck me: 'If I didn't like the food here, I could have gone somewhere else.' It felt so extravagant. Back in Birdsville, if you didn't like the only restaurant, that was just tough.

The next morning our shopping became almost feverish. Not

knowing when we'd get a chance to shop again, we started buying items on the off-chance that we'd need them – this while our departure deadline loomed, based on having a seven-hour drive and a great reluctance to be on the road at night. Despite our best efforts we didn't get going until after lunch, me driving the ute and trailer, Michelle and Teresa (who'd been jogging independently between hairdressers, dentists, shops and banks) sharing the driving in the Truckasaurus.

The light was fading when we reached the border of the Diamantina Shire, and we knew darkness was going to overtake us. At least we'd made it back to the shire, I thought to myself. It certainly wasn't the meadows and curling chimney smoke from the shire in Tolkien's *Lord of the Rings* but even though we'd only been in Birdsville for a month and had to drive another 275 kilometres to get there, it felt like home. Despite the darkness, I was all for pressing on. Then we had an issue with a cow.

I passed the herd first, radioing the girls, who were trailing behind to stay out of my dust, to warn them that there were cattle ahead. As I passed the beasts, the noise of my vehicle made them move away from the side of the road. Little did we know that after I'd passed, at least one of them turned in the darkness and moved back towards the road. It was a tan-coloured cow, the same sandy hue as the dirt on the road.

Teresa was driving the Truckasaurus at the time, travelling at about 80 km/h. Its lights were on high beam, but in country that was utterly featureless and flat it was hard to make sense of objects in the distance. It was only at the very last moment that Teresa saw the cow. She slammed on the brakes. The Truckasaurus began to slide and the animal got closer and closer.

By then I was driving at a crawl, concerned about how the girls were going with the cattle. In my rear-view mirror I could see the lights of the Truckasaurus a long way behind. They didn't seem to be moving. I waited a minute, then a minute more, becoming increasingly worried.

'Everything okay?' I radioed them.

Silence.

'Are you there?' I called again and waited. Nothing.

'We're here,' Michelle radioed me at last, sounding shaky. 'We nearly hit one of those cows. It was very close.'

That clinched it. The cost of a night's accommodation in Bedourie was nothing compared to the consequences of a collision with livestock. Of course, it meant that the Truckasaurus window repair costs had increased yet again. Back in the city, we'd have got it fixed for a couple of hundred dollars. In the outback, repairs included fuel for a 1400-kilometre round trip, plus two nights' accommodation and miscellaneous expenses. It also meant a couple of days off work – all that on top of the actual price of the repair. Plus I made a mental note to get driving lights installed on the Truckasaurus at the earliest opportunity, whenever that might be. We could put it all down to yet another outback experience.

The one compensation was the drive the next morning. To get Michelle and Teresa back to the bakery in time for work we left at the crack of dawn. It was glorious. A faint sliver of red outlined the eastern horizon as we rolled out of Bedourie. We picked up speed, rolling over the first dunes in the pre-dawn glow. Then the sun rose out of an enormous plain. Kangaroos and emus hopped and ran away from the roadside. At that early hour we saw no other traffic. It was just us and the outback.

7

FLOOD

It hadn't rained in Birdsville since January, but that all changed in
June. The first weekend of the month was the running of the Birdsville
Gift, a professional sprint race that the organisers hoped would one
day rival Victoria's Stawell Gift and provide the town with another
event that would attract big crowds of tourists. The Diamantina Shire
Council had organised a bus to bring athletes and officials on a twenty-
hour overnight trip from Brisbane. The town's oval was marked out
with tracks for running and sprinting. Marquees were erected. Sponsors' signs were put up. The Social Club marshalled its catering forces.
When everything was in readiness, the clouds gathered.

The morning of the Birdsville Gift dawned cold and drizzly.
Despite the conditions the first races got under way as a scattering of
locals and even fewer tourists looked on. Community races for men,
women and the town's handful of children were also run. All the
cockies lined up. David Brook, who was on duty frying onions for
the obligatory sausage sizzle, came to the starting line still wearing
an apron. Neale the policeman ran, but not in uniform. Don Rayment manned the microphone as emcee.

Michelle took a break from the bakery to come over for the
women's race. When she found me she told me she'd had a marriage
proposal. A ringer from one of the stations had come in and Teresa
had introduced him to her. The formalities were no sooner complete
than he'd asked, 'Are you married?'

Michelle was taken aback but replied, 'Yes.'

The ringer didn't miss a beat. 'Happily?'

'Yes,' Michelle repeated, a little flustered.

So much for shy country types, I thought.

The most popular event at the Birdsville Gift turned out to be a nearest-to-the-flag golf competition. The athletes got into the spirit of it, along with the locals and a few tourists. Even the town's indigenous people, who largely kept to themselves in a group under one of the marquees, joined in.

Through it all the drizzle kept falling. It wasn't particularly heavy, but it was constant. The ground slowly became muddy and there were mutterings that if the rain kept up the athletes might not be driving back to Brisbane the next morning.

That night country singer Graeme Connors sang a 'Lift the Spirit, Defy the Drought' concert. By then the drizzle had turned to rain. Connors mused that his performance might have done the trick. Outside the Birdsville community hall I saw Geoff Morton and asked if the rain would improve the conditions on his station.

He shook his head. 'It will only wet the surface,' he said. Roseberth was so dry and lacking in feed that he was getting ready to muster stock and truck them out, rather than have them lose condition. It was a story that was being repeated from well down into South Australia all the way up to the Gulf of Carpentaria.

After the concert it rained all night. In the morning, when I walked Michelle down to work, it wasn't too heavy. When I went back at eleven o'clock for smoko, I saw a line of dark cloud sweeping in and obliterating the dunes. My sailing instincts told me that now would be a good time to put on the wet-weather gear, but being in the outback I wasn't so sure. It *looked* like a major rain front, so I increased my pace to make sure I got to the bakery before it did.

Inside I sat down with Bev Morton, Geoff's wife. If you ever want proof of the outback's irrepressible spirit, look no further than Bev.

A slight woman with short wavy hair flecked with grey, she possessed an enthusiasm that I initially found disconcerting. I'd never met anyone with so much energy.

Bev was counting money from a large jar. She explained that she'd just started fundraising for an x-ray machine for the Birdsville Clinic, where with Ross Carter she was one of the town's two Remote Area Nurses.

'How much is an x-ray machine?' I asked.

'Eighty thousand dollars,' she replied. 'But I reckon we'll only need to get half to prove we're serious and we'll get a grant for the rest.'

Good luck with that, I thought to myself. In a town with less than a hundred residents it would take years to raise that amount. I gave her the change from buying my morning coffee. 'How much have you got so far?' I asked out loud.

'We got three hundred dollars at the happy hour in the pub last Friday,' she replied triumphantly.

'That's pretty good,' I said, calculating that it would take two years and seven months to raise the forty grand.

Just then the front hit. As the heavens opened, all the tourists around the tables in the bakery yelled, 'Woooo!' It was a mix of excited and worried – a kind of glass half-empty/half-full reaction. The rain thundered on the tin roof. People came rushing in from outside. I was pleased that my instincts had been proved correct, but that was nothing compared to Bev's display of emotion. She was literally bouncing in her seat.

'I take it this is good,' I said.

'This will bring up winter herbage,' she said, clapping her hands with joy. 'It'll mean Geoff can keep the cattle on and finish them properly. He was looking at moving them off half-finished. Now he'll be able to keep them on until August!'

Bev explained that winter rains bring up ephemeral growth, which will fatten cattle over the cooler months. Summer rains bring up feed that endures even after it dries out. It can provide nutrition that lasts a couple of years.

The downpour dropped 25 millimetres on Birdsville in an hour. This, on top of the rain that had already fallen and was continuing to fall, meant the town was on the way to getting half its annual average rainfall (150 millimetres) in just two days. As the day wore on, vehicles rolled into town covered in mud from their front bumpers to their tow balls.

That day all the unsealed roads out of town were closed. In the afternoon we drove along the sealed road to the racecourse 3 kilometres out of town. It was a lake. The whole track was submerged, with only the rails and signs standing above the water. We ventured out to the other side of town. The road to Big Red was awash and already terribly rutted by vehicles making their way into town across the flood plain. They were finding their way using the guideposts, the only things visible. When we tried to turn around, we had to put a couple of wheels off the bitumen. They immediately sank. The unsealed ground was like a sponge cake. We engaged the Truckasaurus's four-wheel drive and just managed to claw our way back onto the road.

The total rainfall over the weekend was 82 millimetres, a record for a two-day period. It was more than the ground could absorb, yet Bedourie, 200 kilometres north, didn't get a drop. The rain band had been only 300 kilometres wide, and Birdsville was in the middle of it. It made every road impassable. The athletes for the Birdsville Gift were trapped in town, as were a couple of hundred tourists. Vehicles north, south, east and west were becoming bogged and calling to be rescued.

The Diamantina River wasn't flowing on Sunday afternoon, but by the next morning had risen 4 metres. Outside town it swirled beneath the bridge in a brown mass. The semi-permanent billabong below the town was overflowing. The plains that fed it were completely awash. Only seventy-two hours earlier they'd been bone dry. There's a line in the song 'The Diamantina Drover' which suggests it never rains on the Diamantina River. From first-hand experience I could only conclude, oh yes it does.

According to Dusty, this was only a minor flood. Compared to the biggest flood on record, in 1974, it was nothing. He told me that back then Mulka Station, on the Birdsville Track in South Australia, was regarded as one of the driest stations in Australia. It got so much rain that Lake Hope, which is on the station, was completely filled. Before long it was jumping with fish.

'The manager down there applied for a commercial fishing licence,' Dusty said. 'He got a boat, went fishing and started trucking yellow bellies down to the market in Adelaide. Over a few months they pulled $2 million dollars worth of fish out of the lake.'

One consequence of all the rain was that every corella in Birdsville disappeared overnight. With water now pooled in claypans and gibber flats all over the desert, the birds were no longer restricted to the river and billabong. They could spread out over thousands of square kilometres to forage for nuts and seeds.

Seeing so much water flowing down the Diamantina, I assumed it would mean the Birdsville Inside Track would be closed. It had only been opened a couple of days earlier, having been closed for two years by the previous flood. According to Geoff Morton, the water wouldn't even reach the point where the Inside Track crossed the river. 'This won't get past Goyder Lagoon,' he said. 'You go and have a look at Clifton Hills. That whole station is just one big swamp. There has to be a lot of water to get past there.'

It was hard to believe that the immense volume of brown water sweeping under the bridge outside town wouldn't reach more than 150 kilometres downstream. What kind of swamp could swallow up so much water? Here was yet another aspect of the outback I didn't understand.

After the rain, the skies cleared and the sun shone, but in the cool winter days, around 20 degrees, the roads remained quagmires. Grim-faced tourists still rolled into town in mud-covered vehicles. All of them considered inflicting extraordinary damage to the roads a necessity because they 'had to get through'. To them, waiting for the roads to dry out just wasn't an option. The fine for driving on a closed road was less than $200. The cost of repairing deeply rutted roads ran into millions. For locals who had to cope with ruined roads for weeks afterwards, their behaviour was infuriating.

With the athletes and their bus stuck in town, locals were treated to the sight of finely tuned bodies sprinting down the main street as they tried to continue their training on the few hard surfaces they could find. Having got through the mud to Birdsville, the tourists couldn't leave and were buzzing around town like bees in a bottle. Business in the bakery was never better.

'People don't realise what it's like here in a flood,' David Brook told me. 'They get stuck here and just can't accept that's the way it is. We've all got schedules to keep, but sometimes you just have to wait. After a while they start to get pretty tense.'

The road closures also meant that the mail was disrupted, even though the twice-weekly delivery came by plane. The trucks that brought bulkier items (and our groceries) to Birdsville couldn't get through, so urgently needed freight was crammed onto the plane. Since the plane had a freight limit, regular mail bags had to be offloaded in Quilpie, where the truck depot happened to be.

On Tuesday afternoon, at the appointed hour for mail collection, we walked into the post office only to find it crammed with boxes and satchels. Right up the back a beleaguered postmistress Gaffney was peering from between mountains of mail. We didn't have to ask to know this wasn't a good time. One look at her flushed face said it all.

We'd already learned we weren't the only ones who regarded

Narelle as the alpha postmistress. Neale the policeman admitted he watched until Judy Menzies, wife of the owner of the Birdsville Working Museum, went in to get her mail. He described it as 'letting her face the new ball'. If Judy emerged without any mail, which meant it wasn't ready to be collected (and presumably Judy was out for a duck), there was no point running the gauntlet.

To be fair to Narelle, most of the problems with the mail were beyond her control. Even at the best of times the mail plane was notoriously unreliable. It was often late, if it came at all, leaving Narelle in the role of the bringer of bad news. And away from the post office she was as warm and friendly as everyone else in Birdsville.

It took a week for most of the roads to dry out enough to be reopened. Even then they were appallingly rutted and many stretches were still under water. Seven days after they arrived, the runners from Brisbane were finally able to depart. A council grader escorted the bus to clear the way and pull it though the boggier sections.

The poor condition of the road also meant cattle trucks couldn't move. This presented particular problems for the organic beef operators, who had contracts to supply beasts on a fortnightly basis. Floods could disrupt the roads anywhere along the 1600-kilometre supply line to Brisbane, but the critical section was the 300 kilometres of dirt to Windorah.

Once the road reopened, our neighbour Ben, who did most of the baking for Dusty, returned to Birdsville. He'd intended to leave permanently but the replacement baker hadn't worked out. The new baker had flown in on a Monday, started work on Tuesday, pissed Dusty off on Wednesday and threatened to quit on Thursday. To his surprise, his resignation was accepted and he flew out on the Friday. Although Dusty had problems with Ben's reliability, and with 3 a.m. starts it was hard to blame him when he slept in, Dusty preferred the devil he knew to hiring someone else. Ben didn't come back alone. He was accompanied by none other than Zeus.

Zeus was Ben's pig dog, an Irish wolfhound crossed with other breeds of hunting dog. His light brown fur was slightly shaggy, and a small fringe curled down over his deep brown eyes. Although he was still little more than a pup, his head reached my hip. Our trepidation at being savaged by a vicious pig dog was soon allayed, however. He turned out to be the sookiest dog on earth. All he wanted in life was a pat or a cuddle, preferably both.

In the morning, Ben shut him in his backyard where Zeus sat quietly until we came outside. Then he stared longingly at us through the gate between Ben's yard and ours. At first, when we went over to pat him through the fence, we were extremely careful, in case he took our arms off. Instead of trying to savage us, he pressed his head against our hands, trying to get as much contact as possible.

After a few days, I asked Ben if I could take Zeus for morning walks. I made a leash from a length of rope and Zeus came with me when I walked Michelle to work, then we'd do a circuit of Birdsville. Soon he was sitting at the back gate every morning, waiting expectantly.

He never barked, or even moved, until I opened the gate. Then it was like letting loose a small cyclone. He crossed our yard in two bounds, span around then bounded back for a pat. Another bound and he was in my budding vegie patch where the orderly little rows of seedlings were no match for his galumphing paws. 'Zeus! No!' became my morning refrain. Fortunately, as soon as I put his leash on, he fell quiet as a lamb. He'd have been the world's best dog if he wasn't the size of a horse.

*

The road to Big Red was still closed when Dusty rang to ask if I wanted to go with him on a desert rescue twenty dunes out. I did, particularly as it was an opportunity to see the desert after heavy rain, but I wondered when Michelle was going to get her turn. I'd been on two desert adventures already, but she hadn't seen the desert at all.

Just outside town we came upon the first of several long stretches of road that were completely submerged. I was surprised at Dusty's technique for driving through water. When Michelle and I had ventured into floodwater on the now-opened Windorah Road, we'd tackled it at speed, thinking we needed momentum to carry us through. Water had splashed all over the vehicle. Dusty's approach was slow and steady. The vehicle hardly got splashed at all, which meant there was less risk of soaking its electrics and flooding the engine.

Driving over Big Red was a breeze. The rain had compacted the sand and it was almost like driving on a normal road. After that we had to drive 2 kilometres around the edge of a lake that had formed between Big Red and Nemesis Dune. Even Nemesis was a cinch.

The rain meant that everything in the desert was turned upside down. Normally vehicles struggled over the dunes and had it easy across the flats. Now the dunes were easy but there were deep ruts where vehicles had battled through pools of water on the claypans and plains. In places new tracks had been made through virgin scrub to get around the lakes.

As we drove further into the desert I said to Dusty, whose repertoire had now extended to include baker, power station maintenance and outback recovery, 'Mate, this is a bloody long way to go to sell a camel pie.'

He chuckled away. I knew he was thinking he should have brought some.

The vehicle we were rescuing had all the accessories – a huge rack of driving lights, extra-wide tyres, raised suspension, and a snorkel. Spattered with mud it looked like it could go anywhere. The only thing it lacked was a working clutch. The two young men who'd driven across the Simpson Desert only to break down within a few kilometres of Birdsville were acutely embarrassed about what had happened. When they heard I was a writer, the owner asked that I not identify them or their vehicle.

We hooked them up and towed them easily around the lakes and over the dunes back to Big Red. It was only there that Dusty's V8 turbo-charged four-wheel drive found the weight of the vehicle too much. He couldn't get up Big Red so resorted to an alternative route that angled up the slope – the Chicken Track. He got the broken vehicle to within 50 metres of the top before his wheels dug in and he had to cut his throttle. From there we winched and pulled until finally we got them over. Sometime later, Geoff Morton told Dusty that Big Red actually ended about 6 kilometres north of where everyone crossed. A track went around the end without encountering any sand at all. If only we'd known that on our rescues.

On the way back into town, I realised we were approaching a spot on the road where we'd passed a dead fox on the way out. I asked Dusty if we could stop to pick it up.

'Why?' he answered gruffly. 'The bloody things stink.'

'Well,' I explained, 'I'd like to make it into a fox hat.'

'A fox hat?' he asked, taking the bait. 'What on earth do you want a fox hat for?'

'Because when we told people we were moving to Birdsville, some of them said, "Birdsville! Wear the fox hat." '

It took Dusty a while to get the joke ('where the fuck's that?'). Five kilometres later he was still laughing.

The following day, the road to Big Red opened, although the flooded sections made the drive quite an adventure. Nevertheless, after the bakery closed I took Michelle and Teresa out to show them the water. I also wanted to try out Dusty's technique for flooded-road driving.

Armed with cameras, and with no rescue to perform, we made

slow progress as we stopped to look at birds and photograph the pools that had formed at the foot of nearly every dune. In front of one dune black swans were swimming. Avocets waded in another. Spoonbills patrolled the shallows.

In one pool tiny creatures were wriggling about. I caught one and it turned out to be one of the strangest creatures in the desert. Shield shrimps (*Triops australiensis*) are prehistoric-looking creatures with a small shell and a short stubby tail. After rain they hatch from eggs that have endured as many as twenty years of dry, dusty conditions. The larvae rapidly develop into adults that live for a few weeks on rotting vegetation and each other. When the pools dry, they perish, but their eggs remain, waiting for the next good rain.

After I drove nervously through the deepest pools of water, the Truckasaurus slithering in between patches of firmer earth, we reached Big Red. It was an easy climb up the rain-hardened sand. We watched the sun set over the desert and the lake then headed back. On the road into town the moon rose as dusk fell over lakes, dunes and coolabah trees. It took a long time to get home because Michelle kept stopping to take pictures. She eventually had to admit that there was so much beautiful scenery that it was impossible to photograph it all.

*

Michelle and I had been playing tennis on the local courts every Wednesday night since we'd arrived. As we got to know more people in town, we invited all and sundry to join us. In mid-June, our first social tennis night was attended by four – Michelle, Bev Morton, David and Nell Brook. Although I was one of the instigators, I wasn't there. I was out doing another rescue.

This one was a bogged vehicle 150 kilometres down the Birdsville Track. Dusty had got the job once more and as it meant I'd get to see

the famous track in daylight, I readily accepted the invitation to go
for the ride.

The track was in good condition for the first 20 kilometres until
it reached the blacksoil country on Pandie Pandie Station. From
there on it was the most rutted and treacherous piece of public road
imaginable – a result of the flooding, and the destruction caused by
four-wheel drivers who'd ignored the road closures.

I was driving and it was a nerve-wracking experience. One wrong
turn of the wheel could catch a tyre on the edge of a hardened rut
and tear the wall out, sending the vehicle out of control and into a
roll. The only thing that had improved the track slightly was that
Tom McKay had done a run with his road train. While the surface
was firm enough to support the truck, it was soft enough for the double wheels to make two lanes of flat, packed ground for the wheels
of Dusty's ute.

The scenery along the road was classic outback. In some places
there were both red and white dunes, the colour a reflection of the
age of the sand. The older the dune, the redder it gets. Over both
flats and the dunes, however, there was another layer of colour. A
faint green tinge was just discernible. The rain had spurred a surge
of growth, even in the most barren-looking places. Tiny seeds were
lying everywhere, just biding their time. 'You wait and see,' Dusty
said. 'In a month this'll all be up to your knees. Then there'll be flowers everywhere.'

We found the stricken vehicle sitting in the middle of a vast plain
surrounded by lakes that had still not evaporated. They'd become
bogged in the first puddle they'd encountered as they drove up from
the south. They'd made the mistake of trying to drive around it.
Most (but not all) of the outback's dirt roads have had a layer of
rock laid down the middle of them to make a firmer base to drive on,
especially in known boggy stretches. This couple had got into the
soft mud on the side of the road and immediately sank.

They weren't seriously stuck, but had the misfortune of striking a day when another vehicle did not happen by. They'd been forced to call on their satellite phone and cop the $1000 expense of a rescue. It took five minutes to connect a snatch-strap and pull them through to dry ground.

The grateful rescuees were an older couple, retired teachers driving up to Cape York to work as relief teachers in an indigenous community. We started to chat, but the husband quickly excused himself in order to seek relief of a different kind. He stood by the side of the road answering nature's call as the sun slowly sank into the plain. The sun kept sinking. He kept answering.

His wife explained that he'd been dying to go to the toilet for hours. At first he'd tried to get out of the car but didn't want to lose his boots in the deep mud, so he took them off. He'd immediately stood on a patch of bogan flea, incredibly sharp prickles that embed themselves in the soles of your feet. His wife spent an hour pulling them out, after which he'd endured the discomfort of his overfull bladder and his sore feet until we arrived. He'd been extremely relieved to see us, in every sense.

When he was finished we got on the road, but we hadn't gone far before we met another vehicle coming the other way. It pulled out of Tom McKay's tracks to let us pass and paid dearly for the courtesy. It tore the valve out of a tyre on a rut. We stopped to make sure the occupants had a spare and offered to help change the tyre, but they said they'd be right.

Back in town Michelle reported on the success of the social tennis night. 'The Brooks are good players,' she said, 'and very competitive. Though they do it in a sportsmanlike way, they play to win.'

'How so?'

'When the score gets to deuce, they don't just say "deuce". They say "deuce, our way".'

The following week I missed tennis again. I'd thought I'd seen everything when it came to rescues, but then Dusty rang and said, 'Do you want to come out and rescue a forty-seater bus?'

'A bus!' I yelped. Now there was a rescue challenge that was too good to miss. 'I'll be right there.'

We left Dusty's and drove over to the Birdsville Hotel where John Hanna was loading up his ute as well. Corey and the ute from Birdsville Auto were already at the scene (he'd been on his way back from a job towing a caravan to Innamincka and had stopped to help).

The rescue was 100 kilometres out on the Windorah Road, the result of a standard-issue failure to stick to the middle of the road – except that the vehicle involved weighed about 12 tonnes. Three vehicles didn't seem like enough to pull a bus, but it was a start.

We headed out of town and drove for an hour. Then we saw a dune in the distance covered in people. They were elderly tourists who were photographing the desert sunset. As we drove up they started cheering like we were heroes. We smiled and waved back while muttering to ourselves, 'Don't cheer yet. We haven't got you out.'

Then we saw the bus. It was leaning at a dangerous angle where the driver's side had sunk when he'd tried to drive around a large pool of water that covered the road. The wheels had gouged a furrow a metre deep, the mud bringing the bus to a halt.

The front wheel cover was open and Corey was inside, lying face down in the mud, clawing it out with his bare hands. He didn't have a shovel so I gave him one of Dusty's and joined him in the excavation work (I may not have known much about vehicle recovery but I'd already learned how to dig). Dusty and John started hitching up their vehicles using chains, snatch-straps and winches.

A couple of young blokes had stopped in their four-wheel drive to lend a hand, giving us four vehicles for the big pull. Everyone around us seemed confident that we knew what we were doing as we chocked all four wheels of Dusty's ute with large rocks so he could use his winch. John, Corey and the young blokes formed a line of vehicles using snatch-straps.

Experts will tell you that joining vehicles in this way is extremely dangerous, but when you're looking at forty elderly travellers who are watching the sun going down, 90 kilometres from town, and the desert is about to get very cold, that's what you do.

The first pull was a complete failure. When Dusty's winch took up and the other vehicles started pulling, the only thing that moved was Dusty's ute. The winch dragged the ute towards the bus even though I was standing on the brake and the wheels were chocked. We stopped pulling while we got some bigger rocks to put behind Dusty's wheels.

On the second pull the bus moved a couple of centimetres. It wasn't much, but it was better than nothing.

A third try. 'Make this a big one,' Dusty shouted as he signalled to John, Corey and the young blokes. When the tension was taken up on all the lines, I called out to the bus driver to try to drive forward a little bit as well. He couldn't do much because it was important that he didn't spin his wheels and dig them in deeper. Amid the roar of revving engines and winches, the bus edged forward.

'Keep it going!' I shouted, standing on the doorframe of Dusty's ute so I could keep my foot on the brake and see what was happening. At the front of the line of vehicles, the young blokes were spinning their wheels wildly, but the bus was still moving. Then Dusty's winch cable slackened. The winch couldn't keep pace with the bus as it slowly lifted out of the rut and back onto the road. The other vehicles kept pulling. Then, like a cork from a bottle, the bus lurched upright and popped out of the bog.

All the tourists clapped and cheered and took photos while we congratulated ourselves. From the top of a dune John Hanna radioed the pub to tell them there'd be forty more for dinner.

*

After only two months in Birdsville we were beginning to realise that our knowledge of the outback barely scratched the surface. To see Birdsville in the course of a day or two was to experience just one aspect. To see it over a longer time was to appreciate that it was never the same place twice. There was always something new.

One of the biggest surprises was how much there was to do. Before our move we'd feared that we might get bored. Instead, Michelle was being kept busy at the bakery, taking a huge number of photographs and socialising with the locals. When people asked me how my book was going, I told them I needed the town to stop for a few days while I caught up.

One evening we went to a trivia night fundraiser for the Birdsville School. The school, which after the departure of one family was now down to five pupils ranging from year 1 to 6, had more staff than students. There was a principal, Katrina Ireland, assisted by her partner, Jay, and an indigenous teacher's assistant, Fiona Gadsby. Ruth Doyle took care of admin. Neale the policeman cleaned the school while an assortment of people took care of the grounds.

Dusty, Teresa, Michelle and I formed a team for the trivia night and got off to a good start. One of the questions required an intimate understanding of *The Man from Snowy River*, one of the poems I'd been reciting to myself on sleepless nights before moving to Birdsville.

'What was the name of the horse that Harrison made a pile of money on?' the quizmaster asked.

'Pardon,' I said.

'What was the name of the horse that Harrison made his money on?' Dusty repeated.

I started sniggering. The horse's name was Pardon.

Dusty and Teresa couldn't believe anyone would know such trivial information, so I recited the poem from the top.

As it happened, David and Jane Morton from Pandie Pandie were playing with another team that was seated at our table. I'd been told David had a great reputation as a horseman and that he was the best greenhide rope maker in the business but, apart from a few conversations in the pub, I hadn't had much of a chance to get to know him better. As I continued my recital, I noticed David was listening. I got to the description of the horse:

> And one was there, a stripling, on a small and weedy beast
> A trifle like a racehorse undersized.
> With a touch of Timor pony, three parts thoroughbred at least,
> And such as are by mountain horsemen prized.
> He was hard and tough and wiry, just the sort that won't say die
> There was courage in his quick impatient tread
> And he bore the badge of gameness in his bright and fiery eye
> And the proud and lofty carriage of his head.

David was nodding. Clearly he could understand far better than I the qualities of such a horse. Western Queensland equestrian traditions are every bit as strong as those around the Snowy Mountains, where the poem is set. Men from both areas formed the core of the revered Australian Light Horse in World War I. Seeing David's appreciation of Banjo Paterson's description, horseman to horseman, gave the words new resonance.

At the end of round one, which we won easily, Dusty went to bed. He'd decided we were trivia freaks and he had to get an early start in the bakery. Teresa, Michelle and I cratered in round two. Rugby league was a subject none of us knew anything about. Several other teams closed in and then controversy erupted in the final round. Teams had to come up with proper names of things that involved multiples of the letter A, the letter B, and so on. We scored four points for Cooper Creek Cricket Club, which I openly admitted to making up. Our nearest rivals came up with a brilliant answer for the letter X. It was the name of Queensland's favourite beverage, XXXX, so named because Queenslanders can't spell beer. It should have scored four points, but was disallowed. While we were being presented with certificates spruiking our victory, our disappointed opponents slunk away.

The following morning we were doing our usual Sunday morning late breakfast of barbecued bacon and eggs when the phone rang. Teresa wanted me to come down to the bakery and run an errand in Dusty's car.

'Why?' I asked.

'He went pig hunting with Ben.'

'And?'

'He wouldn't say on the radio. He just asked if you'd grab the ute and go for a drive down the Inside Track.'

I started laughing. 'He's bogged, isn't he?'

'He said you should be able to see him in the distance right after you turn off,' she replied, barely able to conceal her own amusement.

We quickly finished breakfast and headed out. Sure enough, a kilometre down the track there was a muddy section. Dusty and Ben had tried to drive around the wet patch and hadn't gone wide enough. The ute was deep in the mud. Zeus was still on the back, wondering what the hold-up was.

When it came to getting bogged, the tracks were completely different. The Outside Track was more like a road, with rocks down the middle, which was where you stayed if you didn't want to sink. The Inside Track was just a track, which meant that if it rained you either avoided the wet bits or sank down to the axles. Nell Brook reckoned the best way to get down the Inside Track was to go with Jimmy Crombie. He'd drive down one side of the track then switch to the other side. With more than seventy years' experience, he knew every soft spot there was.

Two hundred metres down the Inside Track the not-so-experienced

Dusty let me do the hook-up and snatch. My first pull wasn't strong enough. On the second pull I was a bit more aggressive and Ben's ute pulled free. Unfortunately, so did his alloy bumper bar – it clearly wasn't a strong enough connection point. As it turned out it was the only connection point, but they were out of the mud now and hopefully wouldn't get stuck again.

Since we were out with them, and two vehicles are always safer than one, Michelle and I went along for the pig hunt.

Michelle's interest in pig hunting was exactly nil, but she wasn't going to miss an opportunity to do some more photography. I wasn't too keen on it myself and I certainly wasn't happy about Zeus going pigging. It may have been part of the way of life in the outback, and pigs might be feral animals that do a lot of damage to the country, but I was more concerned about the damage the pigs might do to Zeus.

We drove down the Inside Track to the grid that marked the end of the town common (land set aside for townsfolk to graze their horses or use for recreation) and the start of Roseberth Station. Geoff Morton had told Dusty and Ben where he thought pigs might be found. We drove south for a few kilometres then cut across towards the Diamantina River.

When we pulled up, Ben let Zeus off the back and he went bounding down the bank of the river, then flew back up to us. His energy was extraordinary. I turned to Ben.

'You know I've trained him not to hunt pigs,' I said. 'You watch. When he sees one, he'll put his paws over his eyes and bark "run away little piggies".'

'Nah,' Ben replied, brandishing an alarmingly long, double-bladed pig-stabbing knife. 'He loves it.'

We walked through deep gullies for half an hour without seeing so much as an imprint of a pig's trotter. Dusty was starting to wonder if we were in the right place, so we returned to the vehicles and he radioed Geoff Morton.

'Are you on the section of the river where it's running a bit north–south?' Geoff asked.

'We think so,' Dusty replied.

'There should be lots of lignum on the banks?'

'Yep.'

'Okay, come back towards town a bit, and when the river bends a bit more east, that's where you'll find the pigs.'

I was impressed by Geoff's knowledge. 'Amazing. He's got a 5000-square-kilometre property,' I said to Michelle, 'but he knows what's growing on a particular bend of the river.'

Sure enough, when we got to the bend, we found some pig tracks, but no pigs. We searched around for a while then returned to Birdsville unencumbered with pork products of any description.

A few days later Ben found pigs about 100 kilometres from town, on Durrie Station. He started coming back with the bodies of enormous brutes chained on the back of the ute beside Zeus. Both Ben and the dog were often spattered in blood and mud. Zeus sometimes had his ears torn and bleeding. Ben told me these pigs weren't the biggest he'd caught – they were just the ones that were light enough to drag back to the vehicle.

On the days when Ben went hunting, Dusty put up a sign in the bakery that read, 'Sorry, no fresh bread today. The baker's gone pig hunting.' I suggested he add on the bottom, 'Tomorrow's special: pork pies.' Dusty liked it so much he scrawled it on right away.

Ben said I was welcome to go out with him but, given the pigs were killed by hand, I thought it was one authentic outback experience I could do without. Mind you, I was taking the kangaroo hunting scene in Kenneth Cook's *Wake in Fright* as my point of reference. I'm sure Ben's hunting experience didn't involve excessive consumption of alcohol, appalling violence and homosexual rape, but what did a city boy like me know?

I tried to understand the 'sport', but nothing about pig hunting appealed. Ben cut the heads off the pigs and left them in Zeus's yard for a day or so, presumably to give him a taste for pig. To his credit, Zeus just sniffed at them. We always knew when there was a piece of pig about because the whole back fence was lined with a murder of crows. When the crows became too bold, they actually managed to get a woof out of the dog. Just one – deep and loud.

It wasn't long before my worst fears for Zeus were realised – he came home badly injured. 'He saw the pigs before I did,' Ben said, 'and jumped off the back before I could get his protective collar on.'

A pig had turned and attacked Zeus, its tusks slashing his throat. The skin was torn wide open.

'He'll be right,' Ben said. 'He'll heal up fast, won't you mate?'

Zeus was sitting on the back of the ute, very quiet, looking at us with moist sad eyes. The wound was slowly weeping. I looked closer.

'Ben!' I wailed. 'I can see his throat! Call Dr Ross. I don't know if he looks after animals, but someone needs to have a look at this.'

Dr Ross was the nickname for Remote Area Nurse Ross Carter, Bev Morton's colleague at the Birdsville Clinic. He'd done tours of Afghanistan with the International Red Cross and worked in some of the roughest indigenous communities in the Northern Territory. A small, middle-aged bloke with short-cropped hair, he had a laconic manner that was more than matched by a formidable knowledge and competence. He was off duty when Ben called, but came straight away.

'He's in a bad way,' Ross said after assessing the patient. 'I'll do what I can for him, but I doubt that he'll make it.'

Ross was never one to beat about the bush but still, I knew that if anyone could save Zeus, he could. The back of Ben's ute became an operating theatre. Ross bound up Zeus' muzzle so he couldn't bite, then gave him a local anaesthetic. Zeus lay down, perfectly still, while Ross put in stitch after stitch.

As Ross worked on the dog, I couldn't bear to watch. It was just too distressing to see him in such a state. I did some gardening chores, checking progress as I pottered about. As I passed by I said to Ross, 'You know the pig's in the backyard, and he's in worse shape than the dog.'

Ross gave me a look that said 'if I was a triage nurse, I'd send you to the end of the queue' and went back to his stitching. It took sixteen stitches to close up most of Zeus's throat. Ross left a small gap to allow the wound to drain.

In the following days Zeus ran a fever. Ross came every morning and evening to check on him and administer antibiotics. It was a week before Zeus started to come good. I tentatively resumed taking him for a morning walk, but he was very quiet. He couldn't wear a leash so I put him in the back of the Truckasaurus and took him over to the derelict remains of what was once the Birdsville Golf Course so he could have a little walk off the leash. Some days he was full of energy, other days he tired quickly.

While the poor pup recovered, Ben got John Menzies from the Birdsville Working Museum to make up a full-length leather throat protector. After all Zeus had been through, Ben still wanted to take him hunting, and no amount of tsk-tsking on my part would deter him.

8

THE WORKING MUSEUM

In a town full of characters, John Menzies had to be one of the most interesting. His Birdsville Working Museum was located behind our house, but in the two months since we'd moved to Birdsville I still hadn't actually spoken to him. Well, he'd been yelling over the fence, 'When are you going to come and talk to me?' And I'd been yelling back, 'Soon, John. It's just that I'm really busy.'

We'd visited his museum and seen the tour he conducted on our research trip the year before. I thought it had to be the best museum in the outback. Most 'pioneer museums' are little more than storage sheds for decaying junk that is just valuable enough to be saved from a trip to the dump. John's organisation and presentation was proof of his passion. There was an array of Cobb and Co coaches, butter churns and hand-operated washing machines. He had an extensive collection of Furphy water tanks, and another of manual water pumps. A corrugated-iron fence was covered in the iron steps that were used to climb into coaches and wagons. Every one of them was different, many of them gems of industrial design. He had the world's largest collection of horse hames, which are used in harnessing horses. And almost everything worked, which he demonstrated to visitors three times a day, in one-hour shows that moved at a cracking pace.

People came away from the place marvelling at what they'd seen. Many had stories to tell about what John did when people dared to talk or ask questions. John 'hunted them out'. At the beginning of his shows he warned the audience that they should save their questions to the end because there was so much to get through. When little old ladies reminisced about how they'd used such-and-such 'when I was a girl' he gave them short shrift. People reckoned it was the most entertaining part of the show.

John finally cornered me one day while I was pottering around the Truckasaurus. 'I think you're avoiding me,' he said.

'No, John,' I confessed. 'I've just got so much to write up, and if I interview you now I'll just have more. But of course you're on my list.'

It didn't help that John never set foot in the pub or the bakery. Depending on who you asked, it was a case of him having issues with them or them having issues with him. The consequence was that in a town where the social opportunities were already limited, his social circle was restricted to a select few. Surprisingly, he wasn't alone in this. I'd already found that people could be remarkably forthright in expressing opinions about each other. When I commented, 'You'll never die not knowing what people think of you in Birdsville,' the consensus was that I'd hit the nail on the head.

John was yet another Birdsville resident on the other side of sixty. He looked like he'd just come in from mustering, with his work-soiled clothes and old drover's hat held on with a leather strap passing across his forehead. And he wasn't to be put off. He wanted a yarn and that was that. In particular he wanted to tell me what was wrong with Birdsville. For starters he told me he couldn't understand why there were two garbage collections a week. He thought the new $3 million visitor's centre was both a waste of money and completely out of keeping with the character of the town. He didn't have any kind words for the shire council's tourism initiatives and had put up a sign over the museum's door claiming the council had never given him any support.

David Brook found the sign faintly amusing. 'When I was mayor we virtually gave him the land the museum's on. When he first got here I gave him a job.'

John had an opinion on just about everything, and every opinion was a strong one. He went on at some length about the town's hot-water supply, a subject that eventually got me into hot water, too.

In the 1960s, the council sank an artesian bore to supply water for the town. It came out of the ground at nearly boiling point and was eventually used to power a generator that became one of the first renewable energy sources in the outback. (The town now draws power from a thermal power station to supplement the diesel power station, both of them maintained by Dusty and his assistant John Hanna.)

Not surprisingly, the furiously hot water caused problems. The pipes couldn't cope with the heat and kept bursting. Disconcertingly, that meant boiling water could erupt from beneath your feet without warning. Nell Brook remembered her children being scalded when they went to splash in the puddles in their gumboots. She also recalled filling the bath in the morning and leaving it all day so it would be cool enough for her children to have a bath in the evening. Tourists had to be warned about turning on taps and expecting cold water to come out. Progressively, from the 1960s to the 1990s, the council put in cooling ponds and a cooling tower, to reduce the temperature, save money on maintaining pipes and lower scalding rates among the general population.

John wasn't happy. The new arrangement meant everyone in town had to buy hot-water heaters to reheat the water. A further complication emerged in summer. The air temperature was so hot that the water heated up as it was piped around town. When you turned on a cold water tap, it came out warm. People turned off their hot-water systems and the water inside cooled. So hot water came out of the cold taps and cold water came out of the hot. Only in Birdsville? Apparently it was the same situation in many outback towns.

I found what John told me so interesting that I put some of it into a column I wrote for Queensland's *Sunday Mail* newspaper, blissfully unaware that I was about to get a lesson in politics, Birdsville style.

No sooner had the article run than a copy was obtained and distributed to all and sundry in the Diamantina Shire. It turns out that at the time the cooling system was proposed there had been fierce debate. After it was installed, tempers eventually cooled, but all it needed was one spark and it would explode once more.

'I've got a bone to pick with you,' Geoff Morton said ominously when I walked into the bakery for smoko. His tone suggested he'd already chosen the bone he wanted to pick. Mine.

'It wasn't me and I won't do it again,' I joked as I joined him and Bev at their table.

Geoff had read my column. He'd been sitting on the council when the decision to build a cooling system was made. He detailed at length the reasoning behind the decision. It was a sharp lesson in the difference between big city and small town media. In the city you can write something provocative and be protected from the reaction by the anonymity of the crowd, or by the distance between yourself and your detractors. The worst it gets is that angry people write in, and you write back to them. In Birdsville they take you to task while you're having your coffee and a chunky beef pie.

At the next Friday happy hour, another member of the community had a go at me. 'We only want you to write positive stories about Birdsville,' he told me. 'If you write negative stories, we'll move you on. Don't you worry about that.'

'Are you threatening me?' I asked, incensed that he thought he could tell me what I could and couldn't write.

'I rang your paper about it,' he went on.

'Did you get through to my editor?'

'No.'

'Okay,' I said. 'On Monday, when both of us are sober, I'll give you her name and direct number. If you want to make a complaint it will be treated seriously.'

But it was too late, the damage was already done. I'd been judged in some eyes and found wanting. Most of the community was still remarkably open and welcoming, but in some quarters things became decidedly cool.

The curious thing was that my source, John Menzies, was still widely liked. Even some of the people who were on the receiving end of his tirades valued his contribution to the community. 'Opinionated,' was the general verdict, 'but he's great for Birdsville. People rave about the museum and a lot of them stay an extra day to go there.'

Eventually John and I found time to sit down in his museum and have a proper talk. He'd actually been born in Sydney, but had run away to the bush when he was fifteen. His ambition was to work as a drover or a ringer on an outback station. He ended up working in New South Wales, Western Queensland, the Northern Territory and the Kimberley in Western Australia. He also competed in rodeo riding, which took him all over Australia and overseas to New Zealand, America and Canada.

'I was doing rodeos full time for a while,' he said. 'I've got a few broken bones playing up now. Hips are my problem but that could be from station work or anything. I gave it up when I was around thirty, quite a while ago. That was my life: stockman, drover, working for drovers, and rodeo cowboys as they called them then.'

He married and had a daughter, but his wife became ill, forcing him to give up his itinerant lifestyle. He settled in Mitchell, in central Queensland, and found work. Not long afterwards, his wife died. He had two more daughters from other relationships. He later married his current wife, Judy, with whom he also had a son.

'I started collecting things and set up a little museum there but

I never liked the place and I moved back out here as soon as I could. I worked for Brookie [David Brook] on Adria and Cordilla until I got this museum set up. Now I've been opened fifteen years exactly.'

His collecting began with horse-drawn vehicles that he restored in his spare time. As a drover he'd been around older men who still knew the arts of wheel-making and coach-building. His main interest was thorough-brace Cobb and Co coaches, so called because they used an ingenious suspension system based on thick strips of leather. After that he started picking up other items of interest and one thing led to another.

'With my museum I had a plan all the way,' he said, 'even when I was in Mitchell. Once you've got horse-drawn vehicles, you gotta have a wheelwright shop to make your wheels, and a coach-building shop. Then you've gotta fix your harness so you end up with a harness-making shop. When the museum thing come into me head I thought, well, you gotta put everything in their sections where they belong. So you start off with a section, like a shop. You work hard to make sure you get all the things in the sections. So you have butter churns and then you gotta have an ice-cream maker, and then you gotta have a certain sort of butter churn. You work hard to get it and while you're out huntin' that up you find something else that starts you off on another section. Like you get a little bit of shearing gear so you think "I'd better have a wool industry section".' His most recent section is a collection of ship tank lids.

Many of the items in the museum were given to him, including a painting by Winston Churchill. It was donated by an elderly woman who was keen to see that it was put on display, rather than stored in a vault somewhere. She also gave John a small sapphire and diamond crown that he's traced to a Captain Clark, who was aide de camp to Princess Alice, sister-in-law to the late Queen Mother.

Another donation was a Coo-ee Peppermint Cordial bottle. A man simply walked into the museum one day and presented it to

John. They both knew the bottle was quite valuable but the man was happy to part with it, knowing that it would become part of a collection where it would be appreciated.

It was also John's plan to have many of the exhibits actually working. He didn't regard things sitting in cabinets as being particularly interesting, which meant he had to do shows to demonstrate how they operate. It's a unique experience for the visitor/tourist, but he admits he's created a monster. 'When I was thirty I was too old to go ridin' bulls, and now I'm sixty-two I'm too old to go round and round here three times a day.

'Some people make it hard for you,' he said. 'You always get the ones in a group that want to talk. I tell 'em before the show, "I got our rules up there: no questions during the show, and if you've got one, don't tell us about it." Some people are just hopeless. And they're the ones that wear you down; they're the ones that get to you.'

'What do you hope people will get out of the museum?' I asked.

'Understanding what things are about,' he answered. 'Seeing the mules making chaff and those pumps down the back. If you don't see 'em working they don't really mean much. When the people see the water coming up the chain and the spring, you know, that's unbelievable. How can that work? That's defying gravity.'

Every year the museum is getting harder to run and John is looking towards retirement. He says he won't work past sixty-five, but the museum is already up for sale. In the meantime, he works seven days a week throughout the tourist season. Some days he's in too much pain to do the shows, but it hurts him more to turn people away. None of his three daughters or his young son, who's studying a trade, is interested in living in Birdsville and helping run the business.

If the museum doesn't sell, he'll be forced to auction parts of the collection. Whatever happens, once it's off his hands he won't be staying in Birdsville. He'll move on, perhaps taking his mules and training them to pull the Cobb and Co coach he's taken sixteen years to build using original metal he's found rusting in paddocks around the outback.

John has been living in Birdsville for eighteen years, but has been passing through the place since the 1960s. I asked him how it had changed in that time.

'Seen a lot of changes here in that time – for the worse,' he said. 'It's not an outback place any more. All the bushmen are died out or gone. People, families have left. It's just a service centre now. It's not a community any more. When I first come here there was lots of kids at the school. When Nat [his son] was going there we counted thirty kids in the school photograph and what is there here now? Six or eight, and a couple of them are away. You never know who's going to pack up and go.'

I asked him if he kept in touch with any of his droving mates. He sat thinking for a moment, the fans in the roof of the museum slowly turning.

'Jack Tedd, head stockman on Diamantina Lakes, Queensland, in the 1960s. That old man is still alive. When I first went to see him [on the coast] a couple of years ago, me daughter [Melody] took me round. He's got a big house, all on his own. I said to him, "What are we gonna have? A cuppa tea, a rum or a beer?" He said, "I've got a carton of beer. We're havin' a beer." So we sat down and he kept getting beers out of one of them little round fridges and Melody brought fish and chips round for us for lunch and went away and came back at three o'clock. So we sat there for about six hours, seven hours, just drinkin' this carton and talkin'. And he's just so happy, 'cause it's pretty different for him being there from the life he lived.

'There's a couple of people like that I've wanted to catch up with and by the time you're ready to catch up they're . . . well there's one old cowboy I wanted to catch up with in Brisbane but he's gone. They're sort of dyin' off fairly well. Like this place here. You could go in the pub once and you'd have old Frankie Booth and Georgie Flash and Willie Harris and even Joey Harris. But you've only got Jimmy [Crombie] now really. And there used to be all Aboriginal girls working on the other side of the bar and it was the outback. But now what is it? The beer's too dear. The meals are too dear. It's not an outback pub any more. It's a yuppie pub.'

John had an opinion on most things, but what he didn't have an answer for was the question of who would buy his museum. It was a real outback gem, but John was as much a part of its success as anything in it. Whoever took it over needed qualities like John's, but even he admitted that blokes like him are a dying breed. The new owner also had to outlay a substantial sum of money and relocate to a town that's as far from anywhere as it's possible to get. Still, if it was easy, it wouldn't be Birdsville.

9

THE DESERT BLOOMS

It had taken a couple of months for us to realise that what we'd thought we knew about the outback when we arrived was really nothing at all. Of course now we were 'experts' – the only problem being that every day we discovered something new.

At first I'd somewhat dismissively assumed that most people who lived in the outback were there because they couldn't survive anywhere else. On the contrary, our fellow Birdsvilleans lived there because they loved the place. To help them thrive in an environment that could chew people up and spit them out overnight, many had developed great resourcefulness and resilience. The town was full of people who were no strangers to hard work. Dusty and Teresa ground out the hours in the bakery seven days a week, often from early morning until late at night. Barry and Narelle at the post office/petrol station did the same. Judy and John Menzies also worked unrelenting hours at the museum. Part of the reason they all worked so hard was the difficulty and expense of attracting staff. It was no accident Michelle had been offered work within a week of arriving in town.

The longer we spent in Birdsville, the more we understood the social dynamics. 'Do you know,' I said to my gardening guru Harry Crombie one morning when we were comparing notes on why his tomatoes were roaring ahead and mine were sulking, 'I've begun to see that there are three tribes in Birdsville: there's white fellas, black fellas and council fellas.'

He laughed at the description, but understood what I meant. The council was the region's biggest employer (with a budget of $36 million) and its staff were immediately recognisable in their orange shirts and vests. They were all around town (cleaning, mowing, garbage collecting and doing general maintenance) and out maintaining the roads. The apparent dearth of young people in town was in part due to the fact that they were camped out on the roads and only returned home on the weekends.

Unemployment in the shire was practically nil, which meant there were few serious social problems. No-one had the excuse of boredom for falling into bad habits. In some cases, people who had a tendency to go off the rails were discreetly given work on one of the stations to give them a break from the temptations of town, such as they were.

Only one household was a source of unrest. Both adults in the home had lost their council jobs after getting into a fight at the previous year's Christmas party. Since then there'd only been one night of disturbed peace. Neale was responding to the situation as we strolled past on the way to Friday-night happy hour. On the street the male of the household involved was trying to choke Neale and threatening to kill him. Neale and I exchanged a glance. He'd obviously seen and done it all before as he quietly talked the bloke down.

Coming to Birdsville from a major capital city meant there was an extraordinary gap between what I took for granted and what was actually possible in a place with so few inhabitants. There were plenty of people with get up and go, probably more per head of population than in most places, but there was only so much they could do. All around town were the remnants of projects that had fallen over once their instigators had moved on or run out of energy. The outdoor cinema screen near the community hall no longer showed movies. The town's only swimming pool, which was on education department land, was closed and surrounded by barbed-wire fencing. The town's art gallery/cafe was closed. The oval, a council-maintained green sward, was used only once a year for the Birdsville Gift.

Other amenities that Birdsville lacked were less obvious. The town didn't have a chapel, let alone a church. Even for godless heathens such as myself, the lack of a place for quiet reflection, somewhere to contemplate eternity, was surprising. In fact, the town's isolation meant no-one had tended the Birdsville flock for at least six months.

It was the same story in the region beyond the town. At Betoota, the pub that had been shut since Ziggy Remienko died was a business opportunity just waiting for the right entrepreneur. But who would staff such a lonely location, pumping gas and pulling beers for an intermittent flow of tourists during the cooler months and enduring stifling heat and solitude for the other six months of the year? As a result it was a 400-kilometre drive from Windorah to Birdsville without a fuel or refreshment stop in between.

The situation wasn't helped by a gradual decline in the population of western Queensland. Figures quoted in a Draft Central West Regional Plan indicated the population had fallen from 14000 in 1976 to 12500 in 2006. The report talked about the difficulty in planning for a declining population. On the ground we were seeing what it really meant – a slow, seemingly irresistible squeeze on services and amenities.

Meanwhile, Birdsville was visited by no end of consultants who thought they had the answers. One local called them TMWs, Ten-Minute Wonders. He explained, 'They come in here and tell us how we should do everything. After they've gone nothing changes.'

Not that longer term initiatives fared much better. The swimming pool was a case in point. Barry Gaffney told me his children had fundraised for it all through their primary school years. By the time there was enough money to get the pool built, they'd left town to go to boarding school. After all their efforts they never got to swim in it. Eventually use of the pool was restricted to the school, due to concerns about public liability.

Curiously, not all progress was welcome in Birdsville. When the town was asked about getting a subsidised bus service with the potential to put Birdsville on the backpacker trail, it was opposed because it might change the character of the town. There were fears that sealing the roads would have a similar impact. 'You'd have all the riffraff in the world coming down,' one local said.

For the same reason, Birdsville had no mobile phones. I had to admit that after a couple of months, I was beginning to see their point. In the whole time we'd been in Birdsville, we'd never had a conversation or activity interrupted by the infernal things. Telemarketers calling to inform us that we could get a mobile phone couldn't comprehend the fact that we were among the 2 per cent of Australians who didn't have mobile coverage. As time went on, we were proud of it.

Tourists were also dismayed by the lack of shops. To them, Birdsville was a 'destination' but there was no pharmacy, hardware store or newsagent. When a tourist asked for directions to the supermarket, a local told them to head down to the end of the main street and turn right. Apparently the gullible traveller got a fair way along the Birdsville Track before realising the supermarket was 1000 kilometres away.

*

I finally made it to Wednesday-evening tennis when, for the first time in weeks, I hadn't been called out to attend a vehicle rescue. I discovered that David and Nell were as good as Michelle said they were, and keenly competitive. Nell looked like she'd had lessons, with a practised, graceful swing. David may have had lessons but he also possessed plenty of natural talent. One thing I noticed right away was that he didn't have a backhand. He switched the racket from his right hand to his left hand and played forehand on both sides of his body. He was, as a football coach once described a player who could kick equally well with his left and right foot, naturally 'amphibious'.

The four of us were quite evenly matched and it was one of the most enjoyable games of tennis I'd played in a long time. It was a beautiful clear evening. A light breeze brought cool air from the billabong as galahs wheeled and screeched overhead. We swapped partners from set to set and every match was close. And each time the ball hit the synthetic court surface, I couldn't help marvelling at the puff of dust, giving the game that authentic outback feel.

After our game we retired to the Birdsville Hotel to celebrate doing some exercise. Tourists saw our rackets and were dismayed that anyone would play tennis in the desert. They didn't seem to realise that the weather was delightful and the chances of perishing extremely low.

As David and I discovered a mutual affinity for red wine, I expressed some curiosity about the development of the Birdsville Golf Course. I wasn't a keen golfer, but golf struck me as the kind of sport that was ideally suited to the wide open spaces of the outback. There had been previous attempts to establish the course, but they'd all faltered. Council was negotiating with the Queensland government to acquire the land the course was on so it could take over the development.

'How long have you been trying to get the course established?' I asked David and Nell.

'Ten years,' Nell replied.

My jaw dropped. How hard could it be to build a golf course? To my mind, you dug nine holes in the ground and voila! 'I reckon I could knock up a golf course by Sunday afternoon,' I said.

Nell swooped on the suggestion. 'In that case, you should take a look at the master plan,' she said.

The following day I went round to David and Nell's and got a copy. The course had been designed ten years before by a consultant from the Queensland Institute of Technology's School of Landscape Design. It was well thought out, arranged so that players could fan out from a central point and start rounds from holes one, four or six. There were layouts for nine or eighteen holes that traversed sand dunes and claypans. There was even provision for a lake.

One of the perceived attractions of the outback is the high level of personal freedom. Now, here I was, contemplating building my very own golf course. I didn't need 'permission'. I opened my web browser and searched for websites that sold golf cups and flags. I researched hole diameters (108 millimetres) and rummaged around for flowerpots and tin cans that I could use until my order for golf cups arrived in the post.

On Saturday morning I took a shovel, a rake and nine flowerpot 'golf cups' out to the golf course. Using the master plan I worked out the locations for the greens for the first nine holes. At the first green I started scraping away the sparse vegetation. Then I levelled the sand and lightly packed soil with the rake and shovel and put in a star picket to indicate where it was. It wasn't so much a 'green' as a 'brown'.

I'd decided not to buy flagpoles because of the likelihood of wind storms filling the holes with sand, which would then make it difficult to replace the pole after sinking a putt. I planned to attach a piece of irrigation pipe to the top of each star picket to act as the flagpole. I'd also decided on red for the flags, to match those used by vehicles in the desert to alert approaching drivers when they were climbing over dunes. Until the flags arrived, I used strips of orange plastic garbage bag. I soon discovered the crows loved them, pecking away at them until they were reduced to tiny orange shreds.

Digging the holes for my golf cups gave me an insight into the way vegetation in arid regions manages to survive. On the surface, the ground was bone dry, but 15 centimetres down there was still a lot of residual moisture from the deluge six weeks before. The first thing desert plants do after rain is send down a long tap root. Even small plants can reap the benefits by sending tap roots deep underground.

Deeper still, a water table can be found. Even though the country is supposed to be a desert, in places the water table is just 4 metres below the surface. Nell explained how they'd had to water the trees around her son Deon's grave for the first few years after they planted them. They'd drive out with a 44-gallon drum full of water on the back of a ute every week to give the trees a drink. Eventually the roots penetrated deep enough to reach the water table. Since then they've thrived on their own.

It took me a couple of hours to clear the ground around the first five holes. I popped back in to the bakery for lunch with Michelle. When she knocked off work she came out to inspect the Birdsville Golf Course. After a tour of the work in progress we scraped the ground around the last four holes and dug in the cups. The browns were very rough, but I didn't care. I had my very own nine-hole golf course. There aren't many places you can say that. Standing on top of a dune, inspecting the ambitious sweep of my work, I hit upon the course motto: 'Make sand your friend'.

The next morning, I borrowed a set of golf clubs from Gus Daffy, who worked in the pub and was a keen golfer. He'd told me that for want of a proper course, he and a few other people sometimes practised on the oval. They'd once made it interesting by seeing who could hit a ball over the oval, over the road and onto the roof of the national park ranger station. When they succeeded, park ranger (and Aboriginal elder) Don Rowlands came roaring over the oval to give 'em hell. The golfers moved on to the airport runway. They hit over a hundred balls into the sunset. When it got dark they decided to pick them up the next morning. They went out bright and early, but there wasn't a single ball to be seen. The crows had taken the lot. He reckoned that somewhere in Birdsville there was a nest brimming with golf balls.

I decided to combine Zeus's morning walk with my first round of golf. There were no fairways as such, but the greens played better than I'd expected. It took Zeus three holes to work out that we were hunting little white balls instead of big ugly pigs. He trotted up to a ball I was searching for, nosed it, then looked at me as if to say, 'It's here, you moron.' After a couple more holes, he picked a ball up, walked a few metres and then spat it out. Pigs were more fun.

When I finished my round I went back to the bakery for lunch and bumped into Barb Mooney, wife of the council's tourism officer. I bubbled away about the new golf course and she asked where I was getting the money for the cups and flags. Nearly everything the council did was paid for by grants – they were part of the culture. They weren't part of mine, especially if it meant months of inaction while you found out if your grant application was successful.

'I'm paying for them out of my own pocket,' I answered. 'The way I look at it, the cost is half what you'd pay for a year's membership at a reasonable Sydney club. It's a bargain.'

That afternoon, Michelle's mother, Yvonne, and her sister, Lyn, were due to arrive in Birdsville for a week's visit. Michelle was busy making pizzas for Dusty's Sunday pizza night, so I decided to poke along (as the locals put it) the Windorah Road in the Truckasaurus to make sure they got through the boggy bits that were still soft six weeks after the big wet. I spotted them 40 kilometres from town and waved them down.

'Am I glad to see you,' Lyn blurted as soon as she pulled up. 'Our fuel warning light is on.' She'd put a large fridge in the back of her little four-wheel drive and filled it with goodies for Michelle and I. The energy-hungry fridge had raised their fuel consumption alarmingly, but there was nowhere to refuel along the 400-kilometre stretch from Windorah. She was struggling to make it to Birdsville.

'Don't worry,' I said, 'I'll follow you and run you into town if you don't make it.'

They set off, but only 2 kilometres down the road, Lyn pulled over. She and Yvonne became my first solo outback rescue. As the Truckasaurus took diesel and Lyn's car ran on petrol, I drove them into town and borrowed a fuel can from Dusty.

'Why didn't you call into Roseberth?' Dusty asked when he realised it was very near where Lyn had run out of juice.

'I thought about that, but I don't think Geoff has forgiven me for that hot water thing,' I replied. Dusty grunted knowingly. An 80-kilometre round trip was preferable to the wrath of Geoff.

Lyn and I drove back out, and with 20 litres in the tank she finally drove into town. Back at home we unloaded fish, prawns, cheeses, coffee and more from the bursting car fridge. Other delights for us shopping-deprived Birdsvilleans were piled high in the back of the little car. There were extra seeds for our expanding garden and Yvonne's home-baked Anzac biscuits, cakes and fruit loaf.

The following day we took them on a tour of the sights. In the evening we drove out to Big Red. As we approached the climb to the top I made sure everyone was wearing their seatbelts and holding on tight for the bumps ahead.

'Vehicle westbound climbing Big Red,' I said confidently on UHF Channel 10. Then I engaged four-wheel drive and accelerated to the bottom of the dune. We climbed it with practised ease. On top I pulled up at our favourite sunset viewing spot and started unloading the tables, chairs, food and drinks as the others fanned out to take in the scenery.

Once everyone was settled, rugged up against the cool evening air and savouring a selection of cheeses and dips, the beauty of the place began to weave its magic. Yvonne and Lyn grew quiet and sat

ABOVE: A dingo on a gibber plain east of Birdsville. At night their howls are commonly heard around the town. *(Michelle Havenstein)*

BOTTOM: The author and a few of Birdsville's friendly locals check the road conditions. *(Michelle Havenstein)*

TOP: The catcher about to rope a calf during a bronco branding competition. Bronco branding was the traditional method of branding in Central Australia. *(Michelle Havenstein)*

BOTTOM: The Mount Leonard Station ground crew in action. The calf has been pulled up to the bronco branding panel. The front and back leg ropes are going on while the judges look on in the background. *(Michelle Havenstein)*

TOP : My first rescue. David Cox from Mt Dare (centre vehicle) had towed a Nissan with a burnt-out clutch over 20 kilometres of dunes west of Poeppels Corner to the utility and trailer from Birdsville Auto. *(Olivia Corcoran)*

BOTTOM : A tourist's vehicle snapped in half in the Simpson Desert 10 kilometres west of Big Red. INSET: Patrick O'Neill from Birdsville Auto successfully welded the chassis together and the vehicle was driven back to town. It was later written off by insurance assessors. *(Dia Tannock)*

TOP: The author and Corey from Birdsville Auto at the rescue of a bus bogged on the Birdsville–Windorah Road. *(John Hanna)*

BOTTOM: Road trains such as these five taking cattle from Central Queensland to South Australia have reduced the time it takes to move cattle to market. In the droving days, journeys took months with cattle losing condition all the way. *(Michelle Havenstein)*

RIGHT: Tourists watching the sunset from Big Red dune. *(Michelle Havenstein)*

TOP : Ruts on the road to Big Red. Vehicles travelling on closed roads cause extraordinary damage. When the ruts harden the road becomes extremely treacherous. *(Michelle Havenstein)*

BOTTOM : The author photographing Minnie daisies along the Birdsville Inside Track. *(Cathy Gray)* **INSET :** Poached egg daisies and dwarf swainsona. *(Cathy Gray)*

TOP: Birdsville cemetery. Graves of indigenous and non-indigenous inhabitants of Birdsville date back to the 1880s. *(Michelle Havenstein)*

BOTTOM: Dusty Miller towing a vehicle with a burnt-out clutch up Big Red dune. Nemesis dune is in the distance. Between the dunes is a lake formed by rain six weeks earlier. *(Evan McHugh)*

TOP: Bull riding, part of the entertainment in town during the Birdsville Races. *(Evan McHugh)*

BOTTOM: During the races Birdsville Airport doubles as a camping ground. Up to 200 aircraft fly in each year. *(Michelle Havenstein)*

TOP: Fred Brophy's boxing tent has been an integral part of the Birdsville Races for thirty years. *(Evan McHugh)*

BOTTOM: Tourism in Birdsville is boosted by several car rallies that pass through town and take advantage of the surrounding unsealed roads. *(Michelle Havenstein)*

TOP: A dust storm rolls in over Lake Muncoonie, Adria Downs Station. *(Evan McHugh)*

BOTTOM: The country around Birdsville abounds with Aboriginal sites. This framework for a small shelter was originally covered in grasses and is probably about 100 years old. *(Michelle Havenstein)*

TOP: On New Year's Eve the whole town turned up to celebrate in the Birdsville Hotel. *(Michelle Havenstein)*

BOTTOM: Rising waters from the Diamantina River flowing 'upstream' into Birdsville's billabong. When the river fell the channel flowed just as strongly in the opposite direction. *(Evan McHugh)*

PREVIOUS SPREAD : Floodwaters swirl past Birdsville, swamping the billabong east of the town. *(Kay Ezzy)*

LEFT : Floodwaters in Eyre Creek disappearing into Lake Koolivoo (bottom of picture) and flooding back towards Lake Machattie (top of picture). *(Michelle Havenstein)*

TOP : With the town completely isolated by floodwaters for periods of up to three weeks during January and February 2009, the Diamantina Shire Council chartered a helicopter to ferry supplies and personnel in and out of Birdsville. *(John Hanna)*

BOTTOM : The road to Big Red dune cut where the Diamantina River spread over the flood plain west of Birdsville. *(Michelle Havenstein)*

TOP : Gibber country north of Birdsville after heavy local rain. *(Evan McHugh)*

BOTTOM : After the floods, an explosion of life follows, such as this pelican rookery at Lake Machattie, north of Birdsville. *(Lyn Rowlands)*

contentedly looking across the spinifex and dunes as corellas flew across the plains below us.

At last Yvonne spoke: 'Seeing this, I now understand what it is about the place that appeals to you.'

*

Every six weeks the Royal Flying Doctor Service flew in to provide a medical consultation service at the Birdsville Clinic. A plane was chartered for the purpose and after he'd delivered the doctor, the pilot usually spent the day twiddling his thumbs waiting until the doctor finished seeing patients. On his visit in mid-July, pilot Philip Owens tired of twiddling.

'Does anyone want to go for a fly to see the floodwaters?' he asked.

Neal and Ruth Ramm (a retired couple who were caretaking the Old Birdsville Hospital), Lyn and I leapt at the chance. All we had to do was pay for the fuel and Philip would take us anywhere we wanted to go.

Phillip, an older pilot who'd been flying in the outback for years, headed north-west for Adria Downs and the lake Dalene Brook had told me about – Lake Muncoonie. As soon as we took off, we could see that there was still water everywhere, even though it was many weeks since rain had fallen. It was lapping at the dunes. Gibber plains were dotted with pools. In places billabongs were surrounded by silver tendrils of water that snaked outwards through rich herbage.

We flew at low altitude for 100 kilometres, snapping photographs the whole way. Then we started peering into the distance, trying to see the lake. As it turned out, there was no way you could miss it, and in the distance we could see something green.

As we flew in over Muncoonie, we saw that the floodwaters had almost completely evaporated and the vegetation was coming up thick and lush. The lake was, as Dalene had said, grass from one

side to the other – thousands of hectares of it. The edges were surrounded by coolabahs and red dunes. The lake was as unexpected as
finding an oasis on the moon.

Beside Lake Muncoonie, another lake, Selicia, was golden brown.
It still showed signs of where they'd been cutting hay just a few
months before. Hay in the Simpson Desert! Below us the grassy
plains were dotted with fat Hereford cattle. Up in the plane every
impression I'd had of the Channel Country was in disarray. Once
again, everything I thought I knew was turned on its head.

Seeing such giant flood plains also made it clear how floodwaters
from a river system, in this case the Georgina/Eyre Creek/Mulligan,
could be swallowed whole. Lakes Muncoonie and Selicia must take
billions of litres to fill, but they were only two of many.

From Muncoonie we turned north-east and followed Eyre Creek
past the lonely outpost of Tomydonka Waterhole, on Glengyle
Station, then through the dry claypans and dark belts of lignum
surrounding Lake Mipia and Lake Koolivoo. Beyond them was the
vivid green of Lake Machattie, a corner of which was still under
water. It was dotted with cattle and emus. Some of the cattle were
dead. Philip, who also owned a cattle station near Longreach,
couldn't tell us whether they'd died from eating something poisonous or from something that caused bloating. He just said ruefully,
'That's cattle for you. They'll die when times are bad; they'll die
when times are good.'

From Machattie we could see dark flood plains extending far to
the north. They were laced with thousands of channels. To look
down upon them and try to imagine rainwater that could possibly
fill them all, then flow down to Lake Muncoonie and from there on
through the dunes to Lake Eyre simply boggled the mind.

To understand the Channel Country, you have to see it from the
air. It's the only way to get a sense of the monumental scale of the
river systems that bring life pulsing down broad verdant corridors

to even wider lakes and plains. The plants and animals have waited for years and even decades for the chance to burst forth. There is grandeur in the land where boom and bust, plenty and heartbreak rubbed shoulders all the time.

*

Within days of resurrecting the golf course, I had my first players. The Brooks didn't have to be asked twice to come out for a round on a Sunday afternoon. Gus from the pub took it up, as did Neale the policeman. Even Ben from the bakery, with Zeus in tow, came out for a game.

Ben said he'd never played before. I gave him some tips on how to swing, which was really a case of the blind leading the blind. Then he hit his first ball.

'Are you sure you've never played before?' I asked as the ball disappeared into the distance.

'No, never,' he said.

It wasn't long before I was calling him Tiger Ben.

A couple of days after we'd played, he asked if he could borrow some clubs so he could go out and practise. Ben was a fairly quiet guy who spent most of his time off sitting at home alone watching TV – that is when he wasn't out pigging with Zeus. His interest in golf, a healthier option than the couch, made the effort I'd put into the golf course all the more worthwhile.

We were beginning to feel very settled in our outback lifestyle. My clients had all but forgotten I was 2000 kilometres away. Setting up my office had proven that it was both possible and entirely practical to telecommute from the remotest town in Australia. Michelle was enjoying being the bakery rouseabout and was quickly developing a circle of friends with interests in photography and jewellery making. The latter had become a small source of income as Dusty let her sell necklaces and earrings in the bakery, asking only a small commission in return.

There were many things about the city we weren't missing at all – sirens, traffic, jet noise, pollution, bars on windows and doors to keep burglars at bay, drunks vandalising vehicles in our street, to name a few. The only things we really missed were restaurants, shopping and sailing. We were still in contact with all our friends and making many more in Birdsville. On balance we were ahead.

After we finished work each day, we got into the habit of heading out of town to look at the sunset or to explore the new desert phenomenon – the tiny plants that had risen out of the flood plains and dunes were beginning to flower.

Despite the fact that the Inside Track had bogged both Dusty and Ben, we ventured that way one evening to a spot where masses of tiny flowers were turning the flood plains pale green. Five kilometres from town we got out to explore, leaving the car on the track with the keys still in the ignition. We walked across to a small clump of trees and were surprised to discover that they hid a beautiful little billabong. All around the banks the ground was covered in lush herbage. It was a captivating place and we lingered for some time, exploring and taking photographs.

As we walked back to the car I said to Michelle, 'I think we're becoming locals.'

'Why's that?'

'We just abandoned the car in the middle of the road for the best part of an hour and didn't think twice about it.'

'Well,' she said, 'there was plenty of room to go around us.'

*

By the beginning of August, Bev Morton was well on her way to raising $10 000 for the x-ray machine, and I'd had to revise my estimate of how long it would take her to reach her $40 000 target. The work of years was starting to look more like months.

Bev was full of ideas. She was doing plenty of pub raffles, but she also had collection boxes and signs in the Shell and Mobil service stations, the caravan park, the bakery, the pub and anywhere else people might find themselves with a few coins they'd rather donate than put in their pocket. The money kept mounting up.

I'd hit on the idea of collecting empty beer and soft drink cans and selling them for recycling. On trips out to the tip to scavenge irrigation pipe and timber for my garden beds, I'd noticed piles of cans that were going into landfill. Surely if they could be recycled there was a small fortune to be made.

'The freight cost is too high,' she told me, having already been down that road years ago on another of her fundraising drives. 'The money you get for the cans doesn't cover the cost of trucking them out.'

The more I got to know Bev, the more she impressed me. Her energy and enthusiasm were unflagging; her commitment to her goals unwavering. She never pushed herself to the forefront, but she was always around, helping to get the job done.

Her skills were amply demonstrated by one of her best fundraising ideas. In mid-August the Rotary Club of Dubbo arrived in town on its biannual charity fundraising bash. Vehicle after vehicle rolled into town, bringing 160 people to stay for two nights and a day. On the morning that they left, Bev put on breakfast for the lot of them, by way of thanks for the club's $2000 donation. Just to make it interesting, the venue was 30 kilometres outside town, on the side of the road.

She rounded up the usual volunteers: her husband, Geoff, Belinda the cook from Roseberth, Ruth Doyle, Neal and Ruth Ramm. Neale the policeman also turned up to help, dressed in his police uniform. At 6 a.m. I found the team setting up alongside Nappabillie Creek. Gas barbecues were unloaded from trailers, fires were lit to boil water, tables were laid out with boxes of cereal, milk and fruit juice. Trays of chopped tomato and onion were heated on the barbecues. By the time the first vehicles rolled up, they were greeted with the aroma of sizzling bacon. Eggs and toast were on the fry.

Car rallies are a major source of income for small outback towns although the influx of large numbers of people also stretches their resources to the limit. For the next two hours, eight people worked flat out to feed the multitudes. Without the experience and organisation of Bev, and a lot of support from Geoff, it could have been chaos. When I asked if feeding 160 was a challenge, Bev just laughed. 'This is nothing,' she said, 'my record is dinner for 400.'

The Dubbo Rotarians had thoroughly enjoyed themselves in Birdsville. They'd spent their day buzzing around the sights, although one vehicle came to grief on the road to Big Red. It had lost control and rolled.

'We have three kinds of accidents in the outback,' Neale said when he took me out to help him photograph the scene. 'Rollovers, rollovers and rollovers. People have to learn to drive to the conditions. Most people lose it when they try to stay on the road, they have to learn that out here you can often keep going straight and you won't hit anything. And whatever you do, don't hit the brakes.'

In this crash, the driver, the only occupant of the vehicle, escaped without injury. He'd gone to the clinic where Bev and Ross had checked him over and concluded that he was fine. Neale reckoned they gave him a spoonful of concrete and told him to harden up.

Quite a few of the people at breakfast were a little the worse for wear after a long night of partying in the Birdsville Hotel. As the morning wore on some of them came up to Neale and handed him an assortment of items they'd souvenired from the pub. They wanted to return them 'no questions asked'. Before long his pockets were bulging with salt and pepper shakers, beer mats and money for unpaid telephone calls.

When everyone was fed, Geoff Morton got up on the back of a trailer and gave a short talk about Roseberth Station, its history and operations. Geoff was an informative and entertaining speaker. He was quick with a one-liner, too, which he demonstrated when one of the Rotarians asked, 'Given these big stations have hundreds of kilometres of fences and unbranded cattle are ripe for duffing, is it true you've never tasted your own beef?'

He'd as good as accused Geoff of stealing and I expected a response like 'get off my land'. Instead he gave the bloke a grin and said, 'Sure I've tasted my own beef. I've been to my neighbour's for a barbecue.'

It got a huge laugh.

After Geoff was finished, the breakfast broke up and the vehicles set off in leisurely fashion for their next destination. There was an opportunity to talk to some of the organisers, route director Brett McCarthy and event director Peter Scott, about how effective rallies such as theirs could be at fundraising. Halfway into their week-long trip they'd raised $130000. They expected to reach $200000 by the end. It was the tenth of their outback bashes, the first being in 1990. Altogether the trips had raised a total of $1 million for outback projects.

It had been agreed that the Rotarians would donate $2000 to the x-ray fundraising. However, they told me they'd be meeting after the rally to decide how they would disperse all the monies they'd raised. Most would go to the Flying Doctor but the x-ray machine, which had the potential to save $7000 if it meant a plane didn't have to evacuate someone from Birdsville, would also get additional consideration.

*

Every spare moment we had, Michelle and I went out photographing and botanising among the flower-carpeted dunes. We bought a copy of *Plants of the Channel Country* from the Wirrari Information Centre and spent hours identifying the dazzling variety that swathed the once-bare dirt and dunes.

One of our favourites was a bush called the silver cassia. Its Latin name was *Cassia artemisioides*, derived from the Greek goddess Artemis, whose statue was cast in silver. The plant had delicate, thin, silvery leaves, but was covered in small yellow flowers that were shaped like a knight's helmet. Its close relative was *Cassia nemophila* (desert cassia), which used to be called *Cassua eremophila*, meaning desert lover. It also had a beautiful yellow flower.

My golf course was blooming. The fairways were disappearing under a sea of annual yellow top (*Senecio gregorii*), delicately perfumed lavender of wild stock (*Blennodia canescens*) and purple dwarf swainsona (*Swainsona phacoides*). One of the most attractive flowers was the poached egg daisy (*Myriocephalus stuartii*). It really looked like an egg, with a yellow centre surrounded by a mass of white petals. Up on the dunes we found the otherworldly, parrot-faced flowers of the desert rattlepod (*Crotalaria eremaea*).

Having discovered that Zeus really enjoyed going for walks off the leash, every time I took him for his morning walk I ventured further afield, looking for more spectacular areas of wildflowers. Beyond the golf course we discovered a track that was called the Flood Bypass Road. It kept to slightly higher ground that skirted the large plain west of town. The plain and the Big Red Road that crossed it were so far from the river that it would take an immense amount of water to ever render the bypass necessary – a very rare occurrence. I certainly didn't dare hope that I'd see such a thing during my year in Birdsville.

One morning Zeus and I were driving out along the Bypass Road when I noticed a distant line of trees suggesting a possible watercourse and more flowers. I decided to check it out. That's how I came upon the Creek of Flowers.

All along the watercourse the blooms were so thick and the vegetation so lush that when Zeus jumped out of the Truckasaurus he
almost disappeared. The verdure was cool and fresh and before long
he was in raptures. He bounded back and forth, snuffling about and
then lifted his fluffy head above the flowers to see what I was up to.
He charged away while I followed him up the watercourse, thread-
ing through patches of coolabah trees, lignum and desert cassias,
the ground covered in poached egg daisy and stock. Then, beyond
the trees, I saw something that stopped me in my tracks. There was
a large dune rising on the left-hand side of the watercourse, and it
was completely yellow. It was covered in millions upon millions of
yellow-top flowers. In the early morning sunshine, it shone improbably bright. I stood transfixed. The outback had done it again.

And then I noticed the birds. The trees were laden with them – corellas, galahs, larks, crimson chats, hawks. I heard budgerigars before
I saw them. Nearly every book about the outback I'd read had raved
about the flashing green of a flight of wild budgies. To date, the odd
one or two I'd glimpsed had left me thinking such descriptions were
exaggerated. Now, as I walked across the dune, a flight of twenty
or so took wing. Then they darted in a different direction. As they
turned a pulse of light shot from their midst as their feathers caught
the sun. I gave out an involuntary 'oh'.

As soon as Michelle knocked off work that afternoon, I took her
straight out to the Creek of Flowers. As I drove I praised its wonders
while hoping she'd be as impressed as I was. She loved it. As soon as
she got out of the car she started taking photographs, homing in on
one area while I was already trying to pry her away to show her the
next. Beyond the yellow-top dune we discovered a lake. It still had
plenty of water in it and the shallows were being patrolled by a small
flock of Australian bustards (*Arteodis australis*). Bustards are the
largest Australian bird capable of flight. When they do, their flight is
ponderous – slow and majestic, like a squadron of 747s. We watched

them take off and flap over a distant dune, half a dozen birds sil-
houetted against the setting sun – a clichéd image, but spectacular
nevertheless.

The Creek of Flowers became my favourite place for morning
walks with Zeus, and we considered it our little secret. That is until
the morning we encountered another vehicle coming back along the
Bypass Track. As one does in Birdsville I pulled up to say g'day to the
driver. They pulled up as well.

Wolfgang John was at the wheel, with his dog Georgina sitting
up in the passenger seat beside him. Wolfie was a painter, Birdsville's only artist. He knew I was a writer. We eyed each other
suspiciously.

'What are you up to?' he asked.

'Taking Zeus for a walk,' I answered. 'Have you been walking
Georgie?'

'Yes,' he said, with a slight German accent. 'We go out every
morning.'

Neither of us mentioned the Creek of Flowers, which was so close
it was obvious where one of us had been and where the other was
going. We just looked at each other, poker-faced. The outback may
be so vast that there's plenty to go around, but when it came to the
Creek of Flowers, the place wasn't big enough for both of us.

10

MUNGA-THIRRI

Only one thing detracted from the enjoyment of a leisurely round out on the golf course – the human remains. A skeleton, probably of Aboriginal origin and quite old, was buried under a pile of stones near the tee-off area for the sixth hole. A large space around the grave was fenced off. Some locals reckoned it was the discovery of the remains that was the real reason the golf course had never got up and running. Seeing where the grave was (on the edge of the course, rather than in the middle of it) I didn't think that was the case. Nevertheless, every time I looked at it, I worried that playing golf nearby might offend Aboriginal sensitivities. I decided to make sure.

Don Rowlands was both an Aboriginal elder and the ranger for the Simpson Desert National Park. He was another of the grey-haired older generation of Birdsville. He sported a thin white moustache and always had a battered green Akubra pushed back on his head. As with several other members of the Aboriginal community, I'd been introduced to him when we first arrived but we hadn't progressed much beyond polite acquaintance, in part because I didn't think that writing a book gave me the right to barge up and start asking questions. Nevertheless, when I asked if he'd come out to the golf course to have a look at the grave site he was more than happy to oblige.

As we drove out of town I was anxious. If there was a problem, I was prepared to compromise. I figured the outback was big enough for me to be able to realign the course if he thought it necessary. But what if he thought that wasn't good enough? What if he said no location was acceptable because as far as he was concerned every centimetre of the area was and would always remain Aboriginal land?

From what I'd learned about the European occupation of the country around Birdsville, anything was possible. On many stations the process of occupation was relatively peaceful. New landholders with their cattle and sheep had sought to coexist with the original inhabitants. Eventually they had employed them on their properties, often only for rations, but the process of integration meant far less violence and destruction of Aboriginal culture. In other areas the competition for scarce resources, especially water, had led to conflict.

When Cecil Madigan camped at Andrewilla Waterhole, 75 kilometres south of Birdsville, after his crossing of the Simpson Desert in 1939, he noted:

> There were the ruins of a mud hut which had been a police station in the days when blacks were numerous. All that are left of these tribes are now either in Birdsville or Marree, or on the few stations that still survive. The white man dispossessed the black, and now he too is driven out and the country is deserted. Andy [his expedition's Aboriginal guide] himself was a survivor. He told some grisly tales of a certain policeman with a Hunnish name who used to shoot the blacks and then lay them out in rows and poke them with a burning stick to see if they were still alive, for it was a common trick to pretend to be dead.

Madigan had his doubts about the truth of the story, but it resurfaced fifteen years later in George Farwell's *Land of Mirage*. Farwell detailed that and other incidents that probably occurred in the 1880s:

After the Cooninghera cook's head was found in the campoven, savage reprisals were organised. A vengeance party was led by Captain Little, policeman at Bedourie barracks. With a posse of black trackers, he chased the whole tribe all over the country, overtaking the first of them six miles [10 kilometres] from the waterhole, where they were shot out of hand. Others were killed by Coongie Lake, more yet at Coonchere sandhill [both locations are south of Birdsville]. They even shot piccaninnies in their mother's arms.

Farwell estimated the number of dead at 200, but it wasn't the worst incident he'd heard of.

Beneath the big white Coonchere sandhill, near the Diamantina plain, another terrible scene was enacted. A large party of 'salt-water blacks' (so called because they came from desert country where the waterholes grew brackish as their waters evaporated) had come down for a corroboree, making friendly advances to a white man living at Ngappamanna Station, now part of Clifton Hills. But his interest in one of their lubras antagonised two blacks, one of whom wanted her for his wife. One morning, when they had supposedly left for a day's hunting, they entered his tent, clubbing him to death on her breast with boomerangs. They took the woman away, and killed her later.

No remorse was expressed over the seduction, but lynch law was set up. The policeman at Andrewilla, a more clement man this time, sent his trackers to cut out the culprits from the innocent before the white men rode up. He lacked the resources to do more. But the white men came too quickly. Fleeing men, women and children were mustered like scrub cattle, shot down as they ran for cover. Many blacks rushed into the nearby waterhole, swam out amid the rushes with firesticks in their hair. But not one escaped. This is said to have been the biggest massacre known, for several hundred people had come in from the Kallikoopah.

Farwell also referred to Don Rowlands' European grandfather, Artie, coming across a flat strewn with bones while mustering on Coongie Station. Artie thought they might have been from a massacre carried out by an earlier Coongie manager named Wylie. Aboriginal people had given him the name *padimarta,* which meant savage boss.

With that kind of historical context I wouldn't have blamed Don if he'd told me what I could do with my golf course and my golf clubs for good measure. Nevertheless, I pointed out that we were teeing off away from the grave site and that I'd shortened the ninth hole and moved the green so that even a hacker like me couldn't slice a ball into the fenced-off area. I suggested we could put up signs warning golfers not to enter it.

'Mate, that's all fine,' Don said, much to my surprise. 'It's a shame that box [one of the tee-off boxes from a previous incarnation of the course] is inside the fence but if you want, just move it out of there. As long as people stay away from the grave, it's not a problem.'

Too easy, I thought. Don then started hinting that he might be interested in coming out to the golf course for a round or two. That didn't mean he wasn't aware of the terrible events that had all but destroyed his forebears. Some months later I mentioned some of the massacres referred to above. He knew all about them. He described the location at Coonchere sandhill where the worst killings had occurred. 'Some of the people did manage to get away,' he told me. 'But they ended up getting caught. They were trying to escape into the desert but they were starving. So they killed a bullock. The people that were after them found the bullock, they knew who it was that killed it and they tracked them down from there.'

Not long after we'd gone out to the golf course, Don had to go out to Poeppels Corner, on the edge of the national park, to do some maintenance work on the facilities there. Did I want to come?

'He knows the country like the back of his hand,' people told me. 'You'll get to see more than you would with anyone else.'

A journey into the desert with an Aboriginal elder was too good to miss. Once again, poor Michelle had to stay in Birdsville to work in the bakery while I set off on an adventure. It was beginning to rankle with her, but there wasn't a lot to be done. When the tourist season ended, we hoped things would be different.

Don and fellow ranger Ian Andreasen loaded two national parks vehicles with equipment and just before lunch we set out for Big Red. Our route was going to take us across Adria Downs, then into the Simpson Desert. As I rode with Don, I eagerly anticipated rare insights into the culture of the desert's original inhabitants while discovering details of its fascinating flora and fauna. Instead, just after we'd cleared Big Red and Nemesis dunes, we picked up rubbish. All along the road that climbed over a succession of flower-covered red dunes, Don and Ian kept stopping. A beer can here, a chip packet there, we picked up every little thing we saw. All of it had been left by untidy tourists.

'It's not all glamorous stuff like counting bilbies,' Ian said when we stopped to clean up the campsite of someone who'd thought that dingoes couldn't dig up the rubbish they'd buried. We dumped their tin cans, paper towel, plastic bags and bottle of wine into hessian bags brought specially for collecting litter.

It was disappointing to think of people going to so much trouble to visit such a compelling landscape and then defacing it by leaving their rubbish behind. If they wanted to see a garbage dump they could have stayed at home.

After about 20 kilometres of not particularly enriching garbage collection, I had to content myself with admiring Don's uncanny ability to spot pieces of paper hidden under a spinifex bush or poking up out of the red sand.

We eventually reached the boundary of Adria Downs Station and the Simpson Desert National Park and it was there that I witnessed a demonstration of Don's bush skills that was more like what I'd been hoping for. We'd stopped to take photographs of the decaying remains of the century-old rabbit fence that had been built in a failed attempt to check the western spread of the voracious introduced species. We'd just got going again when Don braked.

'Snake,' he said, pulling up and opening his door to get out. Ian pulled up behind us. I waited to see where Don was going, and where the purported reptile was, before following suit.

Don started peering at the ground in front of the ute. All I saw was sand. Don pointed to a series of curved depressions. 'That's where his body presses on the ground to push him along,' he explained. The marks were only just visible and I marvelled that he'd been able to spot them from the car. I was also curious about where the snake had gone.

'He went that way, into that mulga bush,' Don said. He walked right around the bush then said, 'He's still in there.'

There were tracks going into the bush but none coming out. The snake, 'a pretty big one', appeared to have entered a goanna hole. 'There's a tin can there, Evan,' Don said with a mischievous grin. 'You want to get it?'

Sure enough, a tourist had tossed a small can in beside the goanna hole. I thought about doing what he asked and how my willingness might make a good impression. Then I thought of the impression the snake might make on my life expectancy. 'Not for a million bucks,' I replied.

Don chuckled to himself as he got back in the ute. 'We'll pick 'im up on the way back.'

As we drove along Don told me about his life. His father and mother had died when he was young and he'd been raised by his grandparents. 'As soon as I was old enough, about fourteen, I went to work,' he said. 'I was a stockman on all the stations round 'ere.'

He thoroughly enjoyed the work and the life of the cattle camps. There was nothing better than mustering cattle with his mates unless it was playing tricks on unwary new ringers, but there was a down-side. 'Often all we worked for was poor rations and a good flogging. I remember waiting once to be picked up in town to go to work. I waited for three hours in the heat while the boss was in the pub. He didn't bother letting me know he was going to be late, but if I wasn't there when he turned up I'd have lost my job.'

His stories were interrupted when we reached the first channel of Eyre Creek. The country between two high red dunes was lined with healthy-looking coolabahs, a stark contrast to the spindly vegetation we'd been driving through. Coolabahs thrive wherever the country experiences reasonably regular floods. We climbed the next dune and again the space between the dunes was dotted with large trees.

'How wide is Eyre Creek?' I asked.

'From this point, 16 kilometres,' Don replied.

'How could there ever be so much water here?' I said, still strug-gling to understand the scale of things in the Channel Country. 'It must only flood once a lifetime.'

'No,' Don said. 'It comes down every few years, a big flood not so often.'

At the main channel, the four-wheel drive descended a steep deep bank, drove 100 metres across the creek bed, then up the other side. It was difficult to comprehend the volume of water that this series of channels could carry and that such arid country could ever see its like.

'What are the chances it'll flood like this in the next year?' I asked, thinking what an experience it would be to see the Channel Country in full flow.

'Pretty good,' Don replied. 'There hasn't been a flood, a really good flood, for quite a while.'

Beyond Eyre Creek the dunes returned to an endless series of crests and flats. The flowers that we'd seen closer to Birdsville had faded away as we entered country that hadn't received any of the June rain.

Don was telling me how he'd eventually given up working with stock when he'd got the opportunity to become a ranger. He considered it the best job in the world. It allowed him to be a custodian of his country in more ways than one.

We were driving across a flat stretch of land dotted with short, straggly Georgina gidgee trees when we stopped again. I assumed it was another piece of litter that had to be picked up but I was wrong. Don pointed to a clearing among the trees. There was a low structure sitting in the middle of it. Four short logs stood on end in a half circle, leaning inwards to form a peak in the middle. It was all that remained of an Aboriginal shelter, a frame that was once covered with spinifex and branches to provide shade and shelter from the sun and wind.

There were no signs on the nearby road to indicate its presence or to warn visitors away from it. There was no fence around it. Its main protection seemed to be that you had to have very good eyes, or know it was there, to spot it from the track.

'How long has it been here?' I asked.

'People haven't lived out here for at least ninety years,' Don answered. 'I reckon it could be a hundred years old, easy.'

'Can I take a picture?' I asked, mindful that it was always best to ask permission before photographing any Aboriginal artefacts.

'Of course,' he answered. I hurried over. This was more like what I'd been hoping for on my trip with Don. On subsequent trips into the desert I tried to find the shelter again, looking hard in the area I thought it was, and could never spot it. For Don, locating it was as easy as finding the local shop.

We arrived at Poeppels Corner in the middle of the afternoon and immediately set to work on the task at hand. The intense desert heat had warped the synthetic materials used to construct part of a boardwalk from the car park to the concrete post that marked the point where the Queensland, South Australian and Northern

Territory borders met. To repair the affected section, we had to dig up the bearers buried beneath the sand. As I got to work, I wondered if the reason I'd been invited out there was because Don had heard about my skills with a shovel.

During the course of the afternoon tourist vehicles turned up in ones and twos to visit Poeppels, take a photo and drive off. I was surprised when a single vehicle pulled up and an elderly gentleman got out. He was on his own. While it was the middle of winter, it seemed very risky for him to be travelling through the Simpson Desert alone. The chap chatted with us for a while and went on his way. Then, just on sunset, another vehicle pulled up. Once again, an older gentleman got out. He, too, was crossing the Simpson Desert solo. These gents seemed to take the dangers in their stride and presumably preferred their own company. I'd heard several stories of wives who'd arrived in Birdsville after bouncing over the hundreds of dunes of the Simpson Desert and vowed 'never again!'

The light was starting to fade when Don and Ian called it a day. Don invited the solitary traveller to make his camp with us for the night. He seemed a little reticent, but he eventually followed the two ranger's vehicles a couple of kilometres from the work site to a spot Don picked out for a camp.

It was dark when we arrived, but Don and Ian soon had a small fire going. They put water on to warm so we could have a wash and set out camp chairs for everybody. Don opened up the side of a large metal box on his ute to reveal a well-organised camp kitchen. Before long, steaks were sizzling on a hotplate.

Our guest revealed very little about himself, but he did disclose that he was a retired physics lecturer from Tasmania. He wasn't inclined to give us his life story and we thought better than to ask. He seemed to enjoy our company, although he prepared his own meal and preferred to sit on a groundsheet he'd laid down by the fire. It turned out that his reluctance to talk was no impediment to an enjoyable evening. Once dinner was finished and everything was tidied away, Don took the floor. For the next few hours he told joke after joke.

'Do you know how to make mowing your lawn easier?' he asked. 'Sprinkle it with rum until it's half cut.'

'Did you hear about the two European tourists who were eaten by a pair of crocodiles?' he asked, his eyes glinting. 'The Czech was in the male.'

'Did you know that the cowboys in America use dachshunds to muster cattle? That's why they're always saying "get a long little doggie".'

He told us about the time he and Jimmy Crombie were invited to accompany an outback tour as indigenous guides. 'We were supposed to point out cultural things, bush tucker and that sort of stuff,' he explained. 'We were down the Birdsville Track and it was a terrible drought and there was nothin', just nothin' there. But they're payin' us so we thought, we gotta come up with somethin', so we got some eggs from the cook and we took 'em out real early in the morning and buried 'em and made a mound like it was a goanna nest. Then everyone gets up and we said we'd try and find some tucker. Sure enough we found some "goanna tracks" and they're all looking where we've made some marks and they're takin' pictures and we're following the tracks. Then we say, "Oh, here's a nest!" So we dig in there to find the eggs and I pull one out to show 'em and that's when I notice the egg's got a use-by-date stamp on the side. Oh shit! So I'm trying not to let 'em see it and sayin', "Quick, we better not disturb the nest too much," and we're trying to bury the egg before anyone sees the bloody writin' on the side of this "goanna egg". Back in the camp the staff all knew. They thought it was a great bloody joke.'

Someone on the same trip had asked him if Aboriginal people used every part of the kangaroo. He'd replied, 'Oh, yeah, the old people, they used everything. They ate the meat, they used the bone to make things like needles, the skins were used for carry bags or cloaks, the sinews were used for strings. They even used the hops to make beer.'

The next morning, bright and early, we went back to work on the boardwalk. After we finished I took the opportunity to get photos of Don with the information signs that welcomed visitors and identified he and Linda Crombie as elders of the area.

Don then showed me where a new section had been stuck on the sign to cover up a vandalised part. Beneath the new section you could still feel the letters where an obscenity had been gouged into Don's picture.

'You musty have really upset someone,' I said as I felt the letters.

'I don't think it's just one person,' he said with a laugh.

Within days of returning to Birdsville, I was being warned about having anything to do with Don. 'I wouldn't believe anything he says,' I was told. Don also had his supporters. Neale the policeman reckoned he was a 'bit of a rogue', but a likeable rogue.

Don took it all in his stride. It didn't stop him trying to do things to improve the community for both indigenous and non-indigenous members. Like a lot of people in Birdsville he just got on with it, often without much fanfare.

Along with other Aboriginal elders, notably Linda Crombie and her son Jimmy, he had gathered information on one of the most important stories of the Wangkangurru and other peoples of Central Australia – Thutirla Pula (Two Boys Dreaming). They published the story on a poster, hoping it would make it accessible to the general public and promote understanding of Wangkangurru people and culture. Thutirla Pula explains how the spirits of the Dreamtime first crossed the desert they call Munga-Thirri (Land of Sandhills):

The story begins at Dalhousie Springs on the western side of the desert. They had a great ceremony there, a corroboree. At the corroboree it was decided to take feathers as important decorations to their people on the other side of the desert. To get there they needed to create water wells (mikiri) across the centre of the desert all the way to Birdsville and so they engaged the services of the great serpent and also of the two kingfishers which, with their father, were rainmakers and had an affinity with the water. On the first day out the two kingfishers were transformed into the Two Boys and this is where the Two Boys Dreaming began.

They came all the way across the desert, following the serpent (kumarri) who travelled underground. Every time the serpent would find a suitable spot for water he would surface and the boys would identify the place before continuing. The old snake therefore put water right across the desert. There came to be many wells: Parra Parra, Walpurkanha, Boolabutina, Tjilpatha. From Tjilpatha across to Yalkari, Pulawani and Nulla-naringi where they run into the Georgina River and Eyre Creek.

From there they moved to Birdsville where they celebrated crossing the desert at what is now known as the Fish Hole. Not far away they established a ceremonial site on two rocky outcrops, one for women, the other for men. The Fish Hole is on the Diamantina River southwest of town. The rocky outcrops are on the eastern edge of town.

The significance of Thutirla Pula was that it established a direct route across Munga-Thirri, the Simpson Desert. It was a short cut that took 600 kilometres off the journey around the bottom of the Simpson Desert to Lake Eyre, then back up the Diamantina River.

While Aboriginal people had been crossing the desert for millennia, their achievement wasn't matched by Europeans until well into the twentieth century. As mentioned in Chapter 1, the desert defeated explorer Charles Sturt as far back as 1845. It was almost a century later, in 1936, that grazier Ted Colson became the first European to cross the desert from Mt Etingambra via Poeppels Corner to Birdsville, in company with a young Aboriginal boy. In 1939 the members of Cecil Madigan's scientific expedition became the first Europeans to cross the centre of the desert from Andado Station to Birdsville, again with Aboriginal guides. The first European woman to cross the desert, in a four-wheel-drive vehicle, was the late Griselda Sprigg in 1962. Her husband, geologist Reg Sprigg, had bought the car and set out to prove that Cecil Madigan was wrong when he said no motor vehicle would ever cross the Simpson. In later interviews and publicity, Reg never revealed the type of vehicle because he'd been unable to obtain sponsorship from its manufacturer for the journey.

The shorter path through the desert enabled Aboriginal people to connect with other routes through their country and facilitate trade in such goods as stone for making tools, and pituri, a strong drug that gave travellers greater endurance to cover long distances. The new desert route also facilitated cultural exchange and gatherings at locations shared by several tribes, such as Mudloo Well, north-west of Birdsville.

From their slowly disintegrating wooden shelters to the stone circles of their ceremonial sites, evidence of the Aboriginal presence is embedded in the landscape. And startling new sites are still being found. In 2006 station people on Adria Downs alerted Don Rowlands to a peculiar site they'd spotted while out mustering. It took Don and his wife Lyn several weeks to locate it, but what they found was astounding.

It appeared to be a grave, but all around it there were dozens of mourning caps, up to eighty white helmets shaped from gypsum. They were worn by women after they'd shaved their hair to mark the passing of a respected member of their tribe. Prior to the discovery on Adria, only a handful of caps had ever been found at any grave site. Remarkably, those sites were restricted to an area along the Murray–Darling river system, over 1000 kilometres away. None of them is as large or as well preserved as the one on Adria. Its age has been put at between 200 and 500 years. How and why it's there is another of the desert's mysteries.

If indeed it was a grave site, it belonged to someone of great significance. The location is also thought to be on one of the ancient trade routes for pituri, near its intersection with the route of Thutirla Pula. The significance of the site has left the experts guessing.

Don Rowlands and Jimmy Crombie are now the custodians of this site and many others. They preserve the knowledge of its location while trying to pass on an understanding of it to younger Wangkangurru. They are also trying to ensure the site is protected, in the first instance from grazing cattle, but also from the elements and the predations of the curious.

Don has long been a friend of Luise Hercus who, through many years studying Central Australian Aboriginal culture, has often been the last person to document a great deal of the languages, stories and songs that have long since disappeared. Now Don is devoting himself to recording and passing on to his people the knowledge he has acquired over a lifetime.

A few months after I first went into the desert with him, Don rang and asked me for some help with a project he was working on that detailed all the Aboriginal sites he knew about. He was compiling it on a word processor, but was having trouble organising the information the way he wanted it. He'd only got a few pages entered, but I could already see what he was trying to do. I suggested some ways he could structure the information, showed him how to make the word processor cooperate and left him to it.

Later that day, he rang again. He'd shifted a pile of papers onto the keyboard and the next thing he knew everything he'd typed had disappeared.

'Don't touch anything,' I said, fearing the worst. 'I'll be right there.' I went straight out the door.

When I got to his office, I was relieved to see that he hadn't lost everything. He'd simply zoomed out of the document, reducing all the pages to the size of postage stamps. What struck me was the number of pages. In the morning he'd only had a few pages – now there were dozens.

With a click of the mouse I returned the pages to normal size. I couldn't resist the temptation to peek at what he'd been doing. It was breathtaking. Information must have been pouring out of him all day. I didn't need to see much to know that some of it was culturally sensitive and not for eyes like mine. Nevertheless, it was like tearing my eyes away from the treasures of Aladdin's Cave. Don was well on his way to creating an extraordinary resource for the Wangkangurru.

The question was, who would appreciate it? The decline of the Wangkangurru culture that began with the depopulation of Munga-Thirri is ongoing. Several gravestones in the Birdsville Cemetery belong to people who gave 'Simpson Desert' as their birthplace, but ended their days in town: Mintulee of Tharraberree (Joe the Rainmaker, who died in 1955 aged ninety-five), Akawilyika Maudie Naylon (1887–1980), Esther Flash (born at Cooryanna Waterhole, date unknown, died 1988), Jimmy Naylon Arpilindika (1883–1963) and Sally Flash (circa 1889–1964). These days most Wangkangurru claim Birdsville or the surrounding district as their birthplace. As with the European community, many of their children have been lured away to cities and larger towns. So while Don Rowlands struggles to preserve Aboriginal culture for future generations, his sons are working in Charleville and Western Australia.

Out in the desert, Munga-Thirri is uninhabited. Tourists pass through it on decaying mining roads driven arrow-straight from point A to point B. The old Aboriginal wells and the ancient paths that have meandered between them since the beginning of the Dreaming are long since abandoned. The desert is empty in a way it has never been before.

11

THE BIRDSVILLE RACES

At the end of August Michelle and I were driving south from Mt Isa, racing to escape a storm front that was moving in from the west. We'd tackled the 1400-kilometre round trip to stock up on supplies before an invasion of guests arrived for the famous Birdsville Races.

'When are you coming back?' Dr Ross, one of our Remote Area Nurses and Zeus's saviour, had asked before we left.

'Saturday afternoon,' I'd replied.

'You'd better be quick,' he'd said. 'There's rain expected by Saturday night.'

When the savants of Birdsville tell you rain is on the way, I have learned that you ignore them at your peril. Sure enough, as we hurtled down the road on Saturday afternoon, a line of cumulonimbus extended across the western sky. My mind kept running through the fundamental equation of outback travel: Rain = Mud = Stranded.

We were still 100 kilometres north of Bedourie, 300 kilometres from Birdsville, when the weather got even uglier. To the south-west, a large storm cell converged, a solid dark mass of cloud with enormous white turrets billowing skywards. The wind picked up. I could feel it trying to push the Truckasaurus sideways. Long tendrils of sand blew across the road.

'Darling?' I asked Michelle. 'Does that cloud over there look odd to you?'

On the horizon to the south, a dark haze looked like it had been bruised purple and brown.

'I don't think it *is* a cloud,' Michelle said.

It was a dust storm, and it was moving with extraordinary speed. If we were quick, I thought, maybe we could squeeze past before it blew in. As the storm cell loomed larger, we realised the dust storm extended beneath it over a massive front. The Truckasaurus sped on.

.Tense minutes passed. The road kept to a line that stayed just to the left of the approaching cloud. There was still a chance it would keep us out of trouble. Then we topped a rise. Out on the plain below us the road curved right. When we took the curve we would be facing a wall of sand.

'Oh crap,' we chorused.

It was like one of those movie dust storms, 1000 metres high, red-brown and swirling towards us. All it needed was the computer-generated face of an evil genie to appear. Yet face or no face it was frightening. It looked like a solid mass coming to crush us. We'd read of people being smothered in such storms. Having never experienced one, we didn't know whether we were about to suffocate. I slowed down, anticipating fierce winds and zero visibility when it finally hit. For all I knew it might pluck the Truckasaurus from the road and fling it across the desert like a toy.

Then it hit. The wind buffeted the Truckasarus as I slowed to a crawl. Debris and clouds of dust rolled over the road, at times so thick we couldn't see the bullbar. Bright daylight became weird yellow gloom. Looking up, we could still make out shreds of blue between the scud of fast-moving black and silver cloud. Below, it was a vision of hell.

We crept along. At times the wind and dust were so fierce we were forced to stop completely. Then the furious blast would relent and we'd creep a little further down the road. We weren't sure whether we should give up, pull over and wait. Such storms have been known to last for days. If we could just make it to Bedourie we could at least take shelter.

We drove furtively for about fifteen minutes, during which we travelled no more than 5 kilometres. Then, to our complete surprise, we popped out the back of the storm like a cork out of a dusty bottle. Behind us we could see the furious wind and dust. In front the air was clear and clean, and now remarkably cool and fresh. It hadn't rained inside the dust storm, but on this side the road was drenched. Large pools of water lay beside the now-soaked dirt road. The Truckasaurus started slithering through the slush.

As luck would have it, it was only a short distance to a stretch of sealed road that took us all the way into Bedourie. By the time we reached the town, the road had dried. The storm cell was sweeping over broad plains east of the town. In Bedourie the setting sun peeked between clouds, casting the main street in soft golden light.

We'd been lucky to make it that far and with more cloud moving in from the west we debated our next move. Night was about to overtake us and with it more bad weather. The Birdsville–Bedourie Road was no place to get caught on a dark and stormy night, but if we delayed and heavy rain fell, the road might be impassable for days.

We embarked on what became a harrowing drive. In the gathering darkness more storm cells rolled in. Wild gusts of wind hit the Truckasaurus and swirling clouds of dust obscured the road. Sprays of rain turned the dust on the windscreen to muddy streaks. Dark clouds swirled across the fading blue-black sky. By the time we reached the Cacoory homestead ruins, 90 kilometres from Birdsville, the light was all but gone. Still the rain had not set in.

We drove on with our lights on high beam. It was like driving down a brown tunnel. Distance and perspective blurred as the empty road ahead faded into the distance. There was nothing – not a tree,

rock or hill – to give a point of reference. Before we'd come to Birdsville I'd debated having high-powered driving lights installed in the
Truckasaurus. I'd decided we didn't need them because I was sure
we'd never risk the dangers of driving at night in the outback. Now I
had a set in a box in the back of the car and was regretting the lack
of time to have them installed in Mt Isa.

We were within 50 kilometres of Birdsville, and feeling like we
were going to make it, when Michelle started nodding off. Between
the shopping, driving and storms, it had been a long day. Out of the
corner of my eye I noticed her head drop. Unfortunately, out of the
corner of my other eye I noticed a cow. I hit the brakes hard.

Michelle was startled awake and flung her hands forward as I
managed to slow down enough to avoid the beast. It was standing in
the middle of the road. When we got closer it turned out to be not
one but several cows. I'd only spotted one of them. The others were
all but invisible.

'How's your pulse?' I asked.

'I'm awake now,' she said grimly.

We were too stressed to feel relief when we finally made it into
Birdsville. We'd experienced our first real dust storm, but it involved
the hardest drive I'd ever done.

'How was the trip back?' Dr Ross asked when next he saw us.

'For the last 200 kilometres I drove like a frightened rabbit,' I
replied.

He didn't say 'I told you so', but his knowing grin said it all.

                                    *

The storms we'd encountered didn't abate after they were done tor-
menting us. They moved over to the Windorah Road and dumped
25 millimetres of rain on a detour that was in place around a section of new roadworks. The detour traversed a blacksoil plain and,

being temporary, had no rock base. The main route to Birdsville for people and supplies coming to the races from Australia's eastern states promptly turned to slush. There was a report that a bus was already bogged. The road was closed. Driving on any of the roads in the shire was not recommended.

That afternoon, a Sunday, I went out to the racecourse to see how preparations for the big event were progressing. David Brook was out directing preparations in his role as the Birdsville Race Club president. I went over to say g'day and ask about a radio report I'd heard that the races were going to be cancelled because the roads were flooded.

'Why do you think I'm out here?' David said. 'The phone started ringing as I was leaving the house.'

He told me there'd been a report of 100 millimetres of rain at Tanbar Station, near Windorah. David knew the old bloke who'd reported the fall and was sure he'd been using the old system of measuring rain. He'd meant 100 points of rain, or 25 millimetres, as was reported elsewhere.

We'd also heard that Birdsville Caravan Park had increased its prices. While we were in Mt Isa a tourist told us they'd gone from paying $20 per person per night for a powered site to $50. By Sunday the rate had dropped to $35. 'But the damage is done,' Neale the policeman observed. 'The word will have spread that they're overcharging.'

That night the bus that had been bogged on the Windorah Road rolled into Birdsville. It had got stuck at 3 a.m. on Sunday morning, 230 kilometres from town. After being pulled out by a bulldozer from the road construction site, it reached town at 6 p.m.

On Monday, four days before the races, road or no road the town was being transformed. The pub stripped every item of memorabilia from the walls, ceiling and even the roof that might tempt souvenir hunters. Bar tables were unbolted from the floor and taken away. Drinks were no longer served in glass.

All around town the dirt roads were graded. The sections of road out to Big Red that had been under water were filled in, freshly rocked and made ready for hundreds of vehicles to go sightseeing without risking bogging or rolling over.

A portable shower block was set up between the caravan park and the Wirrari Centre. Portaloos were located along the main street. 'Whatever you do,' Neale warned me, 'don't use those portaloos. People reckon it's a great joke to tip them over when someone goes in. Use the toilets in the pub instead.'

Neale was no longer the only cop in town. More than twenty rolled up to the police station in preparation for round-the-clock shifts. They were accommodated in the police station barracks and the old Courthouse. Police from outback police stations swagged it in the grounds.

The bus that had been bogged turned out to be the advance vehicle for the coming onslaught. It parked in the vacant lot behind the Royal Hotel that I'd looked at askance when we'd first arrived in town, wondering why it and other blocks were left undeveloped and apparently unused. Within hours the bus was unloaded and the bare ground was transformed into a tent city, accommodation for the bus tours that would descend if and when the Windorah Road opened.

Out on the town common between the town and the river, another tent city was sprouting from the plain. On both sides of the road hundreds of campers pulled up and pitched their tents for free. The council scattered portaloos all across the area. Brian Mooney, the council's tourism manager, told me of a large group that had contacted him in advance asking if they could hire a portaloo for their exclusive use. Council gave them one for nothing.

For several days in the lead-up to the races I'd been noticing piles of plastic bags dumped on the roadside all the way out to the racecourse. I frowned at the thought of people leaving rubbish lying around until I realised they were put there by the council. They were stamped with the message 'Don't rubbish the outback' and were free for campers so they had somewhere to stow their litter, ready for collection.

Everywhere I turned, it seemed like every conceivable thing that might be needed had been thought of. Over the years, the organisers had learned a thing or two hundred.

Still, it wouldn't be Birdsville without a reminder that it's a bloody long way from anywhere and the services are tenuous, even at the best of times. Sure enough, the Windorah Road still wasn't open when word came through that the Monday afternoon plane from Brisbane to Mt Isa via Birdsville had been cancelled. Once again MacAir, the airline responsible, was proving to be as reliable as a Vietnamese Rolex.

Nell Brook got on the phone. She pointed out to various transport officials, reputedly up to ministerial level, that the town was now effectively isolated. A blowtorch was applied to the appropriate part of MacAir's anatomy and the company chartered a small aircraft to operate the service usually provided by a twenty-seater plane. It arrived in Birdsville six hours late.

On Tuesday morning, three days before the races, I tuned my hand-held radio to the council's UHF channel. It was alive with chatter. Every staff member who could be spared was in Birdsville applying the finishing touches to the preparations. The activity was a stark contrast to the image of council workers leaning on their shovels. Questions like, 'After you've dropped those bags, can you put in those posts?' were answered 'Already done' or 'Be there direckly.'

Ruth Doyle, whose husband Ian worked for the council, got on the two-way and relayed the news that the Windorah Road would be opened at 9 a.m. A queue of vehicles 2 kilometres long had formed at the 'road closed' sign. At the front of the line were the vehicles of Fred Brophy's Boxing Troupe. A fourth-generation showman, Fred has been a permanent fixture of the Birdsville Races for nearly thirty years. Some of the locals regarded his boxing tent as a bigger draw than the races themselves.

Later that morning my sister, Helen, flew in on the returning Mt Isa to Brisbane via Birdsville charter plane. We'd worked out that it would be easier for her to get a flight to Birdsville from there than it would be to fly from Brisbane during race week. Plus, if there was any problem with the MacAir plane, we could always do the now-familiar 1400-kilometre round trip to pick her up.

In the end, because Helen had taken a charter flight, instead of a regular service, she'd flown free of charge. Unfortunately, she was a nervous flyer, and when she got out of the eight-seater that operated the service she was pretty shaky. It was her first experience of a light aircraft flying in turbulent conditions.

I took Helen over to the bakery to say hello to Michelle and get a coffee. While we were there I introduced her to Dusty and Teresa. 'You sure look like brother and sister,' they chorused. 'You're exactly alike.'

We looked at each other. Was it the piercing blue eyes, straw-blond hair or rugged good looks? 'Nah, it's the McHugh nose,' we agreed ruefully.

In the afternoon Fred Brophy's road-weary truck rolled into town. A few hours later the boxing tent was set up on the vacant ground diagonally opposite the pub. Another showground operator was setting up a bull-riding arena next to it.

Now that the floodgates were open, cars were pouring into town. By midafternoon the pub was full. People were chattering on every UHF channel. Some were saying all the best spots on the town common were taken.

All through the next day, still two days before the races began, vehicles constantly rolled in. Barriers were erected and one side of the main street outside the pub was completely closed to traffic. From Fred Brophy's boxing tent to the Wirrari Centre, food vans and tents were setting up. More vans selling fish and chips, burgers, outback memorabilia and keepsakes set up along the main street. For the first time since moving to Birdsville, I could walk around and not recognise a single person.

On Wednesday night, everyone was so busy tennis had to be cancelled. Everyone was getting plenty of exercise anyway, running around getting things ready.

Among the locals there were varying opinions on when the party kicked off at the Birdsville Races. Some said it was the Monday night, the beginning of race week. Others thought it was Wednesday night, when the town was full of people. However, for the serious partygoer it began a week before the races and over 1500 kilometres away. It started with a weekend at the Gympie Muster, one of Australia's biggest country music festivals, 160 kilometres north of Brisbane. After that it was a leisurely two-day drive 800 kilometres west to Quilpie where, on Tuesday night, the town holds a colourful street party. The next day it was an easy 250 kilometres to Windorah for the Wednesday-night yabbie races. After that it was only a 400-kilometre drive to Birdsville on Thursday, to arrive the evening before the races.

Birdsville airport's close proximity to the centre of town (it *is* the centre of town) means another option is to fly in, land and join the festivities. To assist matters, aviators are allowed to camp with their planes. Shower and toilet facilities are also provided in hangars near the MacAir terminal. On the Thursday before the races dozens of planes were landing, taxiing to parking areas off the runways and setting up tents under their wings. Where normally there was only David Brook's plane and maybe the Flying Doctor, there were more than a hundred aircraft of every shape and size, from two-seater microlights to executive jets.

On Thursday evening I began to understand why the Birdsville Races are ranked among the world's top forty parties. Most country towns have their annual festival at their showgrounds, usually on the edge of town. Birdsville has it in the main street. The vacant lots and streets around the Birdsville Hotel were thronged with people enjoying the food and entertainment. The number of people in town had exploded from 60 to 6000. There are few places on earth that could handle a hundred-fold increase in population. Birdsville was doing it with ease.

The first day of the races began with a special event – the unveiling of a bust of the legendary mailman of the Birdsville Track, Tom Kruse. The revered old man even put in an appearance himself, the 94-year-old brought up from Adelaide on a special charter flight. The unveiling was held in the community hall and the place was jammed with tourists eager to get a glimpse of a man who was 'living history'. Locals David Brook, who had a small part in *The Back of Beyond,* the film that made Tom famous, and Robbie Butler, son of Tom's Aboriginal offsider Henry Butler, also took the stage. David and Robbie shared some of their memories, but Tom was too frail to speak.

Not many other locals turned up to see the man who was considered an icon of the outback. Many were gathered instead around Tom McKay and his truck. Tom was still doing the run up the Birdsville Track that had made Tom Kruse an outback icon and he'd just rolled into town. That meant everyone was buzzing around picking up their groceries, last-minute supplies for the races and other equipment.

Tom was a solidly built, knockabout kind of fella who looked uncannily like Tom Kruse in his younger days. Unfortunately, the tourists who were falling over themselves to see Tom Kruse didn't give Tom McKay a second glance. To them he was just some truckie. To us he was a lifeline for almost all our worldly needs (along with Steve Bonsey's truck that did the run from Quilpie), just as Tom Kruse had been for previous generations of Birdsville people.

There was also plenty of activity over at the airport, where plane after plane was landing and being marshalled to the parking areas. We went over there to pick up my sister's friend Therese, who was on the Friday-morning MacAir flight from Mt Isa. Therese and I had been to uni together twenty years before, but while we hadn't kept in touch, she and my sister had remained great friends. Therese, in her mid-forties, was compact and athletic and regularly ran marathons – a bonus when it came to having the stamina to enjoy a good time.

We dropped her baggage at our place then headed for the Birdsville Racecourse. The track was usually three empty, scrubby kilometres from town. Now the fields were dotted with tents, a stream of cars was heading to the track and people were queuing at bus stops that were dotted along the road at regular intervals. The council had only one bus, but all the buses that had brought people to the races had switched to operating a shuttle service from town to the track and back. The fare was a gold coin donation to the Flying Doctor.

Police were conducting random breath tests and making sure no-one exceeded a newly imposed 50 km/h speed limit. One local got pulled up for speeding and complained that the signs had been changed. The police then noticed there was a dent on his bumper.

'Where'd you get that?' they asked.

'It's from the last cop I ran over,' the local replied.

They decided to breathalyse him. 'Take a deep breath and blow here,' they said.

'Why? Won't your wife do it for you?' the local quipped.

The same local had a one-liner for policeman Neale McShane a couple of months before. Neale had been warned that local station owners were so well connected that they had the police commissioner and their local MP on speed dial on their phones. Neale wondered if it was true, and asked the local if he had the police commissioner's number. The man had replied, 'No, just the crime and misconduct commission's.'

Neale had a similar sense of humour. When he'd had to go to Mt Isa to receive a medal for ten years of unblemished service, he told me it was called the Teflon Award. 'Nothin' stuck,' he said.

Out at the racetrack the buses were dropping people at the newly erected front gates, which had arrived in the nick of time on Bonsey's truck from Quilpie. Punters were parking on the flood plain and walking in past the new stables.

Inside the track the facilities were a delightfully rustic conglomeration. Scientists could have studied the buildings like geological strata – new tacked onto old tacked onto oldest, the age of each building calculated using rust instead of carbon dating. Corrugated iron was the construction material of choice.

One of the oldest buildings was the grandstand and jockeys changing rooms that stood at the finishing line. Grandstand was probably overstating it a bit, given that it rose to a mere three tiers. Beside the stands was the judge's box. It looked to be on its last legs, but moves to replace it had met with resistance from those who thought the rickety structure had character.

The betting ring was considerably more modern. It was a large covered area where most of the crowd gathered to have a flutter and seek shelter from the sun. It was only early afternoon and a comfortable 25 degrees, but the shaded areas with a good view of the track were crammed with chairs and tables, picnics and punters.

True to the Birdsville Races' motto that 'the dust never settles', there wasn't a blade of grass anywhere near the track facilities. Over on the dunes the ground was still lush with yellow and purple flowers but on course, it was a dust bowl.

Not much had changed in the previous 126 years. As *The Queenslander* reported in 1882:

The first race meeting held at the newly formed township of Birdsville, situated on the Diamantina River, eight miles [12 kilometres] north of the South Australian border, was held on the 20th, 21st, and 22nd of September [the modern races are held over two days at the beginning of September] and was largely attended, nearly 150 station owners, managers, stockmen, and other employees being present. The weather was delightful, the entrances for the various events good, and the finishes in most of the races close and exciting. Nearly 200 pounds was raised by public subscription, which speaks well for the prosperous condition of the district.

After that first race meeting, the Border Jockey Club was formed. Eventually it was renamed the Birdsville Race Club. For decades the event was almost entirely a local affair, its fortunes rising and falling with the district's cycles of boom and bust. In the 1970s Bedourie claimed to have the larger, better-attended race meeting, but that all changed in 1978 when then prime minister Malcolm Fraser went to the Birdsville Races. The attendant publicity put the races on the map.

Fraser's visit coincided with a surge of interest in outback Australia and the wider availability of four-wheel-drive vehicles to get there. When recreational adventurers discovered the races and the Simpson Desert, Birdsville never looked back. Even when equine influenza forced the cancellation of the races in 2007, the town responded with the slogan 'Who needs horses: let's party!'. The attendance wasn't as high as usual, but locals proudly claim that Birdsville is one of the few places that could get 3000 people to turn up for a non-event.

In the betting ring Helen and Therese found a friend of theirs, Danny, who was working for one of the bookmakers, Terry Picone. The girls were novices when it came to horse racing, but with a bit of help from their friend they got their heads together to study the form and place their bets for the first race, scheduled for 1.05 p.m. By then there were several thousand people at the course and as the horses came to the barrier the crowd could barely contain its excitement.

The Brooklands–Fred Brophy Three-Year-Old-and-Up Maiden Plate, the first of six races for the day, was run over 800 metres. There were six starters. When they burst from the barrier there was a huge roar, an outpouring of anticipation built up by many over several days of travel. No sooner had the race begun than the signature feature of outback racing, a long dust cloud, swelled into the air in a long trail behind the field. There was a lot to be said for taking an early lead – you could see where you were going.

The conduct of the race was as professional as anything to be found at a metropolitan event. Queensland Racing oversaw the organisation and anyone who expected some kind of shambolic hayseed affair was better off turning to an earlier era. Author George Farwell was at the races in 1948 and described the first race:

> The Betoota Maiden Hack was for grass-fed station horses, producing
> a close finish, with the favourite scraping home despite its half-caste
> jockey's bandaged hand. Or perhaps because of it, the wiseacres
> declaring that he had been unable to pull the horse.

Back then, pulling horses (reining them in so they didn't win, thus fixing the result) was a common accusation. Farwell referred to an earlier Birdsville meeting where a Brisbane bookmaker thought he'd fallen victim to the practice. He wrote, 'Packing up his bag after the first day, he said disgustedly, "This here's bushranger country".'

These days, bookmakers return to Birdsville year after year. One of them, Ron Murphy, had a bookie's bag that claimed he was 'registered for 50-odd years on 130-odd tracks'. Ron, a thin, wispy-haired man approaching eighty, was running his stand on his own.

Ron had a sense of humour as dry as the Diamantina in drought. His response to a question about where he was born was typical: 'On the Boulia–Winton Road, probably behind a mob of cattle. I don't remember. I was only one day old.' He told me a doctor once asked how he'd fallen from a windmill. He'd answered, 'Gravity.' He'd also been in a chopper crash. 'The pilot said to me, "Brace yourself! Brace yourself!" When we landed them gidgee trees decided to come straight towards us across this flat. I'm sure them gidgee trees moved towards the chopper. He said, "Why didn't you brace yourself?" I said, "I can only do one job at a time." He said, "Well what were you doing?" I said, "Praying."'

Ron got his bookie's licence when he was twenty-one. 'The first time I fielded in this outback country woulda been at Urandangi in, no, my first meeting was in McKinlay in 1951. I've done the bush for many years, between other jobs. And then I went to Brisbane. An old fella who used to clerk for me, he said, "Ron, these country race meetings, feature ones like Birdsville, the number of people have dropped right off because the stations are employing less people and with sheep going out into cattle you've got less workers. So if I was your age I'd go to the city." So I worked in the city for the best part of twenty years – night dogs, night trots, races – but every betting ring was getting less and less. Even in the city the number of bookies went less and less because people do other things of a Saturday. One time it was traditional. Everyone went to the races Saturday.'

He eventually got back to the bush and bought a cattle property near Longreach. When he got too old to manage the station he sold up and bought a unit in Winton. Now, he reckons, he's never there. He circulates around his three sons and daughter, and the betting rings of the non-metropolitan courses. 'I'd be bored if I didn't come here,' he said. 'I'd have to go to Rocky or Mackay or somethin'. It's just because I was born in the bush. People are sort of different, everyone knows everyone, and even though you haven't seen 'em for twelve months, it's got a different atmosphere.'

Despite his advancing age, he still camps on the town common when he comes to Birdsville. 'It doesn't worry me,' he said.

'I generally stay at some of them bush pubs, wherever. Otherwise I just bring a bunk with me and a swag.'

Bookie Terry Picone, a middle-aged man of quiet intensity, had a similar story. Terry was from Moree in northern New South Wales and had been to the Birdsville Races every year for the last seventeen. He enjoys Birdsville so much he hires a 25-seater bus and brings out fifteen of his staff and friends. They, too, set up a camp on the common and roll their swags out in the dust around the camp fire.

'It's a good fun trip with a bit of work,' he said. 'We enjoy the camping and getting away from normal bookmaking activities. It's my little week's retreat from mainland bookmaking. My staff love it. It's locked in. The first time is a lot different for them, but it's infectious. They all want to come afterwards. They're a bit like me. They're hooked.'

Terry travels up to twenty weeks a year to race meetings from Cairns in north Queensland to Wagga Wagga in southern New South Wales. Yet he particularly enjoys outback meetings. 'They're a bit like the dirt – earthy,' he said. 'The whole meeting's earthy. Noccundra Races [600 kilometres south-east of Birdsville] was fifteen horses, about twenty-five people, and they wanted to get the races over so they could start the rodeo straight after, before it got dark. You feel a sense of community at outback race meetings. That wasn't a profitable experience. I knew I was just going out there for the trip. I just did it because I love it. Took a few mates out and swagged it and had a good time.'

A race meeting like Birdsville attracts entrants from Queensland, New South Wales, South Australia and the Northern Territory. Collating information on horses from such a wide area is the hardest part of his job. 'To access that information for an individual horse is all right,' he said, 'but to put it together is the hard part. So I've got a bit of a network of people I connect to, in South Australia and Queensland, and they'll know if the horses are good. I try to take information from those guys and make my own mind up. It's pretty tricky I must admit. I've had one bad year, but actually most years you don't make much money because of the cost. It's a very expensive trip.'

All through the afternoon races were held for fields of between five and eleven horses over distances of 800 to 1200 metres. While I talked to people and soaked up the atmosphere, the girls made a little and lost a little.

At the end of race six, a fleet of buses was waiting to ferry racegoers back to town. On the road out of the racecourse a squad of police were breathalysing every vehicle, including the buses. It seemed a bit heavy-handed, but it had the desired effect. Over the course of the weekend police conducted 6000 breath tests. No-one was charged with drink driving. With the incredibly efficient bus service running between town and track, no-one had any excuse.

Only a handful of other arrests were made. One motorist was arrested at a breathalyser station when police noticed a UHF radio on the back seat of his car. When the driver was asked where he'd got it, he said he'd just bought it. Police then noticed the driver already had a UHF radio installed in his vehicle. A quick check revealed the radio was stolen from a council vehicle.

Back in town, the main street was revving up for a big night. The area around the pub thronged with people. A band was playing in the beer garden. The lights on the food stalls and souvenir outlets flashed. Loudspeakers were spruiking the bull-riding events and Fred Brophy's Boxing Troupe.

The Birdsville Races had been Dusty the baker's introduction to Birdsville. He'd first visited the place when he and Teresa were operating a mobile food van and they liked the place so much they moved there and set up the business. In previous years he'd tried to run the bakery and cater at the race track but, he said, 'It nearly killed me.' This year he was concentrating his energies on the bakery. In the evening he served pizzas, lit a camp fire in the front yard of the bakery and allowed a visiting bush poet to entertain the diners.

To help him cater for hungry racegoers Dusty had rounded up as many of his and Teresa's relatives and friends as he could. In spite of that Michelle had worked a very long day. She'd started at 7.30 a.m. and over the course of the morning done nothing but make coffees for five hours straight. Now it was evening she was making and cooking pizzas that were being devoured as fast as they came out of the oven. Only when the pizza-munching multitudes abated was she able to knock off. She wasn't exactly thrilled when she found out where I was taking her.

Tum-te-tum-te-tum-te-tum-te-tum-te-tum-te-tum-tum!

Clang-ca-clang-ca-clang-ca-clang-ca-clang-ca-clang-ca-clang-clang!

The tribal rhythm of the drum and bell outside Fred Brophy's boxing tent had an almost hypnotic effect. The boxers, dressed in robes of assassin black, stood in a line on a raised platform out the front. Above them, clouds of moths swirled around a string of bare light bulbs. None of the boxers looked happy. As they gazed out over a sea of people they seemed tense and wary. Unlike me they knew what was coming. Roughly painted screens proclaimed that Fred Brophy's Boxing Troupe was the last boxing tent in Australia, and that this was where champions were discovered.

Fred, in his mid-fifties and wearing a red satin shirt, struck the drum while one of his boxers rang the bell. He was trying to recruit members of the public to step into the ring and attempt to last three one-minute rounds against the likes of the Barramundi Kid, White Lightning and The Cowboy.

'Okay, who wants to have a go?' he said. 'We'll give you a rally on the bells and drums there. We're lookin' for a couple more.'

Tum-te-tum, ca-clang-ca-clang, te-tum-te-tum, ca-clang-clang.

'Okay, that's the national anthem of Birdsville. You'll hear that all weekend. Righto we're lookin' for a couple more. No you're half full son. You gotta be sober to fight here tonight. We're lookin' for another one. Who else wants to earn 'emself a reputation? Okay mate, get up here. Good on ya. That's what they call a fair dinkum Australian when they get up here, whether they win or lose, it's irrelevant. Up you come. Up here. Good on ya mate.'

Tum-te-tum, ca-clang-ca-clang, te-tum-te-tum, ca-clang-clang.

'Clay is it? Clay. And where do you come from? Glengyle Station! We've got a bloke from around here, between here and Bedourie.'

Tum-te-tum, ca-clang-ca-clang, te-tum-te-tum, ca-clang-clang.

'Okay, come up here. You'd have to be a ringer, wouldn't ya? You're a ringer. Okay, you done any boxin' before? What about around the pubs and that? Nah. Well I'll tell you this'll be something you've never seen before. You'll never forget it.'

The challenger looked like he was starting to have doubts.

'No, no, you'll be right,' Fred assured him. 'I've got a little bloke for you, about your size. We've got White Lightning. Put your hands up White Lightning. We've got a little feller. See that little bloke there? That's White Lightning. You got 'im. Okay mate, we're gonna have a bit of fun here tonight.'

When Fred had half a dozen volunteers – builders, factory workers, temporary staff from the pub – the boxing tent opened and the crowd flooded in. Inside, behind the painted signs and bright lights, the boxing ring was a flat space at ground level surrounded by 400 plastic chairs. The tent itself had no walls. When all the seats were filled, the remaining crowd stood around the outside.

In the ring, Fred Brophy was a different man to the one who'd been spruiking on the stage outside. There he'd been a showman. Here he just looked worried. The drum and bell had been replaced with an expectation of impending violence.

After Queensland MP Vaughn Johnson (Birdsville's then local member) and TV personality Rex Hunt were found ringside seats,

Fred explained the rules. 'It they go down three times, it's over. If they get knocked out, it's over. If the challenger wins I'm gonna give him $20 a minute. If he draws he gets nothing. But I'm in a good mood tonight. If he loses, he gets the experience.'

The first round was between Mike, a cabinet-maker from New South Wales, and The Cowboy. It seemed an uneven match. Mike was noticeably taller than The Cowboy, but he was also slightly overweight, particularly compared to his firmly muscled opponent. The Stetson-wearing boxer sized Mike up and didn't look too concerned. The pair squared off and Fred blew a whistle to start round one.

The whistle was still in Fred Brophy's mouth when Mike charged at The Cowboy. His fists were swinging in a vicious flurry. The Cowboy back-pedalled around the ring, but Mike kept coming. The Cowboy's expression quickly turned from complacent to defensive. He knew he was in a fight.

For the first few seconds the fight was all Mike until The Cowboy managed to step aside and the amateur charged past, flailing. Mike had plenty of size and strength, but he had no technique. As he started to turn towards his opponent, he didn't have his guard up. The Cowboy didn't miss.

Mike copped a powerful blow to the side of his head. If The Cowboy was holding anything back, it didn't look like it. Fred blew his whistle when Mike hit the canvas. An excited cheer went up from the crowd. Miraculously, Mike was still conscious and managed to struggle back to his feet. He seemed badly shaken, but after a ten-second count and a correct answer to how many fingers Fred was holding up, the fight continued. Fortunately for Mike, the single minute of the first round was almost up and as The Cowboy came for him he covered up and took everything The Cowboy threw at him in the last few seconds. The bell finally sounded.

Sixty seconds doesn't seem like a long time, but in a boxing ring it was more than enough. Sweat formed a sheen on Mike's torso. His chest heaved as he fought for breath.

Mike was more cautious in the second round and managed to stay out of trouble. He made it through to the bell, but as he collapsed into a chair he didn't look half the brash young man who'd first stepped into the ring. Michelle and I, novices when it came to the subtleties of the fight game, decided The Cowboy would be all over him in the final round.

How wrong we were. Right from the whistle Mike threw punch after punch and chased The Cowboy relentlessly. The Cowboy was trapped on the defensive and had no answer to the onslaught. Half-way through the round he was in trouble. He stumbled backwards, Mike towering over him raining blows. As The Cowboy fell amid the shouts and cheers of the crowd, Fred stopped the fight. He reached for Mike's hand and raised it high.

'Put your hands together for the local bloke. Good on ya mate. Here's your money.' Fred's mouth said one thing. His careworn eyes said another. The crowd might have been entertained, but he didn't seem to enjoy the gladiatorial combat he presided over.

As the round between the ringer from Glengyle and White Lightning began, I thought I understood the expressions of the boxers when they'd been looking out over the crowd. They were preparing to face the unknown. Every time they stepped into the ring, they had no idea what they would be up against. Some of the challengers couldn't box to save themselves. Some were highly skilled. Some were just plain dangerous. In the first few seconds of the first round, all would be revealed.

John Hanna from the pub told me later that there have been times when so many of Fred's boxers have been injured that he hasn't been able to stage his usual two shows a night. As Fred tells the challengers, they're getting the experience of a lifetime. Quite a few of them come prepared. They train for months before stepping into the ring, hoping to go to Birdsville and at least make it through three rounds, or even win.

In the six bouts Michelle and I saw, most went easily to Fred's boxers. In some bouts the boxers played with their opponents. John Hanna told of one bout he'd watched where the boxer entertained by just dancing around the ring while his challenger tried in vain to hit him. After three rounds the challenger hadn't laid a glove on him.

Some of the locals who entered bouts regretted it. Corey, the Canadian ringer who'd been working as a mechanic, said he'd ended up with several loose teeth. His moment of glory was diminished by the thought of what the dentistry he might need was going to cost. His ex-girlfriend, Eve, who'd been working in the general store but had quit at the beginning of race week so she could party, also entered a bout. Fred sometimes has female boxers, but on this occasion another woman in the crowd, a ringer from one of the stations, was matched up against her. The attractive German backpacker reputedly copped a flogging.

The second day of the races, the first Saturday in September, saw the running of the Birdsville Cup. It's been the premier event since Macorbe won the first cup in 1882. The crowds making their way out to the track were even bigger than the day before. Michelle was among them, having managed to get a day off.

At the entrance to the track I noticed David and Jane Morton queuing to get in. Jane had been the Racing Club's Treasurer for years, but neither she nor her husband sought special treatment. Jane got it anyway, later in the day. David Brook organised a special presentation and in front of several thousand racegoers she was presented with life membership of the Birdsville Racing Club. It was hard to imagine a more deserving person. At every Birdsville event she and David were always present, in the background, helping to run things.

Inside the track I got another taste of David Brook's management skills. The previous afternoon he'd spotted me in the crowd and taken a break from an endless list of tasks to ask how I was going. I mentioned that I thought it would be a good idea to get some photographs of the races from inside the track, with the crowd in the background. He agreed and suggested the picture would be even better taken from an elevated position. I hadn't thought much more about it but today, as I looked past the finishing post, an Adria Downs Station ute was parked in the perfect spot.

'It's all organised,' David said, when I caught his eye in the marshalling area. 'Just see the clerk of the course when you want to go out and he'll look after you.'

The feature race, the Birdsville Cup, was the fifth of seven races. The girls and I had our money on Dusty Daniel, for no better reason than it being the namesake for Dusty the baker. Maybe Dusty Daniel was a bit half-baked for the 1600-metre race because he didn't rise to the occasion. We all did our dough. Evading took out the $17 800 prize purse and the winner's trophy, worth $1400.

It was Evading's first time in Birdsville, as it was for one of his owners, Michael Butler from Blackall, in central Queensland. 'He won the McKinlay Cup and the Barcaldine Cup,' Michael told me. 'It was either do a good race in the city or come out to Birdsville. So we [he and co-owner Denis O'Brien] decided Birdsville would be more fun. It paid off. We're very happy.'

Having won the Birdsville Cup, he was definitely coming back. 'I think it's a good set-up,' he said. 'They've done a terrific job here. I think they did a good job maintaining that road, the Windorah Road, that's only dirt.'

By the time the last race was run, by Terry Picone's estimation the crowd had wagered between $400 000 and $450 000 with the bookmakers, which was 'quite substantial for an outback meeting'.

For racegoers with any cash left there were fundraising auctions in full swing back in town. The Royal Flying Doctor Service was the

principal beneficiary, but an auction was also held to raise money for
the x-ray machine for the Birdsville Clinic. Toy-sized stuffed horses
which had replaced the real thing when equine influenza caused the
regular races to be cancelled in 2007 were auctioned. John Hanna
and his brothers, who'd come out to work in the pub during the
races, led the bidding for the most popular horse, called My Face.
There was a joke behind the name. When My Face was in a race his
backers were supposed to shout, 'Come on My Face.' The Hanna
boys' winning bid was $4000. Most of the other horses attracted
much less money, but the tally for the x-ray machine still lifted above
$20 000.

At Brophy's boxing tent and at the pub, there were more auctions.
'A hundred and twenty dollars a bid . . . twenty a bid . . . twenty a
bid. Twenty,' the auctioneers cried. 'Twenty a bid . . . twenty . . . a
hundred and thirty. A hundred and thirty a bid . . . a hundred and
thirty at the back now.' Everything from car fridges to signed photographs of great moments in sport prompted offers ranging from a
few dollars to several thousand. There were some very deep pockets
in the crowd, especially as it seemed there was an auction going on
somewhere in Birdsville all through the evening. Fred Brophy's drum
and bell may well be one of the anthems of the Birdsville Races,
but the auctioneer's cry was another. 'Two hundred dollars . . . two
hundred . . . two hundred and twenty down here. Two hundred and
twenty . . . bid twenty, bid twenty, down here. Two-twenty, two-
twenty – be quick and away. Two hundred and twenty dollars and
all done. Come forward.'

The party went on long into the night. In the crowds young ringers from the stations near and far stood out from everyone else.
While the tourists were in shorts and thongs, the ringers – their faces
deeply tanned from outdoor work – were in best boots and jeans.
Clean long-sleeved shirts had station or company names emblazoned
on the breast pockets. A lot of them also stood out because they

towered over everyone around them. Yet for all their size there was a slight shyness about them. They were unused to being in such big crowds. Flashing lights and throbbing music were a stark contrast to the silence of the stock camps and the stations.

At 5 a.m. the following morning, the music had faded. The chatter of voices, the laughing and shouting, had died away. The only sound was the clattering of beer cans being swept up in the main street.

The plane exodus began at first light. During the races, and particularly on the day after the races, Birdsville feels like one of the busiest airports in the country.

When I walked Michelle down to the bakery at 7.30, people were waiting to fuel up on food and buy a loaf of bread before the long drive home. A stream of vehicles was already on the road out of town. On the common, tents were being taken down and swags rolled up.

Terry Picone's group had packed up and left, leaving Terry and Danny behind. Terry had a vehicle crammed with his bookmaking paraphernalia because he wasn't going home. His next stop was a race meeting in Cairns, but he'd decided to spend another day in Birdsville, swagging it overnight in our backyard. My sister, Therese and I met up with Terry and Danny for morning coffee and they asked what I was up to. I told them I was on my way to court. Of course they all wanted to come.

Over at the school, the chief magistrate of Queensland, Marshall Irwin (now retired), was about to open proceedings. He explained that during the races each year, court was convened so that offenders could have minor matters dealt with on the spot rather than having to travel potentially long distances to have their matter dealt with at a later date.

As it happened, only one person turned up to have his case heard. The defendant, a stocky bush bloke, had set off a flare outside the pub. Neale, as prosecuting officer, explained that when police arrived the defendant was standing in a cloud of orange smoke beside the open boot of his car. In the boot they found a used flare and several unused flares. The defendant entered a guilty plea, but in his defence pointed out that he was a person of good character who'd been in town helping with the auctions for the Flying Doctor and the x-ray machine. He and Marshall Irwin agreed that he'd been foolish and that a fine of $150 was reasonable.

The other cases brought to the chief magistrate's attention were all misdemeanours. Some cases could be heard in the defendant's absence. Neale explained that one defendant had been caught urinating in the main street within 30 metres of a toilet cubicle. His honour kept a straight face while Neale told how the defendant explained his actions by saying, 'I just had to go.'

When the court session ended, I took the rest of the day off and introduced Terry and Danny to the increasingly well-vegetated and flower-covered golf course. When it came to betting, they couldn't help themselves, especially on crucial putts.

'Ten bucks says you won't make this,' Danny said.

'Two to one.'

'Done.'

Between the pressure and the roughness of the 'browns', Terry shaved past the hole, but made it up on the next one.

After the golf we picked up Helen and Therese and took them out to Big Red. While there we saw bush poet John Major with another group. I remembered that my sister hadn't enjoyed her flight from Mt Isa because of the turbulence and that one of the poem's John recited was about a stockman's experiences the first time he flew. I went over and asked if he'd recite the poem for my sister. He came over and gave her a personal performance of *Turbulence,* by Murray Hartin.

It was a riotous ballad. Rather than fasten his seatbelt, the stockman in question mounted his swag and rode the bumpy plane like a rodeo bull. John, a retired Queensland grazier, gave us all eighteen verses. Afterwards, he and Terry got talking. It turned out both of them knew Murray Hartin. John knew him from the bush poet circuit, but Terry nonchalantly admitted that he knew Murray when he was down on his luck and trying to get his first book of poems published. Terry had stepped in and helped fund the project.

That night, back in town, our little house was crammed with people as we enjoyed a lively dinner party. Over the past few months we'd had quite a few dinner parties, sometimes with newly made Birdsville friends, sometimes with people who'd been passing through town – linguist Luise Hercus, maroonees Wayne and Mary, a couple of motorcycle riders whose attempt to cross Australia in record time had ended when they'd shredded their tyres near Uluru, a woman who'd been on an expedition to see the ceremonial mourning caps. The company had proved far more diverse and fascinating than we'd ever have thought possible in a little outback town.

The following morning Zeus gave Terry and Danny the kind of early morning wake-up call that only a dog with a big wet nose can. They and the girls slowly roused themselves while Zeus and I walked Michelle down to work. I had Zeus on his leash so we could go for a walk around town. I was interested to see what Birdsville looked like in the aftermath of the races.

'You wait,' John Hanna had told me. 'On the Monday after the races it'll be like they were never here.'

He was right. All the traffic barriers had been cleared away. All the food stalls had packed up and left. Fred Brophy's truck was loaded and parked outside the pub, ready to go. The main street was completely deserted and only a handful of planes was scattered around the airport.

The Birdsville Races had come and gone, and they'd done so without a hitch. There's plenty of hype about the 'can-do' spirit of people in the outback, but the races were the kind of event that really demonstrated what it meant. This spirit was also the reason the races were such an ongoing success. People wouldn't keep coming if they had a rotten time. At the Birdsville Races every eventuality was planned for and every need met. It was a huge challenge for the small community, but they pulled it off year after year.

By midday there was only David Brook's Cessna 210 left at the airport and soon after, he took off to muster cattle.

At 2.30 we drove Therese to the airport for her MacAir flight back to Mt Isa, from where she'd connect with her flights to Brisbane and Canberra. At the airport Barry Gaffney checked her in. Barry was looking pretty tired after manning the service station on the busiest weekend of the year.

'Do you know the best thing about the day after the races?' he asked me.

I shook my head and waited for the inevitable Birdsville punchline.

'It's twelve months to the next ones.'

12

THE FURTHEST STATION

'You didn't tell me your sister was single,' John Hanna said to me a couple of days after she'd flown home.

'You never asked,' I replied.

John and Helen had become acquainted when he'd joined us for Helen's farewell sunset at Big Red. Somehow he'd formed the opinion she was still married. Now he knew better. 'She's really nice,' he mused.

It turned out my sister had a similar attitude. When she rang to thank us for showing her such a good time, the subject of John came up. 'He's one of those quiet, gentle outback types,' she said dreamily.

I was appalled. How could I retain the appropriate professional detachment from my story if my sister started dating someone in it? I hoped the tyranny of distance would nip romance in the bud, but within a week John was looking like a cat that had swallowed a canary. 'She rang me,' he said. They'd talked for hours.

While their relationship blossomed, spring was bringing other changes to our little outback home. In the days after the Birdsville Races, there was a collective sigh of relief that the biggest event of the year was now past. The flow of tourists slowed to a trickle and Michelle was given increasing amounts of time off at the bakery. Ben started talking about leaving and taking my furry mate Zeus with him.

At the pub there was a change of management. John Hanna's brother, Brian, stayed on after working at the races to take over as the publican. Where the previous publican had a relatively urbane style and manner, Brian was pure country – or pure bikie. He was solidly built, his head was shaved and he had a goatee beard. Instead of his predecessor's white shirts and black pants, Brian favoured jeans and work shirts. He had a relaxed management style, but it was backed by years of experience in bush pubs, including several stints in Birdsville.

Towards the end of September, Michelle got time off to fly to Sydney for a friend's wedding. By now we were experienced enough to know not to attempt flying out on a Friday to arrive in time for the wedding on a Saturday. She went to Mt Isa on Thursday then took a Qantas flight from there on Friday. Even then, the MacAir plane was late. It eventually left Birdsville at 9 p.m. instead of 2.30 p.m. and Michelle didn't reach her accommodation in Mt Isa until midnight.

While Michelle stayed in a boutique hotel in central Sydney (after six months in Birdsville she deserved some pampering), I went to Betoota. The Birdsville Races are actually the first of three weekends of outback race meetings, with the second at Bedourie and the third at the little town of Betoota, population: zero. A day or two before the Betoota meeting bookie Terry Picone rang to ask what I thought the attendance would be like. He was thinking of coming out.

'Well, Geoff Morton [president of the Betoota Race Club] has been on the radio saying they're hoping for 250,' I replied. 'But – how can I put this – that would have to be the best-case scenario.'

Such small numbers meant Terry wouldn't make enough in the betting ring for it to be worth his while, but he decided to come anyway. It was a shame that the attendance was more like a hundred (I counted that many in the betting ring just before the Betoota Cup) because it was a great fun weekend. It was a classic country race meeting with plenty of dust and heat but, as at Birdsville, the organisation was impressive. A couple of people who'd flown in mentioned that when they landed, they were expecting a long walk to the track. To their surprise they'd barely shut down the plane's engines before a vehicle pulled up to offer them a lift.

The following week, with Michelle still lapping up the luxuries of the big smoke, I arranged a visit to Adria Downs Station. I'd been trying to get there for a couple of months to see Lake Muncoonie up close.

'Is there a time I can come when you're not too busy?' I'd asked Don Rayment, the station's manager.

'We're always busy,' Don had replied in his gruff outback way. 'Just come.'

It was a 130-kilometre drive north-west from Birdsville on a rutted dirt road to the homestead. Don was off somewhere with cattle when I arrived, but his wife, Judy, was expecting me. Judy was an attractive, middle-aged woman who'd spent her childhood on the banks of the Georgina, around Urandangie and the northern side of the Simpson Desert, before her parents moved to Longreach. She and Don had been together sixteen years and had a son and a daughter. They each had two children from previous marriages.

Judy proudly showed me around the improvements she and Don had been making since they'd set up the homestead four years earlier. Bougainvillea was flourishing in the garden and the obligatory outback station lawn was well established. A path from the garden led down the riverbank to Judy's pride and joy: a dock. It had a platform that was big enough for entertaining and gave good views up and down the river she regarded as the Georgina. Just north of Bedourie the Georgina joined the Burke River and from there the waterway was generally regarded as Eyre Creek. (When explorers first found bone-dry water courses it must have been hard to throw around words like 'river', so for many outback waterways, it takes two rivers to make a creek.)

The station was a miniature community, entirely self-contained, with power generators, sewerage systems, staff accommodation and kitchens, machinery sheds and the main house. Satellite dishes provided access to TV, telephony and Internet.

After her tour, Judy got one of the ringers, a young Dutchman named Werner, who was visiting the station for work experience, to show me around the improbably green expanse of Lake Muncoonie. From the ground it was easy to see why it's one of the best examples of 'flood-out country' in western Queensland.

At its northern end, the Georgina River flows into the lake. Often the Georgina will flow through its deeper channels on stations upstream, such as Glengyle, without overflowing and spreading over the flood plains. However, once the Georgina reaches Adria Downs, its channels are only 60 centimetres deep. After big rains they soon overflow and spread over a plain that in places is 20 kilometres wide. When its waters reach the lake, the channels are only 15 centimetres deep.

The river has to fill Muncoonie, and Lake Selicia one dune to the east, before it can continue on its way down the channels of Eyre Creek. It does this on average every eight years, but more often than not the Georgina gets no further than Lake Muncoonie, where it spreads out over thousands of hectares of some of the best cattle-fattening country anywhere, bringing up lush grasses (and giving what outback cattlemen refer to as 'relief').

The lakes used to be in the southern part of Sidney Kidman's Glengyle Station. While the Cattle King acknowledged the great ability of this country to fatten cattle, the extremely remote location of Glengyle and adjacent Annandale (Kidman's first Queensland property, purchased in 1896) made management difficult.

In 1921 tragedy struck when two children on Annandale Station died. There are several versions of what happened. One is that the wife of the station manager was left alone for such a long time she went insane and killed her two young daughters. Another is that two boys, aged eight and two, had perished from fever or the extreme heat of summer. According to Don Rowlands' grandmother, the girls had got in the habit of collecting bush tucker with some of the Aboriginal people who were camped near the homestead. One day they'd gone out on their own and collected bulbs from a desert lily. They put them in the onion sack in the station kitchen, unaware that the bulbs contained a powerful and poisonous hallucinogen. When their mother unknowingly used the bulbs, the girls died and the poison sent the mother out of her mind.

Eventually the homestead was abandoned and the property was managed as part of Glengyle Station. In 1939 Cecil Madigan's desert expedition visited the homestead and he described what he found:

> Annandale Station was a sad ruin amid signs of former prosperity. Some outbuildings, a harness room and a store still had iron roofs on and were habitable. In the store room were a stores account book and a great bag of peppercorns. The roof and doors had been taken away from the house, but to our astonishment we found the furniture was still in it. There were beds, wardrobes, chests of drawers, a dining table, account books, garden seats, window glass, a surveyor's chain, a windmill, tools and even explosives. All were covered with dust and now subject to the ravages of wind and rain.

There are many stories surrounding the Kidman company's decision (after Kidman's death in 1935) to let the Annandale lease and part of Glengyle go. One view was that they had fallen victim to Kidman's habit of flogging the country. It was said the fragile desert had succumbed to the predations of cattle and the erosion caused by their hard hooves. Looking at the rich green expanse of Lake Muncoonie, the jewel in the Adria crown, it was readily apparent that this view was mistaken. Of course, you had to see the Channel Country to understand it, and the country has long had opinions expressed about it by authorities who've never been there. Map makers are an obvious example. One map published by the federal government's mapping authority in 1975 describes Muncoonie and Selicia as salt lakes. When it comes to showing where rivers flow and what they're called, the lines are drawn with a hesitation born of ignorance. I know because I can now see where some of the maps in my previous books were a bit vague when it came to detail.

Don Rayment had his own opinion on what happened. He reckoned Kidman was beaten by the lack of water. 'Until David Brook took over Annandale and southern Glengyle and spent a lot of money on waters and bores there was no water here, except for what came down in a flood, and the one bore that Kidman put down. But after about August or September, apart from really good wet years, there was no water here.'

Nevertheless, some Kidman managers now refer to the northern end of Adria Downs as 'Brookies' Gain'. Don recalled a manager from Glengyle flying down to Adria after a small flood. 'He just shook his head and said, "I don't know how Kidman ever sold this or gave it away." We had heaps of feed and he had virtually nothin'. Because in a big flood they get a big area of flood plain, but in a small flood it comes down here and it flattens out on us and we get relief, but up there they don't.'

As Werner and I drove along a track on the eastern side of Muncoonie I noticed a long red cloud over the western horizon – a dust storm. I wasn't as daunted by the sight as I had been the first time I'd faced the dust swirling in over the dunes. It meant I could enjoy the exhilarating spectacle. This time, though, we were surrounded by cattle.

When the storm hit, the beasts panicked and ran chaotically in all directions. They seemed disoriented by the onslaught of howling wind and sand, and we were suddenly glad of the protection of the vehicle as terrified beasts careered around us. It was easy to see what a catastrophe a dust storm could be in the days when drovers on horseback had to risk their lives to prevent such a panic or else lose the entire herd.

We battled back to the homestead as large muddy drops spattered the windscreen. The wild wind and the rolling clouds of red sand had everyone at the homestead – Judy, one of her daughters home from school, a couple of ringers who'd knocked off for the day and tradesmen working on new staff quarters – in a state of excitement. They'd all been scrambling to grab cameras and take photographs. Even after living in the area for several years, the big storms were too good to miss.

As it started to get dark, several vehicles rolled up with station staff returning from various parts of the property. Soon there was quite a crowd in the homestead. It was surprising to see so many young people. The ringers were male and female, Aboriginal and European, and still in their teens, and it was clear that while Don was the boss, he and his wife were also de facto parents of an extended family.

Dinner started out as a ramshackle affair. Before the food arrived people kept coming and going on the large verandah off the main house overlooking the river. Then dishes piled with meat, vegetables and salads were set out on a side table and immediately became the focal point for a dozen voracious appetites. No sooner had a ringer or builder cleaned up their plate than they went back for more. There was plenty for everybody.

After dinner, Don and I retired to his office for a yarn. His desk was covered with paperwork that only got his attention when it was too dark to work around the property. Don was in his mid-fifties, weather-beaten and brown skinned. He was a standard issue out-back type in manner and dress, except for his shoes. He wore trainers instead of the usual leather boots. 'I've always worn 'em,' he said, a little surprised that I'd noticed. 'I just find 'em more comfortable.'

Don was Channel Country born and raised. He grew up on the most eastern property in the Diamantina Shire, Kurran, and was now working on the most western. 'Dad took Kurran up in 1940,' he said, 'and Billy Brook took up the original Adria lease, which was only very small, in 1939.'

Don went to school in Winton and Longreach back in the days when schools had no air-conditioning. He recalled kids fighting to sit directly under the single ceiling fan, desperate for relief from the heat of the classroom. When he left school, in his mid-teens, he went contract mustering then worked a property with his brother.

Adria was the most remote station he'd worked on and by far the biggest. From the homestead at Adria Downs he actually managed two properties. Alton Downs, on the southern boundary of Adria, is part-owned by David Brook and his second cousins, a branch of the Gaffney family. The two stations combined cover 12 500 square kilometres. There are few bigger properties in Queensland, or Australia for that matter. It's a 250-kilometre drive from one end to the other.

'This is the most remote cattle station in Queensland,' he told me. 'There's no-one to the west of us. So we're different from a lot of other areas. When you live this far out, and I don't mean just here, I mean this area, you can't shift your cattle like you can at, say, Winton and Boulia, and put 'em on agistment. We're another 700 kilometres away and the cost is too high. So we've gotta look after our land so that we don't have to shift our cattle.'

The property's remoteness also prohibits bringing cattle in from other Brook holdings to take advantage of good times. They sometimes bring cattle from Kamaran Downs (100 kilometres north), but every kilometre the cattle are moved is another kilometre that's added to the expense of sending them to market. It costs more than $100 per beast to truck them from Adria. For a road train with six decks of cattle, the income earned from one deck pays the transport bill. Add to that the marginal nature of the country the cattle are coming from and it's an extremely delicate balancing act to earn any kind of income, even in a good season.

'When it's good you could put four times the amount of cattle on,' Don explained, 'but if you do that you've lost all the feed. When we get a flood we want to make that feed last for three years. So we've fenced off the lakes so we can control which cattle go in there. Prior to that the cattle just flocked in there and flogged it. Now that we control them, we can run more cattle spread over a longer period of time.'

Fencing has also allowed Don to spell the station's Mitchell grass country, the open plains above the flood levels that bring up golden, straw-like grasses after rain. When he can, he tries to reduce the numbers of cattle grazing it until it's gone to seed. About a third of the station is Mitchell grass, a third is flood-out country and the remainder sandhills.

In addition to the fencing, a lot of work and money has gone into improving the water supply. In the last three and a half years more than 120 kilometres of poly pipe has been laid. 'We did that not to run more cattle but to spread them out so they're not overgrazing,' Don said. 'Our aim, both David's and mine, is to have more consistent seasons. We can't control the seasons, but we can control the ground cover they leave behind. So if we can preserve areas by shifting cattle around and building paddocks it'll give us a much more consistent flow in our cattle aims.'

It sounded like a game of chess, except the game was being played on a board half the size of Tasmania against an opponent who wrote all the rules. It turned out that Adria was one of the last places in the Channel Country to be developed on a large scale. Don Rayment and David Brook might have been taking a gamble, but they'd all but drought-proofed the place.

As Don put it, 'When Judy and I first came here we came in on the end of a five-year drought where we had an average three inches [7.5 centimetres] of rain a year. That was the longest drought since Brooks owned it and it was only in the last six or eight months that we couldn't deliver fat cattle. I've been in a lot of areas in western Queensland and I don't think there's any other country that I know of that cattle hang on as long as this country here, and respond as quickly after rain.'

Don was clearly passionate about the place.

'I love the property. I love it,' he said with real feeling. 'I like big areas. A lot of my time has been in areas of similar rainfall, arid areas, certainly not anything as big as this, but I like the challenges.'

There were plenty of those. The property was being operated as an accredited organic beef producer. Don was trucking fat cattle further to market than any other property in Australia. He was working hard to get them there without a bruise, which required a lot of effort from everyone in the supply chain, from the station hands to the truck drivers and the yards where the cattle spell during the journey. He was employing young people from around the district because he'd been through the experience of bringing people out who thought it was going to be like the TV show *McLeod's Daughters*. He was also quick to admit that he couldn't do it on his own.

'I'm very fortunate that Judy and I work well together and she loves it as much as I do,' he said. 'You couldn't manage places out here if you didn't get on and work well together, or your partner didn't like it.'

We ended up talking late into the night but that made no difference to when we got up the next day. It was a 5 a.m. start. Everyone ate breakfast in the main house while it was still dark. There was a faint glimmer along the sand dune east of the homestead as the ringers prepared to leave. Don was roaring instructions as if everyone was two paddocks away. 'You two go up to Glengyle and walk them cattle down! Don't drive fast! Make sure you got plenty of water!'

'Yes, boss.'

'Werner. You take Evan up on the dune and show him the lakes from up there! Then bring 'im up to the yards at Kaliduwarry!'

Everybody fanned out. I got some shots of the homestead at sunrise and looked over the rolls of hay that had been cut on Lake Selicia. They smelt like caramel. Then Werner and I drove out to have another look at the lakes. After that we headed north to the cattle yards where Don and three ringers were drafting cattle.

Werner climbed through the rails into the yards. I followed and tried to look like I wasn't afraid of being trampled while beasts of all sizes milled about us. Don was in a different yard singling out beasts and prodding them down a race to the drafting pen. He was calling out to Jessica Gilby, standing in the crow's nest above. 'Bush! Breeder! Stranger! Cull! Weaner!' he shouted as each beast bolted down the chute. Jessica was pulling metal bars to open the gates and let the designated beast into the appropriate yard.

Jessica was a pretty young woman and wore aviator sunglasses and a broad-brimmed black Akubra. Her boots were spotless and stylish. Looking at her I was tempted to ask Don, 'Are you sure it's not like *McLeod's Daughters* here?' Instead, I tried to take a photo of the cattle in the yard.

'Don't photograph those ones!' Don bellowed when he saw what I was doing. 'They're rubbish cattle!'

They looked like fine beasts to me – plump and healthy, just as he'd been telling me. 'What's wrong with them?' I bleated.

'They're not our cattle!' Don growled. 'Look at 'em! They're all different colours!'

A motley bunch of Brahman cattle, 'strangers' from other stations, were standing in front of the handsome Adria Herefords. I sighed and put my camera away.

While the ringers continued drafting, Don took me for a drive up to Kaliduwarry Waterhole. It was twenty minutes of fast bush

driving up a station track. When we got close Don pulled off the
road and headed cross country. As he did I was thinking, 'Seen one
waterhole . . .'

Then we topped a rise.

'Oh my god,' I blurted. 'It's blue!'

Don obviously enjoyed my reaction. Before us lay an expanse of
water 200 metres wide. It swept in a broad curve away into the distance in both directions.

'It's not very deep,' Don said. 'But it's permanent water. It goes a
bit salty when the level drops, but the cattle can still get a drink.'

Looking at it with a yachtie's eye for sandbanks, it didn't seem too
shallow. 'You could sail on that and not go aground,' I said. 'How
long is it?'

'Thirty-two kilometres.'

All I could do was gape. Calling a place like this a waterhole didn't
do it justice. It was a lake. I'd imagined the Georgina and Eyre Creek
as a series of dusty gutters. Here the river system formed a broad
waterway with a gently rising far bank lined with green grasses that
turned to gold before the coolabahs started. Behind them a deep red
dune rose to complete the postcard.

We headed back to the stockyards and Don handed me over to
Werner. We got back to the homestead in time for morning tea and
scones. Over a cuppa Judy and I got talking about what it was like
living at Adria. I was surprised to discover that she didn't regard the
isolation of the homestead as a problem.

'I like my space,' she said.

I thought she'd found the right place for that, but no. She mentioned
one occasion when the busy life of the station had got on top of her.

'I was cooking for everyone,' she said. 'There was a mining group
of people that were drilling out here and you never knew when they
were going to turn up. I didn't know what was going on. There were
people coming and going – Don included.'

With a laugh, Judy skirted around the details of how upset she'd become but explained how Don handled the situation. 'He got a bottle of wine and some chocolates and said, "Forget about everyone else, we'll just take time out." We bounced up to Kaliduwarry and had a little picnic and it was beautiful. It was freezing cold and we should've had a thermos of coffee, not a bottle of wine, but it was very nice. You sort of step back and think, "Really, I'm here to do this. I'm here to cook and clean and coordinate. Who do I think I am that I'm going to throw a little hissy fit because I don't know what's going on?" Yeah, so I think Don calmed me down enough.'

When she described what she actually did on the station, it was surprising that she'd only cracked once. At one time she was tutoring three of her children who were doing School of the Air, she was running a household that comprised a dozen or more people with all the logistical challenges that being remote from any kind of shopping outlet involved, she was keeping track of where people were on and off the station and passing messages between them, and she was helping Don with the station's paperwork, including registering and tracking cattle from birth to slaughter under the National Livestock Identification Scheme. Don was also the president of the Birdsville Social Club, which meant Judy was there in the background helping organise events like the bronco branding.

It was a tall order and some of the jobs meant taking on roles she didn't enjoy. 'I'm happy about School of the Air being over,' she said. 'With your own kids you expect more from them than you should. If it was someone else's kid you'd probably nurse them along a bit more, but you think, "No, they should know that." Then when they don't get things done you spend all the time trying to catch up. Now they're off at school and in a classroom again they can come home to me and I'm just Mum instead of being their cranky teacher.'

Yet boarding school presented different issues. It wasn't like the bad old days of children disappearing for up to a year with only an occasional letter. Now they have phones and email and can contact their parents whenever they're not in class, but they're still a long way from home.

'I'm the biggest sook out,' Judy said. 'It near broke my heart leaving Andrew in Dalby the other day, and he's in grade eleven. It was like he was starting school all over again. I promptly burst into tears and bolted because I couldn't talk to anyone, so I haven't seen him again. Well, we've talked on the phone. Someone told me that when you send them to boarding school it's like pulling your heart out and sticking it on a stake and I remember thinking it couldn't possibly be. But I think it is.'

After morning tea I started the 130-kilometre trip down Adria's front driveway. Not far from the homestead I turned off the road and drove down a station track to a dune to steal one last look at the station's remarkable lakes. On my map I could see that the ruins of the old Annandale homestead lay some 20 kilometres further west, hidden behind a succession of tall dunes. As I took in the view of verdant grass dotted with grazing cattle, I recalled something Don Rayment had said the night before.

'If you don't manage this country and look after the land then you won't be here. If you look across the Diamantina Shire, the people that have been in the Shire have been here for a long, long time. They must be doing something right by managing the country or they wouldn't be here. It costs a lot more than anywhere else to get our article out and on the other side of the scale it costs a lot more to get anything in. So you're slugged from both sides. But we're still surviving.'

A few weeks after my visit to Adria there was an incident that highlighted the dangers of working on outback stations. It also demonstrated why the Birdsville Clinic needed an x-ray machine. A family property on the other side of the Simpson Desert had David Brook's permission to muster wild camels on his station. The camels were the descendants of the beasts that had opened up the outback before motorised transport made them redundant. Now feral, they were sufficiently numerous on outback stations that they needed to be kept in check. Some went into the meat trade, others were exported live for camel racing.

One of the family's sons was giving Don and his staff a hand with their mustering when something broke on his motorcycle. The front wheel locked and he was catapulted over the handlebars. When he hit the ground he broke his collarbone. David flew the young bloke back to the Birdsville Clinic where the break was confirmed. His arm was put in a sling and he was given painkillers while he waited for a regular passenger flight out. His condition wasn't considered so serious that he needed to be evacuated by the Flying Doctor.

The Brooks let the lad stay in their staff accommodation in town and we met him one night when we went to their place for dinner. He was a solidly built teenager, tough as they come, but he looked like he was in a world of pain. Nevertheless, in the bush broken collarbones are common. His discomfort wasn't considered remarkable. We found out a week later that when he'd finally got to a hospital that could see him (he'd flown to Townsville, then to Adelaide), the x-ray revealed that his collarbone was fractured in seven places.

It made my blood boil to think how much the poor kid must have suffered. If he'd been in a major city and it had taken more than a week to determine the extent of his injuries it would have made front-page headlines in every newspaper. Angry parents would be demanding action on TV shows. The health minister would be under pressure to resign. Instead in Birdsville there was a grim acceptance that this was just another fact of outback life.

I couldn't join the grim acceptance. Instead, I seized on the fundraising for the x-ray machine. 'We must get that money,' I said to Bev next time I saw her.

'We're trying,' she replied. Bev had got Michelle to design a large

thermometer that was set up in the pub to show how we were progressing. It was now past $30 000. We just needed another $10 000.
It couldn't come soon enough as Michelle and I threw every bit of
loose change that came our way into the collection boxes. We volun-
teered for any fundraising activity going. When a couple of tourists
offered me $20 in return for a game on the golf course, it went to
the collection box.

*

Spring in Birdsville wasn't marked by the blossoming of trees and a
bursting forth of flowers. Instead, October brought the first sightings of snakes around the town.

John Hanna saw a mulga snake over at the thermal power station and called Neale the policeman, asking him to shoot it. Neale
refused.

'I can't go firing a gun in the middle of town,' he told me later.
'What if I only wing it?'

'Neale, you can't wing it,' I replied. 'Snakes don't have wings.
You'll either hit it or you'll miss.'

A couple of days later, Neale found a small snake in the police
barracks and tried to shoo it out with a broom, but it slithered into
a cupboard. He thought it was reddish brown with a black head, but
very thin. He went to see Lyn Rowlands in the Wirrari Centre, and
together they went through a book on reptiles. Lyn verified that it
was an inland taipan, the most venomous snake in the world.

Around the same time, Dr Ross was observed pulling up outside our place on his way to check on ninety-year-old Frank Purser,
a retired air-conditioning mechanic. Ross got out of the ambu-
lance, paused, then got back in and quickly drove off. A minute
later he was back with a long-handled shovel. He got out and started
whacking the road with great vigour. Then he scooped something

up and drove off again. Five minutes later he returned and went in to see Frank.

It turned out that he'd seen a king brown snake (*Pseudechis australis*), also known as an eastern brown, and the second most deadly snake in the world. Someone had run it over outside our townhouse but he wanted to make sure it was dead. He then took the body to the tip.

At the time we had friends from Sydney, Paul and Mardi Brown, and their daughters visiting us for a few days. They were taking a driving tour around the outback and we were on their 'must-see' list. Paul, a sailing buddy, had been on the phone several times to discuss the requirements of outback travel. One of his big worries was snakes. He was particularly concerned that his two young girls might not pay much attention to his warnings.

The following day we were having morning coffee and milkshakes in the bakery with Paul, Mardi and the kids when Dr Ross turned up. I went up to him at the counter and quietly asked if he'd reinforce Paul's messages to the girls about deadly reptiles.

When he got his coffee he came over. 'We've seen snakes over at the clinic,' he told the girls, 'and there was one outside Evan's. It was probably dead, but you can't take any chances with these things. What you have to realise is that they're as dangerous dead as they are alive. There's still venom in the fangs and all it takes is a scratch and you can be dead. That's why I took it away. Kids play up in the cul-de-sac and if they started playing with a dead snake it could be real bad.'

The girls, being only twelve and eight, usually had fairly short attention spans, but they listened in attentive silence.

'There was a case not long ago,' he went on, 'where a bloke came upon a dead snake on the road. He opened its mouth and pulled its fangs forward with his fingers. He didn't even notice that he'd received a small prick. An hour later he was dead.

'The other thing you should remember is that the size of the snake isn't important. The venom is the same. There may not be as much of it, but there's still more than enough to kill you.'

I didn't know if he was making it up to keep the kids away from snakes, but it was working for me. He talked about what to do if a snake bit you. 'The important thing,' he said, 'is don't panic. If you do, the venom will move through your body faster. And you don't try to suck the venom out. The best thing to do is to put on a compression bandage and bind from the extremity towards the heart. Then get medical attention as soon as possible. In town it's better to stay where you are and get me to come to you. Just driving down to the clinic is too much activity.'

Birdsville has the disconcerting distinction of being the habitat for three of the four most venomous snakes in the world: the tiger snake (*Notechis scutatus*), fourth on the list; the king brown (*Pseudechis australis*), number two; and the inland taipan or fierce snake (*Oxyuranus microlepidotus*), at number one.

'You bet they're fierce,' Ross said. 'I saw one once. It crossed a road to chase a little girl on her bike.'

The curious thing about the most deadly snake, the inland taipan, is that although one bite is supposed to have enough venom to lay waste to a third of the Diamantina's population of 300, there's no recorded instance of it actually killing anyone. The reason may have something to do with the method used to test snake venom. Not surprisingly, they don't try it on humans. They use mice. According to Western Australian snake expert Brian Bush, different venoms have different effects on different creatures. So the snake rankings are of great interest if you're a mouse (one of the prey species of taipans, as it happens) but the toxic effects may actually be different if you're a human.

The low population in the outback may also explain why there are so few fatalities. There aren't many people for the snakes to bite.

Not surprisingly, the snakes that kill most people in the world are Asian vipers. Their venom isn't particularly potent but because they inhabit heavily populated areas they're responsible for up to 50 000 deaths a year.

Curiously, the inland taipan was little known to science until the 1970s. Two specimens had been found in 1879, and were held in alcohol-filled bottles somewhere in the Museum of Victoria, except no-one was quite sure where. Then, in 1972, Herb Rabig from Cuddapan Station, between Birdsville and Windorah, sent the head and tail of a snake to Jeanette Covacevich, herpetologist at the Queensland Museum. Did she know what it was? Only after considerable research did she realise it was probably the snake described by the Victorians nearly one hundred years before. It was, she thought, incredibly rare. In September 1972, Herb took Covacevich and a colleague for a drive on his property to show them where he'd found the snake. Along the way they found a large taipan dead on the side of the road. In the next ten days they found thirteen more live ones. The scientists were elated. It turned out that the snake wasn't rare. What was rare was visits by scientists to its habitat.

None of this was news to the people of Birdsville. At a dinner down at Dusty's, Geoff Morton had plenty of stories about encounters with snakes. He told of a stockman who was bitten by a snake far from the homestead. He thought he was a goner so he laid down under a tree and waited to die. He slowly drifted into unconsciousness. Next morning, he woke up. He'd done the right thing to slow his circulation and reduce the effect of the bite.

Another tale was of a stockman bitten while sleeping on his swag. He was so tired he just rolled over and went back to sleep. In the morning, the snake was dead beside him. The stockman survived the bite, but the snake was probably crushed when he rolled on it.

Geoff had a close call himself while mounting a horse in a paddock near town. He'd stepped on a king brown snake which promptly wrapped itself around his leg. He was half on the horse and half off, desperately trying to shake the snake loose while dreading being bitten. Eventually he shook the snake free and it slithered away. He got such a fright that he collapsed on the ground, thankful to be alive. Jimmy Crombie was with him but hadn't seen the snake. Jimmy thought he was just fooling around and really let him have it.

With so many sightings, Neale the policeman gave me some pointers on snakes and the importance of looking around for them when you go outside. One of his favourite sayings was, 'I knew I needed glasses when I picked up a snake to kill a stick.'

When we went out at night, we started carrying a torch to shine around on the ground as we walked. We went to a town meeting one night and felt sure we'd get ribbed when people saw our impossible-to-hide bright yellow torch. When no-one said anything, we started to take the snake threat even more seriously.

While playing a round of golf, Neale asked if I'd seen any snakes on the course. 'No,' I replied, 'but that might say more about my inability to see them before they see me.'

A couple of times I'd noticed lizards taking flight from right under my feet and admonished myself to be more observant. *If that was a snake, you'd be dead by now.* Neale said he'd give me some compression bandages to put in my golf bag. It was probably the only golf course in the world where such things are a recommended part of your kit.

The only other dangerous snake to watch out for was identified by Darren Mills, the policeman from Bedourie. He'd come with me when I'd taken a visiting TV crew out to Big Red to get some dawn shots. While we were out there, we encouraged the crew to take their shoes off and feel the softness of the sand.

Moments later they were wiggling their toes and thoroughly enjoying themselves while waiting for the sun to come up. Darren and I were standing beside them, shoes still on. Down on the face of the

dune we could see long trails of lifted sand that were caused by bur-
rowing beetles.

'Gee, those sand snake tracks are quite high up,' Darren said.

'Yeah,' I replied, 'I thought they usually stayed down near the
spinifex.'

'Snakes?' chorused the TV crew.

'Don't worry,' Darren said while trying to keep a straight face.
'Their bite isn't fatal. It's just excruciatingly painful.'

Suddenly, toe wiggling became toe curling and the crew started
shuffling towards their shoes. Darren and I sniggered quietly among
ourselves.

Back in town, our little prank was more than matched by the
Birdsville Hotel's new publican, Brian Hanna. A tourist came in and
asked if he had any ice. Brian said, 'Yes, but it's only second-grade,
unprocessed, industrial ice. Three dollars a bag.'

The tourist said he'd take it. Brian took his money then went out
the back. He returned with a plastic bag full of water. The entire bar
erupted in laughter and the tourist was so embarrassed he took the
bag and shuffled out. (The pub had actually run out of ice and while
there was a big sign explaining this, people kept asking.)

*

Rumours had been circulating for some months that the station to
the south of Birdsville, Pandie Pandie, was to be sold. In September
the rumours proved correct when the property, which had been in
the Morton family for seventy years, was put up for auction.

David Morton, who was then fifty-four, had lived on Pandie from
the age of one. Jane had been by his side for twenty-five years of
marriage, and together they had endured everything nature could
throw at them. Floods, drought and bad seasons couldn't break
them. In the end it was family conflict. By most accounts David's

father, George, was an extremely difficult man and when it came to passing Pandie on to the next generation, his legacy in death was consistent with the way he'd lived.

The most public demonstration of George Morton's nature was his feud with his brother Lyle over the fence between Pandie Pandie and Roseberth. The two properties had once belonged to their father, Celsus, but he'd passed Roseberth on to Lyle and Pandie to George. The boundary between the two properties ran along the South Australian border.

From the beginning there were tensions over the cost of maintaining the fence, but they came to a head in the major floods of 1974 when large sections were swept away. Lyle told George it was his turn to pay for the repairs. George refused. Lyle went ahead and rebuilt the fence, but he did so 200 metres inside his boundary. George was so incensed he built his own, but did so right on the boundary. To this day along the state border there are two well-maintained fences running parallel, 200 metres apart, for kilometre after kilometre.

Lyle blamed George for the situation. Until his death in 2004, George protested that the fault lay with his brother. Memories linger of the day the two brothers got involved in a wild brawl. One punch had been thrown in the bar at the Birdsville Hotel. Later they'd fought in the street.

When management (and part ownership) of the two properties was passed on to the next generation, Geoff and David continued to maintain their respective fences. However, the bitterness between the families was healed to some extent by their sons. Geoff and Bev's sons Kerry and Steven went to school with David and Jane's son Peter and got along so well that eventually peace broke out all along the fence line.

When I asked David Morton about the feud, he laughed and told me it was worse than I thought. 'The fences got built not long after the war. They got hold of some old mines. Mark my words, boy. You go in there and you'll bloody explode.'

He was probably kidding, but when Michelle and I drove down to the fences 12 kilometres south of Birdsville we were very careful to stay near the road. What we also noticed is that there weren't two fences. There were three.

In between the relatively new Pandie Pandie and Roseberth fences, there was a fence that was much older. It had the remains of what looked like a gate, which suggested it predated Federation, when cattle passed through border gates and drovers paid duty to take their stock from one state to another.

Sure enough, a bit of research revealed the origins of the older fence, and that George and Lyle Morton's feud over the fence wasn't the first time there'd been trouble on the border. In George Farwell's *Land of Mirage*, written in the 1950s, there's this:

> In this unfenced country, the border might well be an imaginary one, for State jealousies ran so high they seldom cooperated. When Queensland wanted to run a dingo fence out to Poeppel's Corner in the Simpson, the South Australian Government refused to pay half the cost. To spite Adelaide, Queensland built its own fence one chain [approximately 20 metres] inside the legal border, and no South Australian fence was allowed to join it. Today, east of Birdsville, you may see two parallel fences exactly twenty-two yards apart, both of them rotten and silted over because their upkeep was too costly.

The fence (and border) Farwell refers to is actually south of Birdsville. And according to Cecil Madigan in *Crossing the Dead Heart* it was a rabbit fence, rather than one for dingoes. He wrote: 'The old rabbit-proof fence south of Birdsville runs along the Queensland–South Australian border ... and from there it runs north along the west side of the Mulligan ... The fence is no longer maintained, and west of Birdsville it is completely buried in sand in places.'

This explanation of the old fence has more of a ring of truth about it. Don Rowlands referred to the badly decayed fence west of Birdsville, which now marks (just) the boundary of the Simpson Desert National Park and Adria Downs, as a rabbit fence. The burial of the fence under the dunes accorded with the experiences related by Geoff Morton.

The auction for Pandie Pandie took place in mid-October. The station, with a total area of 6625 square kilometres, average rainfall of 125 millimetres per year, rated to carry 7800 adult cattle, with potential to be certified organic, was sold to the Oldfield family, relatives of the Morton family, for $7.5 million.

When Geoff Morton was asked if he thought the sale of Pandie Pandie meant the end of the fence feud on his southern boundary he quipped that, on the contrary, he'd have to rebuild it in brick. A couple of days later I saw him at a function and told him there was a bloke in town looking for him. 'He reckons he's a bricklayer,' I said. Geoff chuckled away.

The imminent departure of David and Jane (their son and daughter were employed elsewhere) was felt deeply by the Birdsville community. Their involvement in every aspect of it had been far reaching. I got glimpses of it when Jane resigned as secretary of the Birdsville Social Club and I took over the job after no-one else put their hand up. When she ran me through the responsibilities and showed me through the files, I saw folder after folder filled with letters she'd written to sponsors, authorities, contributors and participants for events like the bronco branding, gymkhana, tennis tournament, New Year's Eve celebrations and more.

Jane had also been treasurer of the Birdsville Race Club for many years. I didn't doubt that her contribution there was just as significant. When the race club had its AGM, which I didn't attend in part because of what I might get elected to, it was decided to appoint an event coordinator because the work involved in organising the races was overwhelming the committee. I wondered whether the loss of Jane's contribution had been the deciding factor.

In the weeks before David and Jane moved away, their friends reflected on their prospects after they left. In Birdsville they were highly respected. Indeed, in the months I'd spent in Birdsville, David and Jane were the only people I'd never heard anyone say a bad word about. However, wherever they went, they'd be starting from scratch to build the deep respect that comes from being part of a community for most of your life. It became something of a refrain. In Birdsville people know who you are. You're somebody. In most other places you're just another face in the crowd.

13

SUMMMER

As the days grew hotter, the tourists in Birdsville grew fewer and the town became more like a community – sixty people on the desert frontier quietly going about their lives. Every day we felt more like we were part of it. People who've moved to small towns often say they don't feel like locals even after living there for ten or twenty years. Perhaps they didn't know the secret – get involved in social and sporting activities. We played rounds of golf and tennis, worked on various fundraisers, and now helped out with the Social Club. We'd formed a circle of friends who made us feel completely at home.

We were enjoying outback life so much that we'd begun to think about what we would do when our year in Birdsville was over. There was no pressing need to return to Sydney. More to the point, there was no desire. We considered extending our stay until the end of the next tourist season, at least another six months. Of course, we'd made such plans without experiencing the hardest time of the year in Birdsville – summer.

Long before December the temperatures were rising. On the first Wednesday in November, Nell Brook rang to check that tennis was on. It was only 3 p.m. but it was a stinking hot 41.9 degrees Celsius. We expected the temperature would drop as the sun started going down, but much to our surprise, at five o'clock, it was 42.2. We decided to play anyway. We took lots of water and headed for the courts.

The curious thing was that on the court it didn't feel very hot. Our faces were quite red, but we didn't seem to be sweating much. In fact we were sweating a lot, but in the dry heat it was evaporating so fast that we didn't notice it. Even our clothes had that freshly ironed feel. We played for an hour, two sets, then decided we shouldn't push things too much.

A week later, after playing in similar temperatures, we dropped into the pub for a drink and met the Flying Doctor Simone Peacock, who was in town conducting one of the RFDS's regular visits. She seemed shocked at the sight of us in our tennis gear. 'We drank lots of water,' I explained.

'In that kind of heat,' she countered, 'you probably need more than water. You've got to get some electrolytes as well. Try drinking Gatorade or Staminade.'

We said we would, but you could see she was thinking an even better idea was to play when it was cool. Still, what's a few agonising cramps, searing headaches and ultimately organ failure among friends?

That week the temperature hit 43.4 Celsius (a more impressive-sounding 110.8 on the Fahrenheit scale). The next day it reached 43.8, the hottest we'd experienced so far. The heat wasn't so bad during the day, but in the evening, when we expected the air to cool, we were disappointed. At bedtime the temperature was still in the high 30s. For the first time, we ran the air-conditioning until dawn, by which time the temperature was 31.1.

The heat all but dried up the flow of tourists and there was no work at the bakery for Michelle. There was nothing for Ben to do either, so I took my best mate Zeus, now fully recovered from his bout with the pig, for a last galumph through the now-fading Creek of Flowers before he and his master left for the summer.

As luck would have it, friends back in Sydney were sending Michelle increasing amounts of freelance graphic design work so she set up office on another table we'd squeezed into our tiny townhouse. Half the dining table was allocated to her jewellery-making workshop. It was pretty cramped, but what made it more difficult was that Michelle enjoyed an interactive work environment with plenty of conversation and exchange of ideas while I preferred solitude and total silence – facing the 'blank page' that writers sometimes talk about. Each day, as she tried to chat and I responded in monosyllables, the tension grew.

There was relief at the end of the day when we knocked off work, grabbed our towels and drove around to Pelican Point, a sandy peninsula that jutted into the billabong, for a refreshing swim. Afterwards we settled back on the beach to watch the glorious fiery red and orange outback sunsets. I couldn't get over how perfect the weather was and how few the tourists were. They seemed to have a terrible dread of temperatures starting with the number four and hadn't discovered the power of a cool swim to deal with them. It felt like we had the entire outback to ourselves.

The heat had no impact on Birdsville's surprisingly busy social round. For the Melbourne Cup there was a lunch, after which Jessica Gilby, the young ringer from Adria, ran a trivia quiz to raise money for the x-ray machine. The Outback Queensland Tourism Awards were held in town and involved two dinners run by the Social Club. We were also planning the Social Club's annual party, a free barbecue for the whole town held at the end of November before people headed off on holidays.

We also discovered the pleasures of barbecues on the verandah of the old Courthouse. Up to a dozen townsfolk brought salads and condiments. Neale the policeman provided the gas barbecue and nipped next door for any odds and ends we overlooked. The Courthouse had a pleasant view across the airport to the Birdsville Hotel. Around the side of the building we could watch the sun go down while enjoying cold beer and nibblies, and it was nicely sheltered from the wind. It hardly mattered that the verandah was where Sub-Inspector Sharpe shot himself back in 1882.

It was at a Courthouse barbie that we first met Neale's wife, Sandra. She'd come out on one of her regular visits from Charleville, where she worked at the Cosmos Centre (an astronomical interpretive centre). She was a warm and friendly person, and seemed comfortable with the dynamics of a relationship that saw her living apart from her husband for weeks at a time. Like a lot of outback people she dealt with the situation with a quiet strength and just got on with life.

The Courthouse was also the venue (in late November) for Dusty and Teresa's farewell barbecue. In Birdsville there are two kinds of people: those who stay for the summer and those who don't. Dusty had done it in previous years and reckoned it was hell. Indeed there was a subtle change in attitude towards Michelle and I when townsfolk realised we intended to spend all summer there. We seemed to have risen in their estimation, although we weren't exactly sure why.

Bound for Adelaide, then a trip to England, Dusty and Teresa entrusted us with the care of their eleven chickens while they were away. I suspected Dusty really wanted to get rid of the chickens and thought leaving them in the hands of a rank chicken novice like me was as good as the kiss of death. I couldn't fault his judgement. We found that when we let the chooks out and left them unattended for the day, the crows discovered easy egg pickings.

Fortunately, there was a wealth of knowledge in Birdsville regarding the care and maintenance of chickens. At a dinner for supporters of the Birdsville Clinic, to which we were invited in my capacity as the Social Club Secretary, Geoff Morton advised that the best way to look after chickens was neglect. 'Just feed 'em and let 'em go,' he said. To deal with the crows he suggested we keep the chooks in their coop until ten o'clock, by which time they'd have laid their eggs. We could then beat the crows to the eggs when we let the girls out. Too easy.

Soon we were getting up to nine eggs a day, far more than we could eat. We distributed them by the dozen to households around town, to Roseberth and Pandie Pandie. The eggs added to the fresh produce we were getting from our small vegetable patch. The broccoli was fading but the silver beet was a wonder of leafy green production. The rocket was living up to its name and we were getting plenty of Italian parsley, rosemary, thyme and basil. The tomatoes were a bit hit and miss. After a winter crop the snow peas sulked in the warmer weather. A second attempt at lettuce was a total failure, as was an attempt at beans. Nevertheless, we were doing pretty well considering Birdsville gardeners reckoned it was one of the toughest places to grow anything.

After six months we'd become accustomed to most of the inconveniences of living in the remote outback but the one thing that still left me frustrated was the mail service. In November I got a phone bill that had taken seven weeks to get to Birdsville. Seven weeks! Fortunately, another letter, telling us the bill was overdue, had overtaken the original bill and so it had been promptly paid. Blue the plumber reckoned such things were nothing new. There was always a risk of getting your phone or power cut off because no-one in a city-based billing office could believe Australia's mail service could be so unreliable.

In Birdsville it was ever thus. In the early days when the mail came up the Birdsville Track or across from Windorah, it was carried by horse or camel and could take weeks or even months. When cars and trucks started running the mail service, they were contracted to deliver the mail fortnightly, and largely succeeded unless floods closed the roads. You'd think that in the days of modern aviation such delays would become a thing of the past, but no.

The air service to Birdsville was one of the running jokes in town. The reasons for SlackAir's delays and cancellations were impressive for their sheer variety. Sometimes the plane was diverted to

Townsville and didn't make it back to Mt Isa in time to do the inward flight. Sometimes the plane had a mechanical fault and there wasn't a spare plane to run the service or the plane didn't have enough fuel to land and take off at every stop along the way. One night the plane that should have arrived at 2.30 p.m. was running so late (it arrived at 9.30 p.m.) that it had to offload passengers bound for Bedourie at Birdsville. Friends drove the 200 kilometres to pick them up. The risk of hitting stock or wildlife at night meant they all booked accommodation in Birdsville and drove home the following morning. On another occasion the plane didn't come because the pilot hadn't had enough sleep since his last flight.

*

When Neale the policeman went on leave for a couple of weeks, he got us to do the town's weather. It meant recording observations at 6 a.m., 9 a.m. and 3 p.m. He showed us how to log on to the weather terminal in the police station, then how to fill in the details of rainfall (such as it was), evaporation and cloud cover. Various instruments (located at the nearby airport) kept track of temperature, pressure and wind, but we also had to note them on sheets as backup in case the communication link failed. The critical things were logging details of visibility, especially when there were dust storms, and low-level cloud (data used by aircraft flying into the area).

Neale gave us a chart of cloud types and left us to study the characteristics of high-altitude cirrus, medium-level altostratus, low-level cumulus and everything in between. It was particularly helpful that we had rain over our first weekend as weather observers. Birdsville received nearly 20 millimetres and with the rain came an abundance of cloud to report. A lot of the time in Birdsville the sky is bereft of the slightest hint of moisture, let alone anything as lavishly showy as a cloud.

While we were at it, he got us to do the daily locust count. This involved a circular pool of water with a light in the middle to attract insects at night. The idea was to go out every morning and count the number of locusts that had fallen into the tank. Alas, locusts were only a small fraction of the prodigious number of insects that drowned on a daily basis. We used a pool scoop to save moths and grasshoppers that were still flopping around in the water. I suspect proper research might reveal that the locust plagues emanating from western Queensland are actually caused by the locust tanks that are dotted about the place. I reckon they drown everything that predates locusts. I dubbed the locust tank the Tank of Death. The name stuck.

John and Judy Menzies from the Working Museum were also getting ready to leave town on a six-week break and John asked if I'd be caretaker while he was away. It meant walking around the buildings every couple of days to check that all was secure. I added it to the daily round of weather observations and chook wrangling.

Doing the weather report at 6 a.m. I quickly discovered that the relatively cool early mornings were the best time of the day to play golf. Michelle had started out doing the early weather report with me, but after three or four starts at 5.50 a.m. her enthusiasm hadn't so much waned as abruptly ceased. Now I was on my own, I did the weather then headed out to play a couple of holes before returning to make Michelle a cuppa at a more humane hour.

November was so hot it left us wondering what we were in for when summer finally arrived. We didn't have to wonder for long. On 4 December the temperature hit 46.3. It was the hottest day Michelle and I had ever experienced. On the Fahrenheit scale the temperature sounded even more impressive – 115 degrees.

Just to make things interesting, in the middle of the afternoon, when the heat was at its fiercest, Tom McKay's truck turned up with our regular delivery of fruit, veg and groceries. Tom's sidekick Stan was driving because poor Tom had been in an accident involving a forklift and was in hospital in danger of losing a leg. Back in Birdsville, as the truck unloaded there was a scramble to get perishables somewhere cool before they succumbed to the heat. In the rush, boxes ended up in cool rooms and houses all over town.

While Michelle drove around town searching for our food order (at the clinic, the pub, the Doyles' and elsewhere), I was at the home of Social Club treasurer Kay Ezzy planning yet another social event. By the time we'd finished Michelle hadn't returned so I decided to walk home. It was only 400 metres, but at 46.3 degrees it was more than enough. On my skin the dry air wasn't too uncomfortable, but as I walked into a headwind, the hot air seared my eyes. I didn't have my sunglasses with me so I was forced to put on my reading glasses to get at least some protection from the burning air.

Elsewhere unwary tourists were still travelling despite the conditions. One group of four German tourists got a flat tyre 40 kilometres from town. They didn't know how to change it. Fortunately, they were only stuck for half an hour before Nigel Gilby (Jessica's father, a cattle-yard builder) came along in his truck and changed the tyre for them. Although they had plenty of water they were already showing early signs of heat stress: paleness and fatigue.

Another group, Danes this time, drove into Barry Gaffney's service station for petrol and directions to the Birdsville Track. While Barry answered their questions he found out they not only lacked a spare tyre, but had no water. He sold them two 20-litre containers of water and sent them to the police station to report their journey. When they ignored his advice Barry called Neale, who then rang the Mungerannie Hotel (300 kilometres south) and Marree police station or caravan park (500 kilometres south), to ask them to keep a lookout. Without the Danes knowing it, their progress was reported all along the Birdsville Track.

It turned out that the day's temperature was the hottest recorded anywhere in Queensland in 2008. Of course, just when I was thinking, 'Well, this must be as bad as it gets,' sure enough on the western horizon an unmistakeable bank of cloud appeared: a dust storm. It blew in just after six. It was a tennis night but even before the storm hit we'd decided to give the racquets a miss.

In the first week in December more people prepared to leave town. The school closed and the teachers, Katrina and Jay Ireland, headed off on a trip to Canada and the US. Wolfgang John, the town's resident artist, was also planning his departure. I went round to have a yarn with Wolfie before he headed off to the Kimberley, where he was intending (wet season permitting) to spend a few weeks with Dia, who'd been working in the Birdsville Auto's general store when we'd first arrived and was now caretaking on a cattle station.

Wolfie had dark medium-length hair and an athletic physique. He looked to be in his fifties, but he told me (a bit shocked himself) that he was about to celebrate his seventieth birthday. He was born in Germany, on the German–Polish border, just before World War II broke out. After the war he studied art and textile design, which led to a well-paid job as a commercial artist. Then, at the age of twenty, conscription loomed and he recoiled from the idea of being trained to shoot at his fellow countrymen in East Germany. Instead, he decided to emigrate.

'When I arrived in Australia,' he recalled with typical irreverent humour, 'I had to borrow a quid from the immigration department to take a taxi to Woolwich. I said to the taxi driver, "I vant to go to Vool-vich." And he said, "It's not Vool-vich, it's Voolich!" He was a Yugoslav. "I vill teach you English," he said. And the taxi fare cost exactly one pound. I still owe the immigration department.'

The people who sponsored Wolfie's emigration to Australia employed him in their textiles business and he stayed there for thirty-four years, eventually becoming a partner. He first painted flowers but in his spare time he also painted Australia's incredibly varied landscapes. He visited Birdsville in 1976 and after returning off and on for the next ten years, he began to stay for up to five weeks at a time, usually at Alton Downs, 75 kilometres south of the town. He moved to Birdsville permanently in 1994.

'I love the outback,' he explained. 'I love the untouched land. It's like the sea. You've got a swell but it's rigid. And you go in a car over the swell. It's like on a boat. I had an old Herreschof [a yacht] which I had twenty years on Sydney Harbour. So I see a similarity, but it's hotter. I also like that you can go sideways, which you can't do in a boat. I like the feeling of being maybe the first human being who ever steps there.'

As he talked about the special places he was drawn to I was glad I'd waited several months to speak to him. If I'd talked to him when we'd first crossed paths at the Creek of Flowers, I would have heard only words. Now that I'd experienced some of what he was describing I knew exactly what he was talking about. For example, some places were only special for a fleeting moment.

'It depends on the light or the time of the day and the weather, the time of year you go there. In the winter you get very low light and at night you get the clouds being lit up from underneath and that's beautiful. I always time myself to come back with the sun behind me because the sand is redder. It's fantastic.'

Michelle had taken hundreds of photographs of the very same sunsets. Driving back from Poeppels Corner with Don Rowlands with the sun setting behind us, not only were the dunes a deeper red, but the desert flowers and plants shone in richer golds, pinks and greens against them.

'The French Line is beautiful,' Wolfie continued. 'That's past Poeppels Corner. You go 300 kilometres that way. I painted it. It's so pristine. The time of the year and the weather was just perfect. It was partially in flower and, you know, it's always different. But I like that rarefied atmosphere. You haven't got gidgee trees there. You've got acacia.

'I like the salt lakes. I like Andrewilla. The desert comes right against the waterhole and you don't expect it to be there. It's like a mirage. You look at this and think, "This is not there. It can't be there." And on both sides I've seen Aboriginal artefacts by the tonne. Where there's water – Eyre Creek, up near Annandale and further north, Muncoonie – you see old fireplaces, lots of them, and you find bits of grinding stones.'

Wolfie's experiences of the desert inspired him to produce vivid images that few people could ever hope to see. The question was: would they believe that what Wolfie was painting was real?

'One typical thing is the flowers come out,' he replied. 'Once I went down the Inside Track as far as where the water started. It was mostly under water. And I went on a purple road. A purple road! *Mimulus prostrates* is a purple flower, very prostrate. It's got a yellow centre but purple is predominant and the whole country was purple. I couldn't believe it. They come out at certain times. You don't know when. The conditions are right for certain things to happen and you have to live here a long time to see everything. Those flowers, I tried to paint. And I didn't feel like it. Who will buy this? Purple. It was a blue sky and purple and it looked like a Monet. Like an impressionist. And *I* didn't believe it. And somebody flew in and bought it. I don't know why. I don't understand these people. They come from Canberra of all places.'

I wondered if being the only artist within hundreds of kilometres left him feeling creatively isolated. 'That's the only problem,' he said. 'I'm not looking for friends – I was lonely all my life – but to have no critic, that's the hardest part. I work on my own. I'm never happy with any painting I ever do. Then I see it five years later and say, "Oh, who did this?" And I will see the signature and say, "Oh, I did it. It's not bad, is it?"'

While I was at Wolfie's we talked a lot about sailing. He gave me the key to his shed and showed me where he stored the masts and sails for two dinghies he kept at Andrewilla Waterhole. He told me I could use them whenever I wanted. The following weekend, I asked Don Rayment's permission to go to Alton Downs, the station Andrewilla was on, and Michelle and I headed down there, lured by the opportunity to go sailing in the desert.

We rigged up one boat even though the wind was gusting up to 25 knots (45 km/h). Michelle went for a swim while I tried to remember how to sail a dinghy. After the boom gave me a solid smack in the head, and the boat capsized, I got my sailing mojo back. Eventually I had something approximating control and sailed over to see if Michelle wanted to come for a ride.

'No thanks,' she said. 'I saw you flip.'

'But you're already wet,' I countered.

'And unbruised.'

She had a point. The wind seemed to be getting stronger as I sailed off up the waterhole. I got a couple of hundred metres away when a little voice whispered, 'It's blowing hard. There's no rescue dinghy and you're 75 kilometres from any assistance. If you get knocked out you'll probably drown before Michelle gets to you.'

It didn't help that there were Aboriginal stories about Andrewilla being the haunt of evil spirits. In the 1950s George Farwell's Aboriginal guide Uley had told him about them.

That bad place, Andrewilla. Plenty coochie there. All same right up to Birdsville. I hear them, the dead singing out to me. I take no notice. They do not harm you. But whatever you do, you not go in that waterhole. There are things in all them holes. I not know what. But they no good.

I turned around and sailed back to shore. Andrewilla was a beautiful waterhole, but this wasn't the time to take risks, sea monsters notwithstanding.

Back in Birdsville I mentioned the old stories to Lyn Rowlands. She nodded and said, 'That's right. And they're in the Fish Hole, just near town, too.'

*

Christmas was fast approaching and we were beginning to wonder what the festive season would be like in the outback. Hot was a given. My sister, who'd been underwriting the phone company's profits with her hours-long calls to John Hanna, was going to drive up with her daughter Emma to spend Christmas with us. Neale's wife and daughter were coming out to spend Christmas with him. Most of the Brooks' and the Gaffneys' children were coming out, too.

A fortnight before Christmas pilot Luke Pedersen took us out on his mail run to Durrie and Glengyle stations. He was training a new pilot, Tom O'Donnell, to take over the job. We'd already got to know Tom, who with Luke was a regular at Wednesday tennis. The Brooks had known Tom even longer because he'd been the music teacher at their sons' school. He'd since found his calling as a pilot and combined flying from Port Augusta on Wednesdays and Thursdays with teaching in Adelaide the rest of the week.

Luke was organising a 'Santa Run' to take presents to the children on the stations he and Tom serviced on the mail run. So, at both stations we visited, Luke checked the correct names and ages of the kids. He had everything planned.

'Tom can fly the plane and I can concentrate on my Santa duties,' he explained. 'I've got my Santa suit organised. I've got a pair of red velvety shorts and thongs because it's just a little hot for boots and pants. I'm going to get all my lollies and things. Tom's got quite a few of his kids' toys that are in very good condition which he thought we might give to the station kids. I'm really looking forward to it and I'm not the most Christmassy person.'

A week before Christmas we drove up to Mt Isa for Christmas supplies. We were now used to a day's drive each way, spending $250 on fuel and as much again on two nights' accommodation, just to go to the shops. On the way back we shredded a tyre just south of Dajarra. I got out to change it and, like a true Birdsvillean, left the engine running so the air-conditioning would keep the car cool. The outside temperature was around 43 degrees. When I lay on the ground to position the jack I was glad of the work boots, jeans and long-sleeved shirt that was the 'uniform' of the outback. The clothing protected me from the searing heat of the road.

Someone once said to me they didn't know exactly when you became a Birdsville local. I'd replied, 'I reckon it starts when you stop wearing cargo pants.'

On Christmas Eve, we put our growing understanding of the way things are done in the outback to good use. John Hanna and I were taking the Truckasaurus to get my sister Helen and her daughter Emma from Windorah to spare her two-wheel-drive sedan the 300 kilometres of dirt road to Birdsville. To make the return trip more enjoyable, Michelle and I employed a trick we'd learned from the station people at Adria and Durrie. We catered.

We filled a chiller bag with cheese and crackers, strawberries and champagne we'd bought in Mt Isa. I stowed them in the back where John couldn't see them. When John and I got to Windorarh, we transferred Helen and Emma's luggage to the Truckasaurus. Emma then got in the front with me, while the love birds, John and Helen, perched in the back seat.

'Have a look in that chiller bag at your feet,' I said to them as we drove out of Windorah. 'Emma, there are glasses in the glove box.'

Soon my passengers were sipping fizz and sharing nibblies as we sped along in the four-wheel drive. True romance, outback style.

It was already dark by the time we'd got going and Emma found the first few encounters with livestock and wildlife alarming. The

Truckasaurus now had driving lights installed and adjusted so they lit up the sides of the road, where the dangers lurked. I could spot animals easily but Emma couldn't see anything until the beasts were close. She couldn't see what I was looking for – eye shine, dark lumps in the distance, grey spots. It took a couple of hundred kilometres for her to get the knack.

I'd also learned from experience that the safest speed for driving in the outback at night was a maximum of 80 km/h. When approaching cattle and kangaroos it was safer to slow to 20 because they had a nasty habit of jumping out in front of the vehicle at the last moment. It made for a slow return trip, but a safe one. The last 100 kilometres of the 800-kilometre round trip seemed to go on forever. Everyone else in the car had long since dozed off, despite the disturbance caused by the occasional manoeuvre to avoid a beast.

It was nearly midnight when at last we rolled into Birdsville. The main street was deserted. There'd been a party at the pub, but now it was closed. I dropped John, Helen and Emma at his place and headed for home. Despite the late hour, the temperature was still in the 30s.

After a long, sound, air-conditioned sleep, Michelle and I woke to our first outback Christmas. We were expecting five for lunch, but during the morning John's brother Brian rang to ask if we could handle two more. John's daughter and her husband were paying him a surprise visit, flying in on MacAir, which had a flight scheduled for that day. It was a minor Christmas miracle when the plane arrived on time.

Christmas in Birdsville ended up being a bit like Christmas in a cold climate. The temperature rose to 42.4 (108 degrees Fahrenheit), which meant a picnic lunch at Pelican Point was out of the question, unless we sat *in* the billabong while we ate. Instead, we had lunch indoors with the air-conditioning going flat out. Even in the evening, when we went round for a get-together at Bev Morton's house beside the clinic, it was still too hot to sit outside.

On Boxing Day we had a golf tournament with the Brook clan. Nell and I had negotiated the tee-off time. I suggested 6.30 a.m., which was when Neale and I had been playing most mornings after he was back doing the weather. All through December we'd found that by 7.30 it was already getting pretty warm.

'I don't think I can get them up that early,' Nell said. Against my better judgement I agreed to start at 8 a.m.

Unfortunately, Christmas night was one of the hottest of the month. The overnight minimum was 30.7. By the time we teed off, in two groups of four, it was 8.30 and close to the century mark on the old temp scale. Foolishly, I'd thought, 'Early morning? Nah, I won't need to take any water.' By 10 a.m. it was over 40 and I was regretting my decision.

It was so hot that Nell and her daughters, all of them very familiar with outback conditions, gave up after five holes. Driven more by bravado than good sense, us blokes played on, sweat pouring off us. Nell, Dalene and Karen drove into town and came back to hand out bottles of Gatorade. On the sixth hole I grabbed one with great relief and drank half. I decided to save the rest until I'd finished my round. Then on the ninth hole, as I prepared to tee off, I didn't feel right. The sun was still shining, but to me it seemed to be getting dark. Lining up on the fairway was like looking down a tunnel. I thought, 'This is where you black out and wake up at the clinic on an IV drip with the Flying Doctor preparing to medivac you out.'

I quickly played my shot. Somehow I still managed a dead straight 220-metre drive. I put my club back in the bag and reached for the bottle of Gatorade. I drank the lot. Now I just had to walk 412 metres to the ninth hole and I'd be safe.

By the time we'd sunk our putts, we were all looking pale. Later, over long drinks of water, there were a few quiet admissions that it really was a bit too hot for golf. That day the temperature reached

44.7. The women had planned to finish their rounds in the late afternoon, but a furious dust storm put an end to that idea.

For New Year's Eve (with a mild top temperature of 40.3) the Social Club organising committee (Michelle, Kay and I) arranged an afternoon and evening of festivities that began with a car rally/observation event around the town, moved to kayak races on the billabong and ended with a sausage sizzle in the evening on the verandah of the Birdsville Hotel. I doubted we'd get much interest, given the total number of people in town was less than fifty, but to my surprise they ended up coming from everywhere. There were people in from the stations; some even drove down from Bedourie. Almost the whole town turned up for the events that started in the midafternoon, and there were still more than seventy people in the pub as midnight approached.

'10, 9, 8, 7, 6, 5, 4, 3, 2, 1,' the crowd chanted. 'Happy New Year!'

Michelle and I kissed and wished each other a Happy New Year. The Brooks came over and wished us a happy 2009, followed by Neale and his wife Sandra, the Mortons, the Rowlands, the Ezzys and everyone else. All around us the well-wishing went on for a quarter of an hour. I took in the extraordinary spectacle as everyone in the pub circulated in the front bar, wishing each other the best for the New Year. No-one was left out. I thought to myself, this is what a real community looks like.

The following morning I got an email from Geoff Morton. 'Thank you for the great day on New Year's Eve. Job well done.' For months he'd been sniping at me. He'd even jokingly tried to run me over when I was starting his team's car in the car rally. (At least, I think he was joking . . .) It didn't stop him giving recognition where he thought it was due.

We'd also raised a couple of hundred bucks for the Social Club. I thought the money could be used for things like the x-ray machine, but by then Bev had already reached the $40 000 threshold for grant applications. Incredibly, in little more than six months she'd done the job I thought would take years.

While Birdsville was relaxing and celebrating New Year's Eve, another drama involving tourists was unfolding. This time it was out on the Windorah Road. Once again the lack of common sense and respect for the conditions had Neale shaking his head: 'The family – dad, mum, two girls – are about 100 ks out of Birdsville when they get a blow-out. It's their second blow-out and they've only got one spare tyre. They don't have a sat phone or UHF so they're stuck there. In the morning another tourist comes along and he says he'll take them into Birdsville. But they don't take the punctured tyres with the vehicle.

'Now they're driving along and the guy giving them a lift sees his fuel light come on. He didn't want to pay the high prices at Innamincka and he thought he'd make it to Birdsville. So he's travelling without enough fuel, out here, at this time of year. What does he do? Unhitches the camper trailer he's towing, which has all their food and water, and keeps going. About 20 k's out of Birdsville, they run out of fuel. So the bloke decides to walk into town. His son goes with him and after an hour he turns back. The bloke keeps going on his own. Fortunately for them someone coming into town finds them both and brings them in.

'So I drive the guy back to his car and he says, "Can you ring up roadside assist on your sat phone? They'll send someone out with two new tyres." I say, "Mate, not out here. And even if they did you'd be stuck out here for at least a day."'

Neale was also checking the progress of a fifty-year-old German–Polish woman who was riding a bicycle between Windorah and Birdsville. A ringer from Morney Station (300 kilometres from Birdsville) had spotted her walking back from a dry dam with empty water bottles. He'd given her all the water he had and found out she was trying to get to Birdsville. She hadn't told anyone what she was doing. The ringer had rung Neale, who'd started keeping tabs on her movements.

After no-one had seen her for two days, Neale went out to find the cyclist. When he did, she was again out of water.

'She seemed to resent people checking on her,' he said. Then with a grin he added, 'She didn't say no to the water, but.'

Neale concluded that the woman knew what she was doing and wasn't in any great danger, but the fact remained that if she hadn't got water from the ringer and Neale, the 400-kilometre ride from Windorah might have been the last thing she did.

A couple of days after New Year's Eve, the same woman was heading down the Birdsville Track, and Neale went out to set up an interview with her and a journalist from the *Courier-Mail* in Brisbane. When he got there Neale couldn't get his sat phone to work, so he called Pandie Pandie on his UHF radio and asked them to ring the journalist. The journalist, Michael Wray, asked questions over the phone which were then repeated on the radio. The woman then responded. When Michael couldn't understand her accent, Neale came on to explain what he thought she'd said. For everyone tuned to Channel 8 the hour-long exchange made fascinating talkback radio, outback style.

After the interview Neale left the woman in her camp by the side of the road and returned to Birdsville. From there he contacted Mungerannie, Marree and stations in between to discreetly monitor her progress down the Birdsville Track. He had good reason, as she was riding through a region that had claimed many lives at the same time of year.

The most terrible tragedy on the Birdsville Track unfolded in late December 1963. Just before Christmas, Ernest Page, a mechanic in Marree who'd emigrated from England four and a half years before, set out with his wife and two young sons, Douglas (twelve) and

Gordon (ten), in their 1958 model Holden for (as he wrote in a letter
to his sister back in England) a 'great holiday adventure'.

They drove north, on the then poorly defined Birdsville Track, to
Clifton Hills Station, where they were joined by their nineteen-year-
old son, Robert, who was working as a drover. From there they set
out for Birdsville, 200 kilometres away, a few days before Christmas. They hadn't covered half the distance when they lost their way.
Accounts in Brisbane's *Courier-Mail* at the time suggested they had
become lost where 'the sanded tracks on the western and eastern side
of [Goyder's Lagoon] were often obliterated by the moving sand and
motorists had to contend with long, confusing S-bends in the sand'.
David Brook suggested that at the time oil exploration was being
carried out in the area and the family may have been confused by a
maze of criss-crossing drilling tracks.

The Pages drove back and forth until they ran out of petrol. They
then stayed with their vehicle for two days, without seeing a soul. They
decided to walk back to Clifton Hills and left a note with the vehicle:

> The Page family of Marree. Ran out of petrel [sic]. Are heading south.
> Have only sufficient water for two days. December 24th.

They carried a 20-litre container of water when they set out. They
may have found a waterhole where they filled it, but not far from the
waterhole it became too heavy for them to carry. They left the water
container and continued on across an almost featureless plain covered in scorching gibber rocks.

On 29 December a rabbit trapper found the car and note. A search
was soon under way. Aboriginal trackers discovered that despite their
stated intention, the Pages hadn't gone south. They were heading
west into pure wilderness. On New Year's Day a searching aircraft
from Pandie Pandie spotted four bodies beneath a coolabah tree
20 kilometres west of the vehicle at Coocheaperoonie Waterhole.

The waterhole was dry but there had been rains in the area not long before and many waterholes in the area still had water. A fifth body, that of Robert Page, was found on a dune another kilometre west.

When Michelle and I drove down to visit the site where the bodies were buried, we logged our intentions with Birdsville policeman Neale McShane. We rang Clifton Hills to ask permission to visit the site, which is on the property. The manager's wife gave us directions, plus we had its coordinates logged into our GPS.

We turned off the Birdsville Outside Track onto a station road that rounded the southern tip of the dune where Robert Page's body was found and buried. A few kilometres further there was a turn-off, and in the distance a single white cross. The gravesite was defined by a ring of gibber rocks. On the cross there was a hand-written message: 'THE PAGES. PERISHED. DEC 1963.'

The grave sat in an area dotted with coolabahs. The air was full of the shrieks of galahs. There was a flush of green herbage in the waterhole that suggested it had held water not long before. It didn't seem like such a terrible place to die. Then we started walking east, backtracking the route the Pages had come.

On the other side of the waterhole the cracked and lumpy black soil ended and the gibbers began. We stumbled and tripped our way onto a slight rise that gave a view across the shimmering heat and mirage of the gibber plain. There wasn't a hint of a tree. To walk across that country, with no water and little hope of finding help, must have been horrible beyond imagination. Every trip and fall, and there must have been many on the uneven slippery gibbers, must have been agony as skin made contact with burning rocks. Somewhere on that plain, the Pages and their children must have realised they were going to die. When they saw the line of coolabahs along the waterhole, did their hopes rise? They found nothing but dust. There was at least one small mercy among the coolabahs: shade. But when they lay down, the flies would have descended.

Kay Ezzy, my Social Club colleague, had a taste of what the Pages went through when she and her husband, Russ, got two flat tyres on the Windorah Road in February 2008. They had plenty of water, they'd told the police in Windorah where they were going and they were on the main road. Theoretically they had nothing to worry about, but they were soon sweltering in temperatures of over 50 degrees in the sun. Kay recalled: 'Temperatures were just horrendous. The flies were awful and then the cat started overheating and we started overheating and we undid the back – got our tarp out, got our chairs out, made ourselves comfortable, pulled an esky out. Our water was starting to get a bit warm by then. Drinking hot water, I started heaving and hyperventilated. I was stressed with the heat and the flies and thinking, "What the hell have we done?" Five hours later, still no vehicles, and of course we didn't have a radio. We had one fly veil that was sort of stiff so we put that over the cat. Poor cat. He was just going crazy. We sort of lay in the shade. We moved around with the vehicle and kept in the shade. There wasn't a breath of wind. Later in the afternoon the breeze got up just a little bit and Russ thought he might walk because he could see a tower and he thought there might be an emergency phone or beacon or something. He got over the first rise and of course the tower was another five kilometres up the road so he just came back.'

Kay and Russ were rescued that evening after being spotted from the air by David Brook, who'd started worrying when they were overdue and flew out to see if he could spot them.

The agonies suffered in the final stages of death from thirst were detailed in a description a cattleman gave author George Farwell in the 1950s:

I've been pretty tightly pushed in my time. I know how it gets you. Your tongue swells up first. You start thinking of all the drinks you ever had. You can see 'em, straight. Right there in front of your eyes.

After a while you begin to go batty. I saw one cove – we just saved him in the nick o' time – he'd torn off every stitch of clothing. Mostly at the very end they start running. Anywhere. They just keep on running till they drop. One time in the sandhills I found a stiff. Sprawled out under a whitewood. I reckon he'd done eight complete circles of that tree, laying on his face – and the bark all scratched off where he'd clawed it. He'd worn quite a track round that whitewood. Generally speaking, they take a while to find. Sooner or later, well, you see a mob of crows somewhere – kitehawks circling over a bush – and there's what you're looking for.

An unknown number of people have perished in the outback, and the country around Birdsville is dotted with lonely graves. One of the strangest deaths occurred in October 1885, 40 kilometres north of town. William Mooney was a fencer who'd come in to town for supplies. When he left he had a riding horse and a packhorse. Among the supplies on the packhorse were two cases of whisky. On his way to his camp Mooney stopped in at old Roseberth. They were the last to see him alive. It wasn't until six weeks later that his body was found in a camp near a dry watercourse just off the track between Birdsville and Bedourie.

In Mooney's camp they found his swag, his riding saddle and his pack saddle. Around him were twenty-two empty bottles of whisky. It's thought he opened the first bottle to slake his thirst and while he was drunk, his horses wandered away. Drinking neat whisky had dehydrated Mooney, but the only thing he had to quench his growing thirst was more whisky. The more he drank, the more desperate he became. To paraphrase Coleridge, 'Whisky, whisky everywhere, Nor any drop to drink.' Mooney was buried where they found him. It's said his grave was marked by a ring of upturned whisky bottles. The locality is still called Mooney's Grave, but the grave itself has long since disappeared.

People have been perishing around Birdsville ever since. Peter Barnes, who's been a mechanic at Birdsville Auto off and on since he established the business about twenty-five years ago (and had been talked into returning when the Brooks couldn't find a replacement mechanic), recalled an incident from 1992.

'I fixed this bird-watching bloke's tyres. It was the hottest time of the year and this bloke was determined to go down to Walker's Crossing [200 kilometres south-east of Birdsville]. On the way back he rolled his vehicle and spent half a day sitting there. He'd run out of water so when someone came along they gave him a drink and drove him back to Birdsville. Along the way he started complaining, "Why have you put vodka in my water?" The people didn't think anything of it. They just thought he might be a bit crazy, and when they got into Birdsville they dropped him at the clinic. Half an hour later he was dead. He'd thought they were making him drunk. He was actually dying from organ failure.'

Peter remembered another couple who'd turned up at the pub. 'They'd broken down and in the heat of summer they sat in their car. They'd been told, "If you break down, don't leave the vehicle." Eventually they were found and they were in a pretty bad way. They came in here and had a beer then they went to their room. She said she was going to have a shower. He said he didn't feel well and was going to lie down. When she came out of the shower he was dead.'

Such stories vividly showed there were plenty of ways to die in the outback, but we thought we'd be all right if we followed the rules. We had a container with 20 litres of fresh water in the Truckasaurus at all times. On trips we took an esky with extra bottles of chilled water. We always told people where we were going and when we'd be there. A couple of times when I forgot to report our arrival, I was chastened when Neale rang to confirm we were safe.

On one occasion a relative worried that we were overdue and began ringing police stations across western Queensland. Someone eventually rang Neale, who had just flown out of town, to say some-one from Birdsville was feared missing. When he asked who, they said, 'Evan McHugh.'

He knew exactly where I was and that I was on my way back to do the 3 p.m. weather report. His reply? 'Nah. We couldn't be that lucky.'

14

THE FACE OF ADVERSITY

For months, speculation that this summer would see a flood in Birdsville had been running around town. 'It's been a few years,' everyone from tribal elder Don Rowlands to publican Brian Hanna said. 'We're due for a good one.' Long-range forecasters predicted higher than average rainfall. The Diamantina Council's monthly newsletter *Desert Yarns* warned that floods might come and people should stock up early. There was even a rumour that indigenous people in the Top End had noticed crocodiles building their nests higher on the riverbanks than usual, suggesting they somehow knew a big wet was coming.

Rain started falling in western Queensland just after the New Year. In the upper catchment of the Diamantina, around Winton, falls up to 200 millimetres were reported. Similar amounts fell over the drought-stricken Boulia Shire. Around the Gulf of Carpentaria, cyclones and tropical depressions brought rains that were even heavier. Road closures began as the floodwaters rose. For a time all the roads into Mt Isa were cut. The local ABC radio station spent more and more time each day listing rising rivers, impassable roads and rainfall readings. There was an atmosphere of growing excitement as the region anticipated the first proper monsoonal wet season in decades. One cattleman in the Northern Territory reckoned it was the best season in fifty years.

Every afternoon, to the east and north of Birdsville, mammoth cloud billows formed, the gigantic storm cells of cumulonimbus floating over the parched landscape. At night lightning lit the horizon. The days became increasingly humid.

The rain began falling in Birdsville on 6 January. The town got 50 millimetres, but nearby stations such as Durrie reported around 125 millimetres. Roseberth homestead received slightly less than 50 millimetres, but elsewhere on the property falls were suspected to be substantially higher.

As it happened, the next day John was due to drive my sister back to Windorah, but the Windorah Road, Bedourie Road and Birdsville Track were all closed. So Helen booked a flight out to Windorah for the following Friday. That evening, the Diamantina, which had been bone dry when we routed the New Year's Eve car rally across it, began to rise.

It was also a tennis night, which meant sweeping water off the courts. Michelle didn't play because she was down at the health clinic. She'd been complaining that she had something in her eye since she'd been caught in a dust storm while swimming with my sister at Pelican Point the previous Sunday.

'It feels like there's something wrong with my eye,' she'd said as we were getting into our tennis gear. 'They're sort of dark blotches swimming in my field of vision.'

'You're having trouble seeing?' I asked.

'Well, yes,' she said, with an 'it's probably nothing' tone.

'Right,' I replied. 'Ring Bev down at the clinic and go and get it checked.'

She started to object but I cut her off. 'Michelle, you can't see properly. It could be something serious. It's best to find out either way.'

She insisted she could drive herself to the clinic and that I should play tennis. I should have skipped the game. As time passed I grew increasingly anxious. When she finally came back I excused myself from the court and went to find out the verdict.

Michelle's cheeks were smudged with eyewash. Bev Morton had rung the Flying Doctor, who'd suggested washing out her eyes. The doctor didn't seem too concerned that Michelle said she was also seeing little flashes of light. She was told to continue washing out her eyes and to return to the clinic in the morning to report if there was any improvement.

Michelle went home to do as instructed, but came to the pub after tennis. She stuck to soft drink. While a general discussion of eye conditions ensued, John Hanna took the tear-off bottle top from her ginger beer and started fashioning it into some kind of artefact. He took his time over it and when he was finished, he said, 'Do you want to see my duck caller?'

I looked at the object on the bar and then at John. This looked suspiciously like another of the Hanna brothers' practical jokes.

'Wait a second,' I said, and tried to get off my stool to escape whatever was coming. Quick as a flash, Brian Hanna, who was sitting next to me, grabbed me. I struggled to get free, but he held me in an experienced publican's grip. At least I'd put an extra metre between me and whatever prank I was going to be subjected to. John already had his I've-got-you grin as he lined up the 'duck caller' on the edge of the bar and bent down towards it.

'Calling all ducks,' he said through the small ring-pull that was standing up from the rest of the apparatus. 'Calling all ducks.'

Brian let me go amidst much chortling.

The next morning Michelle's eye hadn't improved. She rang her optometrist in Sydney to see if the problem might be caused by her contact lenses. She explained her symptoms and he suggested she might have 'vitreous floaters', microscopic fibres that drift in the fluid inside the eye. They were common for people over forty and usually disappeared after a few weeks.

Michelle went to the clinic to talk to Bev. 'She was about to have the RFDS fly me out,' Michelle said when she got back home. Bev was still concerned about the flashes Michelle was seeing, but when she called the Flying Doctor again, the doctor was as reassuring as Michelle's optometrist had been.

Michelle surfed the Internet to find out more about vitreous floaters. On the prestigious Mayo Clinic's website she read that a sudden increase in floaters and flashes of light could mean she had a torn or detached retina and should see a specialist immediately. Failure to do so could result in blindness in the affected eye. Of course, in Birdsville seeing a specialist was easier said than done.

Michelle rang her optometrist again. When he got on the line she explained that she'd forgotten to mention the flashes.

'It's still probably nothing to worry about,' he said, 'but you should probably get it checked, especially considering where you are.'

Michelle went back to see Bev. The Birdsville Clinic might not have a doctor, or an x-ray machine for that matter, but you almost never had to wait to see the nurse. Bev agreed that Michelle should see an optometrist and rang Mt Isa to make an appointment. Michelle booked a seat on the MacAir plane flying out that afternoon.

Michelle packed as little as possible, assuming all would be well and she'd be on the next plane back to Birdsville (the following Tuesday). As it looked like we might be in for a major flood, she left plenty of room in her suitcase to bring back extra food supplies.

The Diamantina River continued to rise. Before Michelle flew out we drove to the bridge to look at the water. The swirling brown mass was only a metre below the bottom of the bridge. Clumps of debris, broken branches and spinifex were being swept along in the stream.

Over at the plane we sat holding hands, telling ourselves it was probably nothing, trying to keep some perspective on things. After we parted and the plane fired up its engines, I thought, 'Well I wasn't expecting this when I woke up this morning.' On the plane, Michelle told me later, she was thinking the same thing.

That evening I picked up my sister from John's and we went out to the bridge again. The water was almost lapping its concrete base. On the way back to town we passed the Doyles heading out to have a look, too. A little further on the Ezzys had stopped on the causeway to photograph waterbirds. While we chatted the Brooks came along. They had a bottle of champagne and were heading for the bridge to celebrate the birth of a granddaughter. In typical Birdsville fashion people stopped their cars in the middle of the road to exchange news.

The next morning my sister said a sad farewell to John and went out to the airport to take the 12.20 plane to Windorah. I wasn't there to see her off. I was waiting by the phone for news from Michelle. Her appointment was at 11 a.m. Narelle Gaffney, who was also the MacAir agent, was ready to book me on the same plane (which flies to Brisbane via Quilpie and Charleville) up until the last possible moment, if it turned out Michelle had to see a specialist in Brisbane.

Michelle still hadn't called by the time the plane took off. At 12.50, the phone rang. 'Do you want the bad news or the not-so-bad news?' she said. My heart missed a beat. The gist of it was that she had a harmless condition to explain the vitreous floaters, but that there was too much material floating around to see if there was also a retinal tear, which would explain the flashes. Once again, it was better to be safe than sorry so she had to see an ophthalmologist in Brisbane.

The earliest appointment Michelle could get was the Monday afternoon. That was three worry-filled days away. After I put down the phone I sat for a moment to consider my options. The plane to Brisbane had just flown out. All the roads out of town were closed. The next plane to anywhere was Monday. The next plane to Brisbane was on Tuesday. Sitting alone, trying not to fear the worst, I felt powerless to do anything. This was one lesson of outback life I could do without.

I had to get out of the house and go for a drive. Not that I could get far. On the edge of town the road to Windorah and the Birdsville Track was awash. While I looked at the water, David McCarthy, the policeman relieving Neale while he was on leave, came along. He'd driven through the water a short while before, but when he came to a deep section he dared go no further.

'I reversed back 300 metres before I could turn around,' he said. 'The first bit was safe but I wouldn't attempt it again, unless you want to get some photos.'

'Are you looking for encouragement?'

'No,' he said, with an adventurous glint in his eye, 'not exactly.'

I jumped in the police car and together we braved the flood. It was there that I witnessed first-hand how rivers in the Channel Country can flow in both directions. The Diamantina River had risen to a level higher than the town's billabong. The stream that ran between the two usually flowed from the billabong to the river (fed by the overflow from the town's artesian water supply). Now the stream was flowing from the river to the billabong. And it wasn't just flowing. It was a torrent. Upstream, where the creek broadened, a pelican was cruising on the new waterway, pursuing all the creatures flushed out by the flood. In the shallows four spoonbills formed a neat line as they worked up and down the shore sieving the water.

Back in town, the flood wasn't a source of worry. Excitement gripped everyone in a way that only an immense body of water pouring through normally parched country can. By Saturday afternoon the billabong had burst its banks. Pelican Point was under water. The water was spreading over the flood plain west of town. It crossed the Birdsville Inside Track, then the road to Big Red. From our kitchen window the normally dusty plain was covered in water studded with trees.

At sunset I drove out to the bronco branding yards where the plain was alive with the deep-throated chorus of frogs. Across the flood plain, the foliage on the trees was already a lustrous deep green, flushed with the first pulse of life that the waters brought. Once again, it was one of those changes you wouldn't notice if you were only in Birdsville for a day. And by now I knew enough to understand that this was just the beginning.

On Sunday morning I got a call from Ruth Doyle. Did I want to come to morning tea? It was a kind gesture considering I was fending for myself, although I suspected she thought I was 'cooking-challenged' and wanted to check up on me. I strolled over for a cuppa and it wasn't long before Ruth got down to business.

'You were in the shop yesterday and only bought two cans of food,' she said. 'What were they?'

'Beetroot,' I replied, a little taken aback. There really were no secrets in a small town. 'I thought I'd make hamburgers and needed beetroot. Then I thought, there's a flood, better stock up, and bought an extra can.'

My answer appeared to be satisfactory. 'Just so long as you're eating well,' she said, offering me a slice of cake.

On Monday afternoon the waiting game began anew. Michelle was due to see the ophthalmologist at 1 p.m. I tried to work, but as time wore on the worries grew. At two I was reduced to waiting for the phone to ring. My greatest fear was hearing her say, 'If only I'd got here sooner.' I couldn't help thinking how different things would be in Sydney. Michelle's optometrist was five minutes from home. Around the corner from his office was the Royal Prince Alfred Hospital, with wall-to-wall eye specialists. What had taken six days and counting would have been dealt with in an afternoon.

Finally, Michelle called.

'Well,' she said, her voice sounding shaky, 'that was one of the most unpleasant things I've ever been through.'

'What's happened?'

'I've just had laser surgery on my eye,' she replied. 'I had a retinal tear that had to be treated immediately. The floaters weren't just vitreous material. Some of them were blood. The doctor said if I'd got there twenty-four hours later, I'd have been in real trouble.'

The details of the operation were harrowing, but the good news was that she wasn't going to go blind. We'd been right to be concerned and very lucky that her condition was caught in time.

The follow-up to her eye surgery presented more logistical problems. The ophthalmologist wanted Michelle to come back in a week to check that the retina was healing properly. That would have meant staying in Brisbane, where she was being looked after by very kind friends of ours, or flying back to Birdsville then to Brisbane then back to Birdsville.

Driving the 1600 kilometres to Brisbane still wasn't an option. The river had peaked at 6.7 metres over the weekend then dropped just enough to make the road over the bridge passable. However, the flood had swept away part of the Windorah Road and it was still closed. There was also the risk that if I drove out to get Michelle, neither of us would be able to get back. The flood that had come through was from local rain, but a great deal more water was still to come down from the upper reaches of the river. When it arrived it was expected to cut the roads for several weeks. Everyone in town was ordering up big in expectation that the next food delivery might be the last for some weeks. Michelle had sat at her laptop in the middle of Brisbane doing the same, a somewhat surreal experience given she was surrounded by shops at the time.

In the end the doctor agreed to see Michelle after only two days, so she could get the next flight to Birdsville, on the Thursday. Fortunately, Michelle was given the all clear. She'd already booked her flight and was keen to come home.

The plane that flew in from Brisbane on 15 January marked something of a turning of the tide in Birdsville. People were coming back to town from their summer holidays. Along with Michelle, the Ramms and Irelands were on board. John and Judy Menzies had also returned.

They were all just in time to feed the sandflies that descended on the town as the floodwaters receded. Michelle's first night home was spent swatting the tiny insects, which somehow managed to get through the fly screens to attack us. By morning, our legs and arms were covered in bites.

That night the much-awaited Adelaide truck reached town and began unloading the following morning. It was carrying the biggest shop Michelle had ever done in her life. She'd gone from a shopper who bought groceries four times a week to one who could order enough food for six weeks. But there were problems. Russ Ezzy rolled up at our place with his forklift carrying three boxes of our 'dry' groceries and two bags of chook food. He told us that was all there was for us.

'There should be boxes of frozen food,' Michelle told him.

'I didn't see any,' he answered.

There was also supposed to be a separate order of fruit and veg. We went in search of the truck. By the time we got to the Shell service station, Stan, Tom's offsider, had already finished unloading and gone. Around at the pub we found two boxes of our fruit and veg. At the Doyle's there was more of our veg, but we were still short one box of fruit and veg and couldn't find any of our six-week supply of frozen foods.

Michelle went back to the pub and after considerable rummaging discovered the missing box of veg. We never found 5 kilograms of sweet potatoes. Michelle rang Jo McKay, Tom's wife, in Adelaide, to find out what might have happened to the frozen foods. Jo rang the supermarket where we'd placed our order. A quick check revealed that they'd forgotten the frozen items. The supermarket people said they were sorry and would send the order box by the next truck. That might be in three weeks. It might be six. With the vegie patch really struggling in the heat, I knew we'd run out of green veg long before that.

There was now no doubt the big flood was coming. Up in Bedourie, they were already cut off. Eyre Creek, fed by the Georgina, was over the road on the edge of town. The information from upstream indicated it would keep rising and stay high for the next month at least. It prompted a curious email from the shire council:

> Due to the oncoming flood, the Australia Day Awards to be held in Bedourie on January 26, 2009, have been postponed until March 16 2009.

Postponed? *Australia Day?* Bedourie was one of the few towns in Australia that would contemplate doing such a thing. It was probably the only town that had to, although all across western Queensland towns large and small were being cut off by the floodwaters.

For Australia Day in Birdsville the pub was organising a cricket match and the Social Club was planning another sausage sizzle. Kay and I met at the Brooks (where she worked as the housekeeper) to work out the catering arrangements. While we were there David was on the phone dealing with major problems getting cattle in from Adria Downs. It had rained out there and one of two trucks had got bogged picking up 250 head of cattle. It took hours to get the vehicle out. Now, in Birdsville, it was overcast and there were spots of rain.

A large part of David's life seemed to be spent dealing with trucking cattle incredibly long distances to market. There was almost always something playing on his mind. I mentioned that it reminded me of Shakespeare's merchant of Venice worrying about the trading vessels he had on the high seas. When I got home I emailed him the passage.

My wind cooling my broth
Would blow me to an ague, when I thought
What harm a wind too great at sea might do.
I should not see the sandy hour-glass run,
But I should think of shallows and of flats . . .
Should I go to church
And see the holy edifice of stone,
And not bethink me straight of dangerous rocks . . .

I added, 'As we watch the passing showers, we've got our fingers crossed for you.'

The next morning David emailed back with the subject line 'Cross 'em 'arder'. They'd got the trucks out of Adria and on their way to Windorah. Then they'd hit another soft patch of road. David emailed:

Truck stuck 6.30pm 5km into Barcoo Shire in light scud. Perhaps pray as well.

The bogged trucks caused a scramble as Don Rayment and ringers from Adria drove over to unload the cattle and make sure they were fed and watered while efforts were made to pull the truck out. They eventually got the cattle on their way, in the nick of time. Rain deluged the entire region on 20 January. I was out on the golf course when the huge black clouds rolled in, floating less than 300 metres above the plain. Curtains of water descended, veiling the land.

The next morning, David rang at 6 a.m. to ask if we'd like to come for a fly to see how far the floodwaters of Eyre Creek had reached. We scrambled out of bed and got to the plane by a quarter to seven. David and Peter Barnes were already there. We were in the air minutes later.

The overnight storms had drenched the landscape. To the north of

the town we flew over previously dry country that was now an archi-
pelago of outcrops amid countless pools of water. Broad channels
were flowing, flecked with foam and debris. There was an extraordinary mixture of colours as red gibbers, green grasses, brown waters
and pools reflecting blue sky spread to the horizon.

'I didn't realise there was that much rain last night,' David said as
he flew north. Peter was sitting beside him. Michelle and I were in
the back of the plane, with our cameras, taking picture after picture.
Then we got to the sea.

In the preceding months we'd driven across Cuttaburra Crossing and flown over lakes Mipia, Koolivoo and Machattie when they
were dry or only partly full. Now they were all joined together, inundated by an immense body of water through which a line of trees
indicated the normal course of Eyre Creek. Here and there the Birdsville–Bedourie road emerged from the water then disappeared again.
On an island, Glengyle Station had water lapping at its outbuild-
ings. Here Eyre Creek was between 10 and 20 kilometres wide. The
amount of water was utterly mind-boggling.

As we circled west of Glengyle I looked down on the flood plain
and with a shock realised that it wasn't just under water, the entire
body of water was moving, visibly flowing on a front so wide the
volume involved must have been astronomical. And from the reports
of river heights all the way back to Camooweal, hundreds of kilometres north, this was just the vanguard of the immense amount that
was still coming.

David had intended to fly north to Eyre Creek then follow it down
to see how close it was to the homestead and lakes on Adria Downs.
Seeing so much water, he decided to fly a little further and take a
look at Bedourie as well. The water was up to the town's levees. The
road south was completely under water until it reached a sandhill,
which it followed until it crossed the King Creek flood plain. In
places Eyre Creek was 60 kilometres wide. Only the Amazon could

compete with this breadth, but 1000 kilometres from the sea not even the Amazon was as wide.

From Bedourie we turned south-west, passing lyrically named waterholes like Pippagitta and Tomydonka. All were now lost beneath the waters spread across the flood plain. In places the only landmarks were sandhills, a kilometre or more apart, extending out into the flood for hundreds of metres. They ended where the creek's main channel had cut away the dune and all the waters gathered to rush past. Here long skeins of debris traced the water's flow and coolabah and gidgee lined the drowned banks.

Just after crossing the boundary of Glengyle and Adria, we reached the flood's advancing headwaters. It poured over a vast network of lignum-lined channels, anabranches, rivulets and billabongs. Its pace was slowed as it filled every hole and crack, but once that was done, across a front kilometres wide, its waters poured inexorably forward.

The time between floods determined how fast the waters moved through the country. Land that was still wet allowed floods to move quickly over it. Land that hadn't seen moisture for years soaked up much more and the waters came down slowly.

We passed over cattle yards that were awash, but we saw few cattle. David later explained that unless cattle were weakened by drought, they were usually strong enough and smart enough to find their way to higher ground. They could easily swim channels. After a couple of good seasons on Adria, he wasn't worried about them.

Eyre Creek's channels were almost dry by the time we reached Muncoonie. The main river had water in it, and the overnight rain made landing on the airstrip impossible, so we flew down to circle over the lakes and contemplate the benefit they were about to receive.

'There's no question both lakes will fill,' David said. 'It should even back out into Eyre Creek.'

I had no doubt. Seeing the flood rolling down through the country, I could now understand how all those channels of Eyre Creek I'd crossed in the four-wheel drive with Don Rowlands many months before could be filled. You just had to think big – incredibly big. It also put the flood we'd experienced in June (and I'd flown over in July) into perspective. That was nothing. This was the real deal.

The day after we went for a fly with David, the Diamantina River broke its banks at Birdsville for the second time in a month. This was still only the local rain from the storms two nights before. As the water spread over the flood plain it drowned the sandflies as it went. The roads south were cut again, but the water was only up for a couple of days before it subsided. About 200 kilometres upstream, still rolling towards us, was the big flood. We were now facing an unprecedented three floods in a row.

*

On Australia Day the road between the Birdsville Hotel and the airport was closed off and the local community turned out for the Birdsville versus the Pub cricket match. Play started with the temperature (measured under the pub verandah) at 43 degrees. The humidity was something ridiculously high. Kids, parents, young and old took the field with the primary object of having fun.

Each team batted ten overs, a maximum of two overs per batsman. If you hit the ball over the pub or into the airport it was six and out. Policeman Dave McCarthy and I opened the batting for Birdsville, mainly because no-one else wanted to do it. We both fell early. I hooked a ball into the airport. Dave walked after an extremely doubtful run-out decision. He was home by an outback mile.

Michelle and the school principal, Katrina Ireland, then played chanceless innings as they ran singles on almost every ball. After four overs, drinks were taken, and not a moment too soon. Everyone piled into the pub for refreshments and the relief of air-conditioning. Back at the crease, local mum Fiona Gadsby had clearly played backyard cricket before and the run rate accelerated as she cut and drove with style. On her last ball I called out to her to hit a six. She hoisted the ball into the airport. Teresa Booth's children and cousins gave our batting depth. We had to retire them early so every kid got a bat. Bev Morton, with her leg in a cast after a fall, was saved the necessity of batting with a runner. Birdsville managed to field ten players and we pushed our score to a formidable 100 by the end of the tenth over.

The Pub started badly. After four overs the kids and relatives of various pub staff had only put on 15. Then Lynton, partner of Kate the bookings manager, took the match by the throat. He was the first player who looked like he could actually play cricket. Every shot was a four. Only when he hit a single did we get a chance to 'arrest' the run rate. We brought Dave the copper on to bowl.

Dave pinned down Gus the barman then he fell to a brilliant catch by Jay the relief teacher. Brian the publican also lingered at the crease before being caught without scoring. When Kate came in to bat she scored a single that brought Lynton back to the crease. Two more fours ensued then he had only one ball left before he retired. Taking a leaf from Fiona Gadsby's book, he belted his last shot deep into the airport. Six and out. Dave the policeman went to get the ball. When he threw it back it didn't reach the fence. 'So much for the long arm of the law,' a spectator quipped from the pub verandah.

Drinks. At the bar one of the spectators told me of the days when Birdsville had a proper cricket team. He remembered when the army came to town and a match was arranged. The army won the toss and elected to bat but when Birdsville took the field the army's opening batsmen were nowhere to be seen.

'Where are they?' the army was asked.

'They'll be here,' the army answered.

Then, in the distance, the heavy thud of a helicopter was heard. The chopper appeared, flew in over the oval and landed next to the pitch. The doors opened and out stepped two men in their cricket whites, wearing pads and carrying bats. The army's openers had arrived in style.

After drinks the Pub had two overs to go and 25 to get. As Birdsville prepared to defend its honour there was a distinct falloff in the number of players. Cricket and heat couldn't compete with beer and air-conditioning. To cut off singles, we brought what field was left in close. In the penultimate over we took three wickets and conceded five runs. In the final over the Pub had six balls to get 20. Housekeeper Kym was pinned down for two balls, then turned a ball away for four. Then came two singles.

'One ball left, 14 to get!' I cried, tasting victory.

Jess the barwoman/umpire turned from the scoreboard and looked at me, 'Three balls to go.'

I was starting to suspect the match was rigged.

Six balls later Jay was tired of bowling and wanted someone to finish the over for him. We were no longer sure of the score. I told Jay that at this rate he was bowling himself into form and should keep going. Sure enough his next ball took another wicket. The Pub had now gone through all its batsmen, so one of their previous batsmen was allowed to return to the crease for the last ball. They chose Lynton.

Jay was exhausted but he dug deep and shuffled in again. He put the ball on a good length outside off stump. To no avail. Lynton stepped inside the line, judged the bounce perfectly, and swept the ball over the airport fence for six.

'Tie!' Jessica shouted. The Pub was alleged to have scored 14/100. Birdsville had managed a heroic 10/100. The kids kept playing while the grown-ups retired to 'the pavilion' to cool down and discuss the rules.

As the sun set we had a golf chipping competition, followed by a sausage sizzle. When everyone had eaten, there was an informal Australia Day award ceremony for the participants in the cricket match – Best All Rounder, Best Player, Best Young Player and Best Senior Player.

The only thing that diminished one of the most enjoyable Australia Days I'd ever experienced was the heat and humidity. After several hours outside, my clothes were soaked with sweat.

'That's got to be the most you've sweated in your life,' Narelle Gaffney commented as I stood in the middle of the pub's front bar, trying to position myself between a ceiling fan and an air-conditioner.

'You're not wrong there, Narelle,' I said, sweat dripping from my brow. Once we'd tidied up the sausage sizzle and Bev's raffle for the x-ray machine had been drawn, I called it a night. All I wanted was a cool shower and dry clothes. At home I turned on the cold water tap and jumped into the shower to get some relief before the town's 'cold' water heated up the pipes. The novelty of Birdsville's heat was starting to wear pretty thin.

After my shower I opened the back door to see if the night was any cooler. It was like a sauna outside. I stepped onto the back verandah and heard as much as saw the entire back garden moving. The place was alive with insects – beetles, sandflies, grasshoppers, locusts and mosquitoes. There was something crawling on every surface. From every corner came sounds of scratching and scurrying. I'd heard of the outback's 'pulse of life' but this was going too far.

The day after Australia Day, the Flying Doctor came in to medivac a young bloke I'd seen in the pub the night before. He and his mate had tried to drive to Windorah on the closed road under cover of darkness. They'd hit a washout, a section of the road that had been completely washed away by floodwaters. They'd dropped a metre, smashed in the front of the vehicle and bent the chassis. The vehicle was a wreck. The young bloke who was driving had broken his neck

a year before and Bev wasn't taking any chances. To make matters
worse, because he'd had the accident on a closed road, and therefore
was breaking the law at the time, his insurance company didn't have
to pay a thing.

At the end of January, the big flood finally arrived. On the 29th
the river started rising for the third time. Like a lot of Birdsvilleans,
we went for a drive to watch it come up. In a couple of places it was
over the road. We drove through the first bit of water without any
trouble. Then came a stretch that was 200 metres long. There was no
flood sign so I assumed it was shallow. As we drove into the water, it
slowly got deeper. Then it got quite deep. I started steering towards
the upstream side of the road to buy space should the vehicle start
to be pushed sideways. The water got deeper still. The Truckasaurus
became strangely quiet.

It ploughed forward, slowing occasionally in the faster flowing
currents. My pulse rate rose with the water level. This was starting
to feel like a bad idea, but I couldn't see how stopping and reversing
was any better. Nervously we pushed on, hoping the water would
get shallower soon. It eventually did, but not soon enough for my
liking. It was probably less than 40 centimetres deep, but that was
10 centimetres out of my comfort zone. At the time, half a dozen
Queenslanders had died after being washed off river crossings.

On the dry road on the other side of the water I turned around. If
the water was rising, I wasn't about to dawdle. Back in we went, and
the knowledge that we'd just got through made no difference. It was
a nerve-wracking drive.

The next day the road out of town to the south was closed and we
were cut off for the third time in a month. This time we were expecting to be flood-bound for three to four weeks. It had already been
two weeks since a grocery delivery had been able to get through.

For us the floods were still a novelty. Bev Morton had seen it all
before. She told us, 'When the kids were young we used to go to Mt

Isa twice a year. Like clockwork it always rained. One time I was determined we were going anyway. I got up near Glengyle, on the old road, and it was all black soil then. The car was slithering from one side of the road to the other. The trouble was it had power steering and I had it on full lock and I thought, any moment this car's going to grip and then we'll be in real trouble. The kids were in the back saying, "Turn around, Mummy. We want to go back. Turn around." The police were out looking for us, the stations were out looking for us. Then we got past the rain and onto some firm ground. We made it to Bedourie and the kids are going, "You did it! Keep going!"'

The day the road was cut was a Friday. We were about to leave for happy hour at the pub when the news came on. The lead story was about MacAir. The company had just announced it was going into voluntary receivership. The Queensland government was scrambling to organise charter flights for stranded passengers all over western Queensland.

At happy hour the conversation revolved around the fact that Birdsville was now cut off by land and air. That didn't present big problems if we weren't planning to go anywhere, but it did put a big question mark over mail deliveries. I realised how lucky I'd been that the last plane to Birdsville had delivered a care package from my mate Jamie back in Sydney. He'd sent some fertiliser for my embattled zucchinis and 6 kilograms of bread flour to go with two bread tins he'd sent me the week before. If it came to the crunch we could live on zucchinis, eggs and fresh bread until the supply lines reopened.

Typically, the attitude in the pub was pretty relaxed. Something would be worked out somehow. The flood wouldn't last forever. The roads would open eventually. It was a little disconcerting that some people were predicting floods until June.

What was more of a worry was the fact that this time the rising waters weren't making a dent in the insects. At home, we'd left the back light on. The lit area was thronged by thousands upon thousands of sandflies. It was impossible to go outside. The thought that anyone might camp or sleep outdoors in such conditions was incomprehensible. Under the circumstances the Aboriginal technique of sleeping between two smoky fires made a lot of sense, even if it carried the risk of rolling over in the night and being burned by hot coals.

In a radio interview about the floods, John Hanna referred to the insects as being like a dust storm. He'd hit the mark. Between the heat and humidity and the bugs, I was beginning to get a clearer understanding of what had killed explorers Burke and Wills. In 1861 they'd been struggling through this very country in these relentless conditions. Travelling day after day must have sapped their energy.

An unexpected consequence of the floods was that we could no longer go swimming at Pelican Point. It was under water. Swimming in the river we ran the risk of being swept away. The barbed wire surrounding the pool was making a lot more sense as the thought of a refreshing dip became an obsession. The lack of swimming pool access prompted a town meeting where we learned that it could only be opened if someone with a bronze medallion was in attendance. That meant someone, or several people, travelling away to get the necessary qualification, and then paying the $180 fee for the privilege of supervising the pool. It ended up in the too-hard basket.

The sandflies were now becoming a major concern. Michelle and I were covered in bites. We'd evolved a strategy to keep them at bay. Whenever we went outside we slathered on insect repellent. At night we closed all our windows and curtains, blackout style. We avoided turning on any bright lights. We left the bedroom lights off until we were ready for bed. Then we turned on our reading lights and read for a couple of minutes until a few insects appeared. As the numbers started to increase we turned off the lights and tried to sleep. On bad nights we dreamed of mozzie nets.

While our strategy was reasonably effective with the sandflies, it didn't do a thing to keep the centipedes at bay. Bev Morton had warned us that their sting is incredibly painful, and the effects can last weeks. One night we were just going to bed when Michelle saw one in the bedroom that was nearly 150 millimetres long. When she whacked it with a tennis shoe, it didn't die. She had to hit it twice.

The Monday after MacAir went into receivership, a curious scene played out at the Birdsville airport. When the plane chartered from Skytrans to replace the MacAir service flew in, half the town turned up to watch. Everyone seemed to need reassurance that they still had a link with the outside world.

The river was still rising. When it reached 7.0 metres the water was almost lapping the cattle grid on the edge of town. We were in no danger of being inundated as the town stood on ground that was higher than any known flood level. After a week the river peaked at 7.2 metres. It was now 2 kilometres wide, and for most of that width more than a metre deep. By my rough calculations it was flowing past town at about a million litres a second. The area where thousands had camped during the races was now a lake studded with coolabah trees, a beautiful water park of lush green trees amid the constantly moving brown water. From the dunes at the golf course there was water to the south and west as far as the eye could see.

In the midst of the flooding a rumour came through that the grant application for the x-ray machine for the Birdsville Clinic had been successful. Not only that, it was for a sum of about $320 000, which meant an x-ray machine for Bedourie as well, plus training and incidentals. It was extremely good news, and a tribute to the incredible efforts of the tireless Bev Morton. I was eager to congratulate her, but she and Geoff had navigated the floods and escaped on a holiday to Western Australia.

After the second fortnight of the third flood our food stores were helped when Brian Hanna made a deal with Skytrans to get a grocery order for the townsfolk brought out from Quilpie. Skytrans generously footed the freight bill. If they hadn't, Brian and the pub would have had to wear it. Michelle scrambled to place an order which gave us an enjoyable half-hour at the kitchen table compiling a list of fresh veg that would be delivered within twenty-four hours. We felt as excited as kids in a lolly shop.

The water level was slowly falling around the town, but as it was dropping only 5 to 10 centimetres a day it was going to take a while before the roads reopened. I'd got in the habit of checking the river height bulletin on the Bureau of Meteorology website every day and by my calculations the waters would take two weeks to subside. Then, on the same website, I noticed a new flood rising in the upper catchment. There'd been even more rain. At Oondooroo, 700 kilometres to the north-east, it looked like a wall of water had gone through. The river had risen a metre in an hour and was still rising.

In the ensuing days it became clear that the river was going to drop, but that we would then get a fourth flood. Such a thing had never happened before, at least in recorded history.

Throughout western Queensland community after community was in the same boat, in most cases an SES flood boat. Most of them uncomplainingly took the floods in their stride. The road reports broadcast on ABC local radio took on a rhythm that was almost like poetry: 'Birdsville to Windorah, closed. Birdsville to Bedourie, closed. Birdsville to South Australia via the Birdsville Track, closed. Birdsville to South Australia via Cordillo Downs, closed. Bedourie to Windorah, closed. Bedourie to Boulia, closed. Boulia to Winton, closed . . .'

The river height bulletin had a different rhythm: 'The Diamantina at Diamantina Lakes, 5.4 metres and steady, 3 metres over the crossing. The Diamantina at Durrie, 1.4 metres and rising, 1 metre over the crossing. The Diamantina at Roseberth, 5.4 metres and steady. The Diamantina at Birdsville, 6.2 metres and falling slowly, 0.8 metres over the approaches . . .'

With the roads around us closed and not much to do, we started going out on trips through the dunes with park ranger Don Rowlands and Neale the policeman, who'd returned from leave. Don and Neale had to check local conditions in order to advise tourists and four-wheel drivers on where they could and couldn't go. They were happy for us to tag along. On one trip out to see where Eyre Creek was flooding through the dunes, we took Jimmy Crombie with us. The old Aboriginal drover was pointing out things along the way, like the original Birdsville Track on the edge of town, but he kept saying, 'Don't you put this in your book.'

Despite this, the knowledge he had wasn't something he could bottle up. When we got to the first channel flowing down between the dunes at Eyre Creek, he took me a little way off and pointed out a distant waterhole. We were on Adria Downs, a station he'd worked on since he was a boy. He told me it was permanent water, useful knowledge if you were in danger of perishing in dry times.

On the way back to Birdsville we struggled to get back over Big Red. No-one had been over the dune in weeks and the crest had built up. Neale took several goes in the police car then gave up and tried using the Chicken Track. He almost made it before he got seriously bogged and the police car slewed down the slope on a precarious angle.

Jimmy enjoyed Neale's predicament immensely.

'You gonna put this in your book?' he asked.

'You bet,' I replied with a chuckle.

As luck would have it, Don pulled Neale out without incident.

It was such a good trip that we were all eager for more. When I suggested I'd like to see lakes Muncoonie and Selicia now that they had water in them a patrol was organised in a blink. We rang Adria to get permission to go out there, then Don and his wife, Lyn, Neale, Michelle and I headed out with swags and tucker. We camped on the dune that separates the two lakes and looked out in both directions over enormous bodies of water spreading across what was supposed to be desert.

The next morning, when we dropped in to say g'day at the homestead, we had to stop a kilometre away while Don Rayment came out in a boat to pick us up. The homestead was completely surrounded by floodwaters and had been since mid-January, shortly after we'd flown over in David Brook's plane.

When we got to the homestead, wading through the shallows and mud for the last bit, Judy welcomed us with tea and pikelets. Flood or no flood, the Adria hospitality never faltered.

At the beginning of the third week in February, the Diamantina was down to 5.75 metres, which meant the water was only 0.35 metres above the approaches to Birdsville. The Birdsville Track was opened on Sunday afternoon. The feeling of freedom as we drove out to the bridge was surprising. We'd always thought the hundreds of kilometres of dirt road gave Birdsville its isolation, but it felt even more isolated when the only way out was by plane.

On Monday morning, the ABC announcer was loping through the usual report of road closures: '. . . Birdsville to Windorah, closed. Birdsville to Bedourie, closed. Wait a moment. Birdsville to South Australia via the Birdsville Track, open! Well, doesn't that make a pleasant change. Birdsville to South Australia via Cordillo Downs, closed. Bedourie to Windorah, closed. Bedourie to Boulia, closed. Boulia to Winton, closed . . .'

It had been unbearably hot and humid for nearly two months and we'd all but forgotten what cool weather felt like. The insects were at times insufferable. One night at tennis I'd endured 45 minutes of flies and sandflies swarming all over me, even though I was covered in insect repellent. Then I'd cracked.

'I don't know about anyone else but I can't take any more of this!'

'Yep, let's call it a night,' the others chorused without a moment's hesitation.

'It has been a pretty bad year,' Barry Gaffney admitted a couple of days later when I dropped in to the post office to get our mail.

And yet, we'd come through it. We hadn't quite spent a year in Birdsville yet, but as February turned to March and the temperatures began to drop ever so slightly we thought we were going to make it. It was still very hot during the day, but the nights were a little bit more comfortable. We'd survived the summer. We'd survived the flood. When we escaped Birdsville for a week to take a break in Adelaide, it felt like we were in the home stretch.

15

PARADISE

As predicted, when we returned to Birdsville after our break down south, the Diamantina had cut the road again. No worries, we thought. When we got to the bridge we called up Ian Doyle on the UHF radio and he came to get us in the big SES flood boat. Ruth Doyle, Neale the policeman, John Hanna, and Neil and Ruth Ramm came along for the ride. A bloke from a mining site out near Windorah happened along and we took him into town so he could see the sights of Birdsville. Everyone helped us load the extra supplies we'd bought knowing we might be cut off for another fortnight. Too easy.

For Michelle and I, the tables had turned. I was now chained to the computer churning out chapters of the book while she was taking trips into the desert having the kinds of adventures I'd had while she'd been working in the bakery. She flew with the Brooks and Kay Ezzy to an art exhibition in Winton, taking photos all along the way. She came back with stunning images of the flood-out country now that the water had receded. It looked like God had swept a gigantic green thumb through the landscape, leaving vivid swathes of succulent verdure with parched red and brown desert on either side. She'd helped form a Birdsville photographic group with half a dozen members and they were busy organising an exhibition of flood pictures.

Both of us were too busy to take up an invitation from Don Rowlands to visit the pelican rookery that had appeared overnight on the shores of Lake Machattie. The lake was teeming with fish and thousands of breeding pairs were raising hatchlings on its shores. Don and Lyn came back with dozens of great photographs of the rookery. They'd also taken a photographer from *The Australian* newspaper with them and his photos ended up on the front page.

Not that we had to go far to see the abundance of birdlife. The Diamantina was thick with fish and yabbies, and now that levels were dropping, thousands of birds – nankeen night herons, straw-necked ibis, pink-eared ducks, teals and egrets – were clustered along its shores and shallows, gorging themselves on food. Kites and hawks swooped down and snatched fish from the surface.

Michelle hadn't been able to go to Lake Machattie because she'd had to bake a cake for Wolfie's seventieth birthday party. She'd also made him a card using one of her aerial photos of the flood country. At first Wolfie thought it was a painting. When he realised it was a photograph he said, 'Art is dead,' and asked Michelle to sign the picture. Wolfie's party was one of six social engagements we attended that week.

As word spread that the waters were flowing down to Lake Eyre, 350 kilometres away by plane, tourists descended on the town by road and air. Dusty and Teresa had returned in mid-March. They reopened the bakery for business at Easter, and did a roaring trade. Soon they were asking Michelle to give them a hand. The town was changing back from small local community to tourist destination. The pub was often full of strangers.

It was now cool enough for barbecues on the Courthouse veran-dah. Tennis on Wednesdays and golf on Sundays were no longer sweat-soaked affairs.

Nell and I were playing a round of golf one afternoon when David flew in from drafting cattle at Cordillo. He circled the golf course looking for us. We waved to him. When he saw us he waggled the plane's wing in greeting.

'That's so Birdsville,' I said to Nell as we resumed our game. 'This is probably the only golf course in the world where people fly over and say g'day with a plane.'

The weather returned to being sublime, and the landscape revealed the abundance of the Channel Country after flood. We went for a drive down the Birdsville Inside Track and were astounded to see it lined on both sides by metre-high grasses. At a barbecue at Bev Morton's, Geoff said he was confident that he had enough feed to get through the next two years, even if there wasn't another drop of rain.

Wolfie took us down to Andrewilla, and we found an enormous patch of *Mimulus prostrates*, the purple flower he'd told me about in our interview. In another spot the ground was carpeted in yellow billy buttons. Everywhere, the flood plains were the most extraordinary vibrant green. The dry, bare country we'd seen when we first arrived in Birdsville was completely unrecognisable.

*

A similar transformation had been wrought on our perceptions of the outback. After nearly a year, I'd more than filled a book about our life in Birdsville. I'd planned to base my stories on interviews and research, but it wasn't long before I was being surprised by dimensions of outback life I hardly knew existed: being welcomed by a generous community, making new friendships that felt strong enough to last a lifetime, and sharing the challenges of an environment that operates on such a grand scale it leaves you awed and humbled.

I'd discovered that when people in the bush say people in the city really don't understand what life is like in the outback, they're absolutely right. The outback has its frustrations, like the lack of shops and restaurants. It has its hardships – it nearly broke me when Michelle was in danger of losing sight in one eye. It seriously tests a lot of families when they have to send their children thousands of kilometres away to school. Yet it also has its rewards. The quality of life is vastly superior to the pollution, crowds, noise, crime and stress of a modern city. And surprisingly, it's never boring. Before we left Sydney we'd been asked, 'But what will you do?' We knew the answer now: 'Try to keep up!'

Like many communities in outback Australia, Birdsville faces an uncertain future as young people are lured to the cities where services and amenities abound. Many of the older generation are approaching retirement. The slow decline has been going on since Federation. In 1901 western Queensland's population was 8 per cent of the state's total. In 2008 it was 0.4 per cent. If the outback becomes a 'failed state' (a possibility suggested in a prospectus for remoteFocus, a concept for revitalising remote Australia published in 2008), the consequences for national security in a world filled with overpopulated countries may be felt by every Australian.

Many outback communities are struggling. It's a battle getting anything, from x-ray machines to Internet and telephony. Life in the outback is infinitely better than it was 100 years ago, but as the quality of life in the rest of Australia improves, the outback has to go flat out to avoid being left too far behind. People end up sounding like a broken record as they argue endlessly for support. There seems to be no other way.

It costs 55 cents to post a letter from Birdsville, just as it does from everywhere else in Australia, but there's no profit for Australia Post in a letter sent from the outback. All services – education, energy, transport, health – cost significantly more to provide than they do elsewhere in Australia. It would probably be cheaper to shut Birdsville down and give every man, woman and child $100 000 a year for the rest of their lives to live somewhere else, except it's estimated that cattle and tourism in the Diamantina Shire contribute $60 million a year to the national economy – $200 000 per head of population. Add to that intangible benefits like maintained roads and medical help, police assistance and rescue services close at hand for those who will always be drawn to explore the outback, and the argument for sustaining a vibrant community is still compelling.

Rather than give up, many people in the outback are constantly on the lookout for ways to improve their communities. The shire council was exploring options for building the job base in the region, and doing so with little outside help. It had looked at building local abattoirs. It was considering a scheme to mothball obsolete aircraft.

One thing Michelle and I proved during a year in Birdsville is that a professional couple can telecommute with relative ease from a place so remote. Our clients, ranging from boutique companies to multinational corporations, enjoyed the same quality of service they did when we were in Sydney. With the right incentives, more people like us could be encouraged to do what we'd done, bringing new people, employment and skills to outback communities. It's worth noting that the Arts Council of Australia maintains apartments and studios in Paris and Rome for the purpose of enriching the experiences of young Australian artists and writers. It's time they gave priority to establishing a studio in the outback. Surely getting to know your own country is as important to a young artist as anything in France or Italy.

At the end of our year in Birdsville we were surprised at how much we cared about the town, its people and its future. When Michelle was offered a job in the Hunter Valley, north of Sydney, where we could continue to have chickens, a vegie patch and a sense of space, we couldn't escape a sense of disappointment at the thought of moving 'closer in'. The one consolation was that the outback had now become part of us. 'It gets inside you,' the locals had said. After a year we knew that we could leave the outback, but that it would never leave us. We loved it. We would always love it.

Birdsville
1 May 2009

ACKNOWLEDGEMENTS

It would be impossible to thank every individual who assisted with the writing of this book without risking many sins of omission. However, many thanks are due to the staff and representatives of the Diamantina Shire Council, to friends and family around the country for their support and care packages, and to the staff and management of Penguin for their support for the project and their understanding and professionalism in bringing it to fruition. I owe a great debt of gratitude to all the people of the Diamantina Shire, in particular the people of Birdsville and the surrounding stations, who were generous with their time, incredibly welcoming to Michelle and I, patient with my endless questions, and trusting with my handling of the details of their lives. This book would have been impossible without their willing support. Finally, special thanks to one individual who put so much at risk and gave such unwavering support through the thick and thin of an extraordinary year in our lives – my wife, Michelle.

Michelle's blog on her year in the back of beyond and lots more photos can be found at birdsvillelife.blogspot.com.

Also by Evan McHugh

Outback Heroes

The men and women you'll meet in this fascinating book come in all shapes and sizes, from convicts and engineers to cattleduffers and anthropologists. These remarkable Australians share an extraordinary ability to survive the rigours of the bush.

In *Outback Heroes*, Evan McHugh brings together his favourite ripping yarns from the Australian frontier. He begins with escaped convict William Buckley, who emerged from the forest after thirty-two years in the wild; re-examines the legends of the Man from Snowy River and Waltzing Matilda; recounts one of the most stunning rescues in Australian history; and relives the 2000 Olympics Opening Ceremony.

These and other true stories of courage and ingenuity remind us how the Australian character was forged – through encounters with the bush, desert and outback.

RED CENTRE, DARK HEART

A journey into Australia's heart of darkness, where life is lived by a different set of rules and it is easy for criminals to disappear into the vast landscape – and yet it can be difficult to remain anonymous. Some of the most shocking and fascinating crimes in our history have been committed in its harsh surrounds.

Beginning with the chilling tale of convict and cannibal Alexander Pearce, *Red Centre, Dark Heart* explores historic and recent true-crime in the outback, including the Belanglo State Forest murders and the disappearance of Peter Falconio. Read these stories and you'll discover that Australia's dark heart is frighteningly close to home.

Winner of the 2008 Ned Kelly Non-Fiction Award

'It's enough to make you run for the beach.'
SUNDAY HERALD SUN

OUTBACK PIONEERS

Here are the enthralling stories of the men and women who opened up the Australian outback, and in the process discovered the beauty and terror of this extraordinary country.

We meet the little-known convict explorer John Wilson, the first European to cross the Blue Mountains (though history favours the proper English gentlemen Blaxland, Wentworth and Lawson); we follow Australia's greatest drover, Nat Buchanan, as he blazes stock routes from one side of the country to the other; and we marvel at the genius and grit of the men who overcame political treachery to build the Coolgardie Pipeline and the Trans-Australian Railway.

'*A fascinating collection of stories about our lesser-known achievers.*'
SYDNEY MORNING HERALD

'*McHugh tells the stories of these great achievers simply and without romantic or other embellishment, which is how these characters would have wanted it.*'
COURIER MAIL